AF594015

The Words of War

By

Donagh Bracken

History Publishing Company, LLC
PO Box 700
Palisades, New York 10964-0700

The Words of War

Published in the United States by
History Publishing Company, LLC
Palisades, New York

Publisher's Cataloging-in-Publication

Bracken, Donagh
The Words of War/
by Donagh Bracken.
p.cm.
Includes bibliographical references and index.
LCCN 2006938438
ISBN-13: 978-1-933909-32-5
ISBN-10-1-933909-32-3

1.United States–History–Civil War, 1861-1865–Press coverage. 2.United States–History–Civil War, 1861-1865–Campaigns. 3.United States–History–Civil War, 1861-1865–Journalists. 4.Journalism–New York (State)–New York–History–19th century. 5.Journalism –South Carolina–Charleston–History–19th century. 6.American newspapers–New York (State)–New York–History –19th century. 7.American newspapers–South Carolina – Charleston–History–19th century. I Title.

E609.B733.2007 973.7
QBI06-600707

Printed in the United States on acid-free paper

9 8 7 6 5 4 3 2 1

First Edition

Contents

Acknowledgments

In order to properly acknowledge all those who contributed to this book, it is necessary to reach back fifteen decades to those in American journalism whose work is contained on these pages. There are men whose contributions, unfortunately, are anonymous at this point: the newspaper compositors and the telegraph operators and all the others on the technical end who made the *Charleston Mercury* and *The New York Times* possible. Then there are the names we remember: Henry J. Raymond and Robert Barnwell Rhett, whose identities with *The New York Times* and the *Charleston Mercury* will forever be linked. So, too, the gentlemen whose writings made newspaper history: Franc Wilkie, L.L. Crounse, Sam Wilkeson, and William Swinton, all of the *Times*, and George William Bagby who wrote under the pen name, *Hermes*, for the *Mercury*, and Robert Barnwell Rhett, Jr., the actual editor of the *Mercury*, who toiled in relative obscurity in his father's shadow.

To those with us today who put the battles contained herein into historical perspective, much is owed. In 1993, the Civil War Sites Advisory Commission brought together prominent civil war historians for their knowledge, input, and analysis of civil war battles. The resulting summaries provided a more clear understanding of each battle, qualities that might not have been so evident to the early war correspondents.

Many thanks are due to Beatrice Agnew, Marie Firestone, and the staff of the Palisades Free Library, in Palisades, New York. For their reach into the inter-library loan system on my behalf, a special acknowledgment goes to Joanna Lo and Mary Beth Darnobid of the reference desk. My appreciation goes also to Dr. Libby Chenault and Gary Patillo of the University of North Carolina's Wilson Library and Davis Library, respectively, and Tom Nix of the reference staff of that great university. Thanks, too, to Katie Gray of the Charleston County Public Library in Charleston, South Carolina, and Susanne Christof and Elaine McConnell of the Special Collections Section, and Nick Battipaglia of the Reference Section of the United States Military Academy at West Point.

And to those who took my compilation of information and turned it into the attractive book it is, I am very much indebted: Tom Cameron, Senior Editor of History Publishing Company, whose artistic typographical touch and editorial skills are superbly demonstrated, and whose insightful suggestions brought a bright polish to areas in need of a glow; Ann Walter for her tireless eye and interesting thoughts on the English language of the Civil War era; and Blair Sutphen who designed the eye-catching cover graphic that captured everything in the book. A note of thanks, as well, to Marcia Carlson, who compiled a thorough index of a rather complicated subject.

And, of course, to my sons Chuck and Don and daughter-in-law Elizabeth, whose interest in my progress never wavered, goes my deep appreciation. To my special friend, June Starke, whose carefully phrased questions relating to the progress of the book were really more prod than query, I owe a heartfelt sense of gratitude.

Introduction

A Note to the Reader About Newspaper Style During the Civil War

When the *Charleston Mercury* and *The New York Times* reported on the Civil War, they captured the fever of that great war and the flavor of the era. The language used by both newspapers was influenced by their European counterparts, the *London Times* specifically, which was then the preeminent newspaper.

> *Of particular note is that the articles reproduced here are original, unaltered, battlefield reports as sent from the nearest telegraph station. They include all the typos, convoluted syntax, stylistic peculiarities of the era, and perhaps inaccuracies one might expect from inexperienced and rightfully frightened reporters. The reports, as written, were immediately sent to press, without review or editing.*

Dispatches from correspondents like Franc Wilkie, in the West, and L.L. Crounse and William Swinton, in the East, were printed verbatim. Telegraph companies charged by the word. To save costs, reporters would join two words into one. So Lee's Army became Leearmy, and, when it came to stating the time of action, just 12 'o would suffice because everyone knew the next word should be clock.

There is one other jounnalistic aspect to this book, the war artist. The technology of photography was too cumbersome to capture the actual battle scenes. Because of the daily nature of the newspaper, illustrations in the newspapers were limited to rough line drawings of maps and diagrams of the war. Often they showed unfamiliar terrain with unfamiliar names. But there were periodicals other than newspapers, the weekly journals, *Harpers Weekly* and *Frank Leslie's Illustrated Magazine,* that dispatched artists such as Edwin Forbes, the brothers William and Alfred Waud, and Theodore Davis to sketch events as they happened. These drawings would then be sent to the magazines and turned into line engravings. In company with the correspondents' writings of the *Times* and *Mercury*, some of the artist's renditions are presented, many with the artist's notes – snapshots of events as they occurred.

When the Civil War started, American journalism was put to the test. It was the start of the modern age of journalism, and it was a rough start indeed. Newspapers had to wrest themselves from an unsavory past with propagandistic objectives to the dissemination of information relatively free of propaganda. In this objective they were not entirely successful; but in the restructuring of their nature, they did achieve lasting success.

Newspapers were instrumental in teaching Americans how to read. For most Americans, newspapers were their only reading material; and, to a great degree, their thinking was shaped by published reports. Publishers, for their part, influenced the political thinking of their followers—sometimes with negative results. Political differences, in some cases, were often resolved with duels, horse whippings, and ransacking newspaper offices.

In its dark and formative days, the American newspaper was largely a propaganda organ, owned by or rented by subsidy to some political personage or party. Fierce in their opposition to contending interests, newspapers respected no bounds.

In the early 1830s, Alexis de Tocqueville wrote: "The spirit of the journalist in America is to attack coarsely, without preparation, and without art, the passions of those whom it addresses, to set aside principles in order to grab men, to follow them into their private lives, and to lay bare their weaknesses and their vices."

The French aristocrat had a keen eye. The politically slanted newspapers, North and South, were written to satisfy the partisan prejudices of their subscribers. As a usual practice, news content was formed by lacing a few "heresays" or rumors with an abundance of editorial comment, which was often spiked with vituperation and accusation.

But now with the Civil War, the reader wanted more than partisan vituperation and the latest news of their neighbor's peccadilloes. Much more.

In the North, this demand to know the news as it happened in places far away, forced the newspapers to expand exponentially. As the scope of the War widened, and its fierce intensity increased, the amount of reportage exploded, as did the payroll for the number of correspondents required to cover the growing number of battles and expanding theaters of war. In doing so, many newspapers incurred great financial strain. Newspapers in the South, never as large or as cash-flow blessed as their Northern counterparts, suffered pains, too, but of a different nature. As armies advanced, newsprint supply was often cut off; and as Union Armies settled in occupied cities, the more outspoken newspapers were usually shut down.

At the outset of the War, New York City, which boasted seventeen dailies, was the newspaper capital of the country. Not all had a Lincolnian perspective; only five showed degrees of loyalty to him during the War. Many were pro-South in their sympathies, some even pro-slavery.

The strongest supporter of Abraham Lincoln and the preservation of the Union was *The New York Times* and its editor, Henry J. Raymond, a bright, industrious, young man who was born in the upstate New York town of Lima in 1820. Educated in New England at the University of Vermont, Raymond was a young man of considerable talent, whose proclivities were the Siamese twins of American public life: politics and journalism. In 1851, he was a principal founder of *The New York Times* and used its editorial pages to promote Whig interests until he left that party in 1856 to help found the Republican Party. In 1860, he accepted Lincoln's nomination and supported him throughout his presidency, even in the darkest days of the war. It was during this crisis of war that Raymond and his competitors, Lincoln advocates or not, wrought the change so often fostered by crisis that elevated American journalism to a degree of respectability.

In the South, newspapers constantly struggled to balance the books. The population was more sparing than in the North, and circulation was limited, but their influence was significant since they were the only source of information. In 1860, the citizens of the states that would make up the Confederacy had access to over seven hundred political journals and newspapers; but the total population, according to the 1860 Census, was only 5,579,000; while the remainder of the nation was 25,996,000, an indication of the difficulties Southern newspapers faced.

In South Carolina, its paltriness of numbers did not dissuade the *Charleston Mercury* from preaching secession and achieving a result far exceeding what its small circulation numbers might indicate. Guided by Robert Barnwell Rhett, the *Mercury* was his organ for secession, and he used it well.

Rhett was a man destined to bring a flame to the fabric of the American Union. He was raised comfortably in an isolated cocoon of the slave-plantation culture. His formative years were spent devoid of formal education save for two preteen years. His education was self-applied, and eventually he entered the practice of law, which led him to politics where he had intermittent success, with greater degrees of failure, in the U.S. House of Representatives, U.S. Senate, and the South Carolina legislature. He was quick of mind, brash and self-confident, and of the latter, annoyingly so to some. Given to syllogistic reasoning and quick to act on his conclusions, however, flawed the basic premise; he believed that the South was economically subservient to the North, and, if it remained so, would never achieve its true level of economic well being. Free from the bonds of the Union, South Carolina, in concert with other southern states, could become prosperous while maintaining its independent, self-governing ways in a confederation of other like-minded southern states.

For twenty eight years, Rhett's words of defiance, censure, and criticism were ever ready for usage. Flowing from the lectern, the platform as a member of government, and the editorial room of the *Charleston Mercury*–the newspaper his family would come to own and he would influence–he brought discomfort, disapproval, and disquietude to many as he brought a blood rush to others. His reasoning, usually free of concern for subtleties and complexities, would take him on a straight line to the heart of the issue and then to a "logical" conclusion. Once reached, it was time for action, and action in troubled times usually meant more trouble. And Rhett was never out of it, for his constant call for action was abrasive to the more moderately disposed. Even in the southland drifting toward disunion, there were some who resented his extremism, but there were not enough to prevent disunion or to foster some sort of compromise. The sparks from Rhett's fiery orations and writings over the years had singed enough minds to create enough burning embers of discontent. But when disunion came, they were enough to thwart his ambition for high office in the new government of the Confederate States of America. Denied a significant role, he took to Charleston and the *Mercury*, and reported the war with a bitterness not only towards the hated Yankees but to the Confederate government in Richmond, arguably bringing to the Confederate cause a demoralization that impacted significantly on the home front, the place that would inevitably become the scene of battle.

A Few Particular Terms of the Era

Debouche – emerge from a confined area into a wide clearing; a passage or opening thrugh which troops may debouche.

Enfilade – a volley of gunfire directed along a line from one end to the other; a position of earthworks, troops, etc., subject to a sweeping fire from along the length of a line of opposing troops, a trench, or a battery.

Factious – inclining towards dissension; *a factious group was trying to undermine the government.*

Fascines – bundles of bound sticks used to reenforce the side of a trench; used in building earthworks and batteries and in strengthening ramparts.

Hors de combat – put out of action; no longer able to fight.

Investing – to besiege a town or an area; to surround a place with military forces or works and thereby prevent approach or escape.

Qui vive – a sentry's challenge (Who goes there?); on the alert; watchful.

Resaca – Sherman's first battle in the Atlanta Campaign (May 13-15, 1864).

Revetments – Facings of sandbags, stones, felled trees, etc. to protect a wall.

Sideling – moving to the side while approaching stealthily.

Toades – a contemptible individual.

Secession

It may have been the fastest report of breaking news in the history of American journalism. When South Carolina seceded from the Union in the building that would become known as Secession Hall on December 20, 1860, the *Charleston Mercury* had an extra edition on the streets of Charleston five minutes after the Convention adjourned.

The broadside's announcement of South Carolina's secession was the culmination of Robert Barnwell Rhett's efforts to wrest South Carolina from the Federal Union since the nullification days of Andrew Jackson. He was the father of the editor of the *Mercury*, a key player in the South Carolina delegation, and a volatile force in the writings of the family owned newspaper.

Several states to the north, *The New York Times*, in one of its pieces on the following day, was rather haughty in its understated reportage of South Carolina's actions. In the piece headlined "The Secession Movement," it said: "South Carolina passed the ordinance of secession yesterday at 1 o'clock P.M. by the unanimous vote of the Convention and her action was greeted with a salvo of a hundred guns. As this step was universally anticipated, it will create no special uneasiness. It does not change the relations of South Carolina to the Union in the slightest degree . . . ," then, as if reconsidering its thoughts added. . . " though it will very possibly be followed by acts that will have that effect."

CHARLESTON MERCURY

EXTRA:

Passed unanimously at 1.15 o'clock, P. M., December 20th, 1860.

AN ORDINANCE

To dissolve the Union between the State of South Carolina and other States united with her under the compact entitled "The Constitution of the United States of America."

We, the People of the State of South Carolina, in Convention assembled, do declare and ordain, and it is hereby declared and ordained,

That the Ordinance adopted by us in Convention, on the twenty-third day of May, in the year of our Lord one thousand seven hundred and eighty-eight, whereby the Constitution of the United States of America was ratified, and also, all Acts and parts of Acts of the General Assembly of this State, ratifying amendments of the said Constitution, are hereby repealed; and that the union now subsisting between South Carolina and other States, under the name of "The United States of America," is hereby dissolved.

THE

UNION

IS

DISSOLVED!

1

Fort Sumter

Initial Engagement of the Civil War

Author's Commentary

There was a carnival-like atmosphere in Charleston, South Carolina, as the count down marking the instant of the first cannon burst approached. When the muzzles roared at Fort Sumter, cheers arose as if the hometown favorite had scored a winning point in a sporting match. A frenzy of good fellowship embraced the Charleston citizenry.

Others watching the event did not enjoy that fellowship. Indeed, they were fearing for their well-being. Northern newspaper correspondents were told that they might be hung if they were caught. One such was George Salter, a physician and a native of Charleston. Often sympathetic to the South in his correspondence to *The New York Times,* written under the pseudonym "Jasper," he was still viewed in South Carolina with suspicion. As the *Charleston Mercury* reported on April 13, 1861, Dr. Salter, in fact, was thrown into prison.

The follow up to the story is that Dr. Salter, after being relieved of his personal effects, was imprisoned in a rather foul place reeking with odor where he was taunted by the guards with threats of being hung or being shot from the mouth of a cannon as an example to Northern newspapermen.

After an uncomfortable night and the passage of twenty four hours, Dr. Salter was released, put on a train, and sent on his way.

It was later reported that Dr. Salter's composure was not restored until he got to Wilmington, North Carolina, which was still in the Union, where he was befriended by a fellow newspaperman.

Jan.10, 1861: From the *Charleston Mercury*

Special to the *Charleston Mercury,* the Ninth of January, 1861. Great Events crowd rapidly one upon another. Three short weeks ago, and the greatest event of the century upon the Western Hemisphere was transacted in Charleston. The Union of the States of North America was dissolved by the action of the State of South Carolina.

It appears to be a decree of history that upon all great revolutions or changes of the Government of a people, the red seal of blood must be set. Yesterday, the 9th of January, will be memorable to history. Powder has been burnt over the decree of our State, timber has been crushed, perhaps blood spilled. South Carolina will maintain her liberties and her independence whilst there is a single shot in her lockers. Blind infatuation is driving our enemies forward, and stroke by stroke the liberties of the South are being welded and cemented together.

The expulsion of the steamer Star of the West from the Charleston harbor yesterday morning was the opening of the hall of the Revolution. We are proud that our harbor has been so honored. We are more proud that the State of South Carolina, so long, so bitterly, so contemptuously reviled and scoffed at, above all others, should this proudly have thrown back the scoff of her enemies. Entrenched upon her soil, she has spoken from the mouth of her cannon, and not from the mouths of scurrilous demagogues, fanatics and scribblers. Condemned, the sanctity of her waters violated with the hostile purpose of reinforcing enemies in our harbor, she has not hesitated to strike the first blow, full in the face of her insulter. Let the United States Government bear, or return at their good will, the blow still tingling about her ears – the fruit of her own bandit temerity. We would not exchange or recall that blow for millions! It has wiped out a half century of scorn and outrage. Again South Carolina may be proud of her historic fame and ancestry, without a blush upon her cheek for her own present honor. The haughty echo of her cannon has ere this reverberated from Maine to Texas, through every hamlet of the North, and down along the great waters of the Southwest.

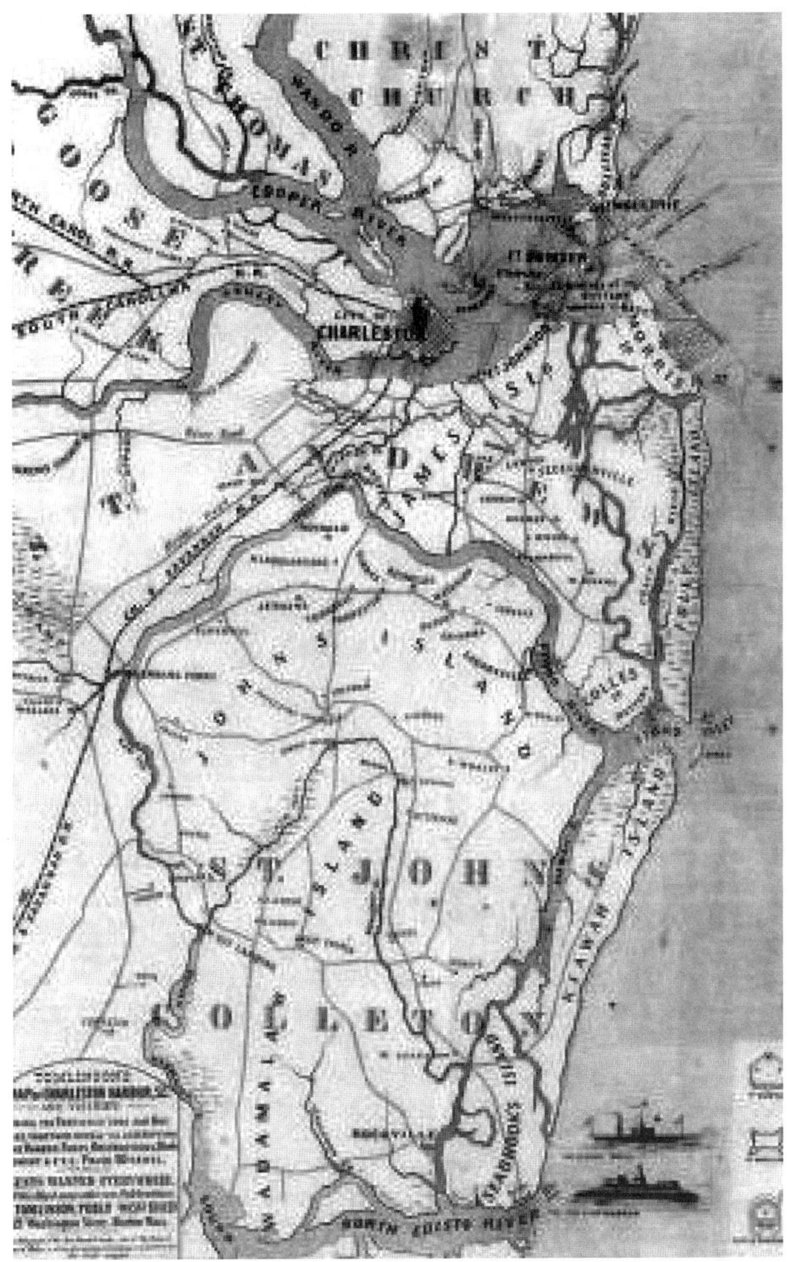

CHARLESTON HARBOR, SHOWING THE SCENE OF THE NAVAL BATTLE BETWEEN THE IRON CLAD MONITORS AND THE REBEL BATTERIES (TOMLINSON, G.W.). LIBRARY OF CONGRESS.

The decree has gone forth. Upon every acre of the peaceful soil of the South armed men will spring up, as the sound breaks upon their ears; and it will be found that every word of our insolent foes has indeed been a dragontooth sown for their destruction. And though grisly and traitorous ruffians may cry on the dogs of war, and treacherous politicians may lend their aid in deceptions, South Carolina will stand under her own Palmetto tree, unterrified by the snarling growls or assaults of the one, undeceived or deterred by the wily machinations of the other. And if that red seal of blood be still lacking to the parchment of our liberties, and blood they want – blood they shall have – and blood enough to stamp it all in red. For, by the God of our Fathers, the soil of South Carolina SHALL BE FREE!

The *Charleston Mercury*

April 12, 1861

War News, The Times – Charleston, April 12, 1861 – Yesterday was an exciting day in Charleston. Men met in crowds at the various corners of our thoroughfares, and the only topic was the all-engrossing one of WAR. Every moment the names of BEAUREGARD, ANDERSON, Sumter, Moultrie and Morris Island, would reach the ear, and the low, earnest conversations of the people gave evidence of their interest in the subject, and determination to proceed. At an early hour a large crowd congregated in front of THE MERCURY office to learn the latest news which appeared on the bulletin board, and the party only dispersed at eleven o, p.m., when it was understood that the bombardment would not commence immediately.

On the Battery several hundreds of persons, principally ladies, were promenading until near midnight, anxiously gazing at the dim lights, barely visible through the haze, which indicated the position of the batteries, where fathers and sons, brothers and lovers were willing to sacrifice their lives for the honor of South Carolina. And yet there was but one regret expressed, and that was at the delay and procrastination of hostilities. A detachment of the Citadel Cadets are stationed here for night service, with some heavy pieces of artillery.

Among the exciting rumors of the day was one that Major ANDERSON had fired into the steamer Gordon, which was, of course, without any foundation.

A Pilot boat reported the steam cutter Harriet Lane, Capt FAUNCE, off the Bar, which also created a sensation, but it was one of rejoicing, as it was hoped that hostilities were then certain to commence.

The reliable events of the day, however, were that about three o a demand for the evacuation of Fort Sumter was made by Gen. BEAUREGARD, through his Aids, Col. CHESNUT, Col. CHISHOLM, and Capt. LEE, and that Major Anderson replied he could not, consistently with his honor as an officer of the United States Army, retire from his post without instructions from his Government. At half past eleven, p.m., Gen. BEAUREGARD'S final reply was borne to him by the same officers, but up to the hour of our going to press, we have not had any further information.

Among the noticeable incidents visible from the Battery last evening, were a number of rockets let off, a private signal no doubt, by the steamers on duty in the harbor; also the fiery appearance of the three schooners in the neighborhood of Sumter, with pine wood and tar burning for the purpose of lighting the harbor in that vicinity.

THE FLOATING BATTERY AT CHARLESTON, S.C., INTENDED TO ASSIST IN THE CAPTURE OF FORT SUMPTER, WITH DR. DE VEGA'S HOSPITAL ATTACHED. FROM A SKETCH BY OUR SPECIAL ARTIST NOW IN CHARLESTON. (FRANK LESLIE). LIBRARY OF CONGRESS.

The *Charleston Mercury*
April 13, 1861

Charleston, April 12, 1861 – We stated yesterday that on Thursday, at three o, p.m. General BEAUREGARD had made a demand upon Major ANDERSON for the evacuation of Fort Sumter through his Aids, Colonel CHESNUT, Captain LEE, and Colonel CHISHOLM, and that Major ANDERSON had regretfully declined, under the circumstances of his position. It was, however, understood that unless reinforced he would necessarily yield the post in a few days – say by the fifteenth. An effort was, therefore, made to avoid an engagement, without incurring greater risk of reinforcement.

At one and a half, a.m., Colonel CHESNUT and Captain LEE reached Fort Sumter from General BEAUREGARD, and, we gather, were prepared to enter into any arrangement for non action as to Fort Sumter, if no assistance were given to the efforts of reinforcement; but postponement merely to mature hostile plans was impossible. No satisfactory agreement being proposed, and time being important, at three and a half o a.m., Major ANDERSON was notified that, at the expiration of an hour, the batteries would open their fire upon him. The Aids then passed thence in a boat to Fort Johnson, and Col. CHESNUT ordered the fire to begin. Precisely at four and a half o a shell was fired from the signal battery on James' Island, which, making a beautiful curve, burst immediately above Fort Sumter. Within fifteen minutes all the Carolina batteries were in full play. The inhabitants of Charleston forthwith thronged to the East Bay Battery and other points of observation, and excitement prevailed through the day amid various and stirring rumors put afloat from time to time. Major ANDERSON, no oil to light up his casemates, and the morning being slightly murky and drizzly, did not respond until broad day. At a quarter before six he opened his fire by a shot at the Iron Battery on Cumming point; then at Fort Moultrie, the Floating Battery, located at the west end of Sullivan Island; the Dahlgreen Battery, the Enfilade Battery, Major TRAPIER Battery, and Fort Johnson, interspersing his attentions by paying respects to the numerous mortar batteries, by which he, encased in brick, is surrounded. Hour after hour has the fire on both sides been kept up, deliberate and unflagging. The steady frequent shock of the cannon boom, accompanied by the hiss of balls, and the horrid, hurtling sound of the flying shell, are now perfectly familiar to the people of Charleston.

While the early sun was veiled in mist, we saw shell bursting within and illuminating Fort Sumter, or exploding in the air above, leaving a small thick cloud of white smoke to mark the place. We saw solid shot striking the dark walls, and in each instance followed by a fume of dust from the battered surface. One man was visibly stricken prostrate on the wharf, and carried in the fort; and several guns were dismounted. The walls, too, in several spots, were damaged. And while Sumter has certainly and manifestly been injured, no loss is yet sustained on our part. Fort Moultrie is intact, so far as fighting capacity is concerned. The Iron Battery is ready for continued work, after a full and fair trial of its powers of resistance; also the Floating Battery. The practice of our soldiers, as marksmen, has been excellent and highly satisfactory to officers of science and experience; and, great gratification, at the last accounts, six o, p.m., not one man of our army has suffered injury.

The Pawnee and Harriet Lane are lying off North Channel bar, with another ship, supposed to be the Baltic; at ship bar a war ship, judged to be the Illinois. Whether they will attempt to reinforce Fort Sumter in barges tonight, or land troops on Morris Island for an engagement, or will try to run the gauntlet of our channel batteries and Fort Moultrie, remains to be seen, and we will see.

BOMBARDMENT OF FORT SUMTER BY THE BATTERIES OF THE CONFEDERATE STATES (HARPER'S). LIBRARY OF CONGRESS.

The *Charleston Mercury*
April 13, 1861

Incidents – Two companies of volunteers passed THE MERCURY office at three o yesterday, with their banners flying, and tendered us a salute, for which we return our compliments.

Two members of the Palmetto Guard paid fifty dollars cash for a boat to carry them to Morris Island, to join their company.

The Battery, the wharves and shipping in the harbor, and every steeple and cupalo in the city, were crowded with anxious spectators of the great drama. Never before had such crowds of ladies without attendants visited our thoroughfares.

Business was entirely suspended. The stores on King street, Meeting street and East Bay were all closed.

Dr. SALTERS, the 'Jasper' correspondent of *The New York Times*, was arrested, and locked up in the Guard House, where he yet remains.

One of our special reporters to Fort Moultrie brought a trophy of war, in the shape of a 32 pound ball, which ANDERSON had fired at Moultrie, and which lodged in the sandbags. It may be seen at our office.

Another of our reporters has circulated the number of pounds of balls fired by both sides up to seven o, the hour at which Fort Sumter ceased firing. He gives as a total 75,000 pounds or over thirty-six tons of iron.

It was currently rumored that the Harriet Lane was crippled by the Star of the West Battery, while trying to run in yesterday morning, but that the Harriet Lane pursued the course of her predecessor, and put back to sea minus one wheel.

The *Charleston Mercury*
April 15, 1861

Serenade to Gov. Pickens – On Saturday evening last, after our citizens were entirely satisfied of the capitulation of Fort Sumter, a large crowd assembled in front of the Charleston Hotel, and honored the Governor with a serenade. He acknowledged the compliment in a brief and appropriate speech, in the course of which he congratulated our citizens upon the happy termination of the bombardment.

The *Charleston Mercury*

April 16, 1861

Incidents of the Bombardment and Surrender – Fort Sumter was delivered up on Saturday to Capt. FERGUSON, one of Gen. BEAUREGARD'S Aids, despatched to receive it, and raise upon its walls the Confederate Flag. Previous to leaving, Major ANDERSON carefully pointed out the location of the mines which he had laid to defend his post; also the powder magazines, with the danger to which he might be exposed by the progress of the fire, etc. After performing these offices, he delivered up the keys.

It is understood that Major ANDERSON had intended to fire a salute of one hundred guns before striking the United States flag, both the national salute of thirty four or thirty six guns, and the President salute of twenty one guns. This not being particularly agreeable to the captors of the fort, he determined to fire a full salute, but one without special point. The accident which happened to his gunners put a stop to his intention. Immediately upon seeing the fatal effect, Major WHITING wrote an order for the Confederate troops to bury the body in the parade ground of Fort Sumter with all the honors of war, and sent a copy to Major ANDERSON, who was visibly affected by this token of respect towards his brave garrison by their victorious enemies.

The Confederate flag and the ensign of South Carolina were hoisted simultaneously on the ramparts looking towards Charleston. Capt. FERGUSON, in charge of the former, was assisted by Maj. JONES. The Palmetto Flag was raised by Cols. F. J. MOSES, JR., and J. L. DEARING, assisted by Col. CARROLL. The two flagstaffs, upon which the colors had been raised, had been lashed to two guns near one another by Commodore HARTSTENE, and rose some fifteen feet above the parapet.

It is stated that ANDERSON flagstaff at Fort Sumter was touched by balls seven times before the final shot which cut it down. The halyard was cut below the flag on the morning of the 12th. At Fort Moultrie, where floated both the Confederate and State colors, the folds of the former were pierced by four balls, the latter by three.

USS Harriet Lane (reproduction of Clary Ray) Naval Historical Center.

Our readers may not have remarked the auspicious circumstance that on the nights of the 12th and 13th, the moon showed the silver crescent, which stands on the flag of the State. A gentleman also informs us, on the morning of the13th, as an omen of victory, that he saw a gamecock mount the tomb of CALHOUN, on Church street, flap his wings and crow. The superstitious will make a not on.

The *Charleston Mercury*
April 16, 1861

Morris Island , Saturday, April 13 – Up to this time, after thirty hours of bombardment, at 11 o, no one at Morris Island has been injured. It is believed here that Sullivan Island has been almost as fortunate. The fact is as wonderful as it is providential. With this promise for the relief of your many anxious readers, I hasten on to make a brief statement of the engagement as it appeared from this point.

At five o, on the afternoon of the 11th, the officers were informed that the bombardment would be opened on Fort Sumter at 9 o, p.m. Orders were issued, in accordance, to the several regiments, as to their particular duties. Men slept, arms in hand, all night. At half past four in the morning of the 12th a shell was thrown up from Fort Johnson, and the ball opened, with shell and shot from some eight or ten batteries. The sight of the whizzing shell in the grey morning light, bursting in every direction, above and around the solitary grey mass in the harbor, was beautiful indeed. I have but ten minutes to write only a word – interruptions innumerable. Not until after six o did ANDERSON reply at all to their delicate hints suggested to him. At that time, however, he began to let himself out loosely, like forty bees in a barrel, right and left. But he couldn't hold his hand long, and was driven from the parapets to the next tier of guns. The shell and shot pouring in from the iron battery, the rifle cannon, and the Trapier Battery, and from Fort Moultrie, the Floating Battery, the Butler Battery, and others on Sullivan Island and James Island and Mount Pleasant, drove him below. The Major then drew in his horns, and paid his especial compliments first to the Iron Battery and the Shell Battery here, and then to the Sullivan Island batteries. During the morning he paid his respects to all, and had tested the Floating Battery and the Iron Battery, and made nothing for the trouble. The last two or three hours before dark he devoted himself exclusively to Fort Moultrie, and the two fortresses had a beautiful little duello. Game to the last, though much more exposed, Fort Moultrie held her own, and, it is believed, a little more than her own. This battery has here received universal applause and admiration, as we suppose it has on all hands. The Iron Battery and Shell Battery, in charge of Capt. CUTHBERT, were under Major STEVENS' command. The rifle cannon has also been most admirably managed. The practice of BUTLER'S Battery and HALLONQUIST'S Shell Battery have been excellent. Indeed, where there is so much to praise every where, it is difficult to discriminate even where there is advantage. Wish I could write more, but the time is up. All have slept four nights on the open ground – storm and sunshine – were under arms in rain all night. Will be again tonight.

The *Charleston Mercury*

April 16, 1861

The Battle of Fort Sumter. HEADQUARTERS PROVISIONAL ARMY, C.S.A. CHARLESTON, S.C., April 14th, 1861. General Orders No. 20 – The Brigadier General commanding is happy to congratulate the troops under his command on the brilliant success which has crowned their gallantry, privations and hardships, by the reduction of the stronghold in the harbor of Charleston. This feat of arms has been accomplished after a severe cannonading of about thirty three hours, in which all the troops have indicated, by their daring and bravery, that our cause must and shall triumph.

Fort Sumter, which surrendered yesterday, about 1:45 p.m., will be evacuated at 9 o a.m. today; and to show our magnanimity to the gallant defenders, who were only executing the orders of their Government, they will be allowed to evacuate upon the same terms which were offered to them before the bombardment commenced. Our success should not lull us into a false security, but should encourage us in the necessary preparations to meet a powerful enemy, who may, at any time, attempt to avenge this, their first check, in the present contest.

The commandants of batteries will promptly send in their reports through the proper channels, giving a journal of the firing of their batteries against Fort Sumter, and of the fire of Fort Sumter against their batteries – furnishing the names of those who particularly distinguished themselves, and other incidents relative thereto, in order that the General commanding may be able to make known to the Confederate States Government, in a proper manner, their bravery and gallantry. The General is highly gratified to state that the troops, by their labor, privations and endurance at the batteries and at their posts, have exhibited the highest characteristics of tried soldiers; and he takes this occasion to thank all – his Staff, the Regulars, the Volunteers, the Militia, the Naval forces, and the numerous individuals who have contributed to the surrender of Fort Sumter.

By order of Brigadier General BEAUREGARD.

D. R. JONES, A. A. General.

From *The New York Times*

Charleston, Friday, April 12 – The ball has opened. War is inaugurated. The batteries of Sullivan's Island, Morris Island, and other points, were opened on Fort Sumpter at 4 o'clock this morning. Fort Sumpter has returned the fire, and a brisk cannonading has been kept up. No information has been received from the seaboard yet. The military are under arms, and the whole of our population are on the streets. Every available space facing the harbor is filled with anxious spectators. Of the nineteen batteries in position only seven have opened fire on Fort Sumpter, the remainder are held in reserve for the expected fleet.

Two thousand men reached this city this morning and embarked for Morris Island and the neighborhood.

Charleston, Friday, April 12 – The bombardment of Fort Sumpter continues. The Floating Battery and Stephens Battery are operating freely, and Fort Sumpter is returning the fire. It is reported that three war vessels are outside the bar.

Charleston, Friday, April 12 – The firing has ceased for the night, but will be renewed at daylight in the morning, unless an attempt is made to reinforce, which ample arrangements have been made to repel. The Pawnee, Harriet Lane, and a third steamer are reported off the bar.

Troops are arriving by every train.

Later Dispatches: Hostilities Still Proceeding

Charleston, Friday, April 12 – The bombardment is still going on every twenty minutes from our morters. It is supposed that Major ANDERSON is resting his men for the night. Three vessels-of-war are reported outside. They cannot get in. The sea is rough.

SCENE ON THE FLOATING BATTERY IN CHARLESTON HABOR DURING THE BOMBARDMENT OF FORT SUMTER (FROM A SKETCH BY AN OFFICER).LIBRARY OF CONGRESS.

Nobody is hurt. The floating battery works well. Troops arrive hourly. Every inlet is guarded. There are lively times here.

Charleston, Friday, April 12 – The firing on Fort Sumpter continues. There are reviving times on the "Palmetto coast."

Charleston, Friday, April 12, - 3 A.M. – It is utterly impossible to reinfo[f]ce Fort S[hr]npter, to-night, as a storm is now raging. The mortar batteries will be playing on Fort Sumpter all night.

From Another Correspondent

Charleston, Friday, April 12 – Civil war has at last begun. A terrible fight is at this moment going on between Fort Sumpter and the fortifications by which it is surrounded. The issue was submitted to Major ANDERSON of surrendering as soon as his supplies were exhausted, or of having a fire opened on him within a certain time.

This he refused to do, and accordingly, at twenty-seven minutes past four o'clock this morning Fort Moultrie began the bombardment by firing two guns. To these Major Anderson replied with three of his barbette guns, after which the batteries on Mount Pleasant, Cummings' Point, and the Floating Battery opened a brisk fire of shot and shell.

Major Anderson did not reply except at long intervals, until between 7 and 8 o'clock, when he brought into action the two tier of guns looking towards Fort Moultrie and Stevens iron battery.

Up to this hour – 3 o'clock – they have failed to produce any serious effect.

Major ANDERSON has the greater part of the day been directing his fire principally against Fort Moultrie, the Stevens and Floating Battery, these and Fort Johnson being the only five operating against him. The remainder of the batteries are held in reserve. Major ANDERSON is at present using his lower tier of casemate ordnance.

The fight is going on with intense earnestness, and will continue all night. The excitement in the community is indescribable. With the very first boom of the guns thousands rushed from their beds to the harbor front and all day every available place has been thronged by ladies and gentlemen, viewing the spectacle through their glasses.

EVACUATION OF FORT MOULTRE AND BURNING OF THE GUN CARRIAGES ON SULLIVAN'S ISLAND (FRANK LESLIE'S ILLUSTRATED NEWSPAPER). LIBRARY OF CONGRESS.

The brilliant and patriotic conduct of Major ANDERSON speaks for itself.

Business is entirely suspended. Only those stores open necessary to supply articles required by the Army. Gov. Pickens has all day been in the residence of a gentleman which commands a view of the whole scene – a most interested observer. Gen. Beauregard commands in person the entire operations.

It is reported that the Harriet Lane has received a shot through her wheelhouse. She is in the offing. No other Government ships in sight up to the present moment, but should they appear the entire range of batteries will open upon them.

Troops are pouring into the town by hundreds, but are held in reserve for the present, the force already on the island being ample. People are also arriving every moment on horseback, and by every other conveyance.

Charleston, Friday, April 12 - 6 P.M. – Capt. R.S. Parker brings dispatches from the floating battery, stating that up to this time only two have been wounded on Sullivan's Island. He had to row through Major Anderson's warmest fire in a small boat. Senator Wigfall in some manner bore dispatches to Morris Island, through the fire from Fort Sumpter. Senator

Chesnut, another member of the staff of Gen. Beauregard, fired a gun, by way of amusement, from Mount Pleasant, which made a large hole in the parapet.

Quite a number have been struck by spent pieces of shell and knocked down, but none hurt seriously. Many fragments of these missiles are already circulating in the city. The range is more perfect than in the morning and every shot from the land tells.

Three ships are visible in the offing, and it is believed an attempt will be made to-night, to throw reinforcements into Fort Sumpter in small boats. It is also thought, from the regular and frequent firing of Major Anderson, that he has a much larger force of men than was supposed. At any rate, he is fighting bravely.

There have been two rain storms during the day, but without effect upon the battle. Everybody is in a ferment. Some of those fighting are stripped to the waist.

Important Correspondence Preceding The Bombardment

Charleston, Friday, April 12 – The following is the telegraphic correspondence between the War Department at Montgomery and Gen. BEAUREGARD immediately preceding the hostilities.

The correspondence grew out of the formal notification by the Washington Government, which is disclosed in Gen. BEAUREGARD'S first dispatches.

[No. 1.]

Charleston April 8
L P. Walker, Secretary of War:

An authorized messenger from President LINCOLN, just informed Gov. PICKENS and myself that provisions will be sent to Fort Sumpter peaceably, or otherwise by force.

(Signed.) G. F. Beauregard.

[No. 2.]

Montgomery, 10th
Gen,. G. T. Beauregard, Charleston:

If you have no doubt of the authorized character of the agent who communicated to you the intention of the Washington Government to supply Fort Sumpter by force, you will at once demand its evacuation, and if this is refused, proceed in such matter as you may determine, to reduce it. Answer.

(Signed) L. P. WALKER, Sec. of War.

[No. 3.]

Charleston, April 10
L. P. WALKER, Secretary of War:
The demand will be made to-morrow at 12 o'clock.
Signed, G. F. Beauregard.

[No. 4.]

Montgomery, April 10
Gen. BEAUREGARD, Charleston:

Unless there are especial reasons connected, with your own condition, it is considered proper that you should make the demand at an early hour.

(Signed) L.P. Walker, Secretary of War

[No. 5.]

Charleston, April 10
L.P. WALKER, Secretary of War, Montgomery
The reasons are special for 12 o'clock.
(Signed) G. F. BEAUREGARD.

[No. 6.]

Charleston April 11
L.P. WALKER, Secretary of War
Demand sent at 12 o'clock. Allowed till 6 o'clock to answer
(Signed) G.F. BEAUREGARD

[No.7.]

Montgomery April 11
Gen. BEAUREGARD – Charleston
Telegraph the reply of Maj. ANDERSON
(Signed) L.P. WALKER, Secretary of War

[No. 8.]

Charleston, April 11
To L.P. WALKER, Secretary of War
Maj. ANDERSON replies:

"I have the honor to acknowledge the receipt of your communication demanding the evacuation of this fort. And to say in reply thereto, that it is a demand with which I regret that my sense of honor and my obligations to my GOVERNMENT WILL PREVENT MY COMPLIANBCE." He adds:

"Probably I will await the first shot, and if you do not batter us to pieces, we will be starved out in a few days."

Answer. G.F. Beauregard

[No. 9.]

Montgomery, April 11
Gen. BEAUREGARD – Charleston:

We do not desire needlessly to bombard Fort Sumpter, if Major ANDERSON will state the time at which, as indicated by him, he will evacuate, and agree that, in the meantime, he will not use his guns against us unless ours should be employed against Fort Sumpter. You are thus to avoid the effusion of blood.

If this or its equivalent be refused, reduce the fort as your judgment decides to be the most practicable.

(Signed) L.P. Walker, Secretaty of War

[No 10.]

Charleston, April 12
L.P. WALKER, Secretary of War

HE WOULD NOT CONSENT. I write today.

G. F. Beauregard

Mr. Fox's Visit to Fort Sumpter
Charleston, Friday, April I1

Intercepted dispatches disclose the fact that Mr. Fox, who had been allowed to visit Major Anderson on the. pledge that his purpose was pacific, employed his opportunity to devise a plan for supplying the fort by force, and that this plan had been adopted by the Washington Government, and was in progress of execution.

The Kentucky Volunteer Regiment
Louisville Friday, Apr-1 12

Dispatches have come here to hold the Kentucky Volunteer Regiment in readiness to move at a moment's notice from the War Department at Montgomery.

Excitement in Mobile
Mobile Friday, April 12

There is intense excitement and rejoicing here. Fifteen guns have been fired in honor of the attack on Fort Sumpter.

The Confederate States Congress
Montgomery, Friday, April 12

An extra session of the Confederate States Congress has been called for April 29.

The New York Times

April 15, 1861

Fort Sumpter Fallen, Particulars of the Bombardment

Charleston, Saturday, April 13 – Evening – Major Anderson has surrendered, after hard fighting, commencing at 4½ o'clock yesterday morning and continuing until five minutes to 1 to-day.

The American flag has given place to the Palmetto of South Carolina.

You have received my previous dispatches concerning the fire and the shooting away of the flagstaff. The latter event is due to Fort Moultrie, as well as the burning of the fort, which resulted from one of the hot shots fired in the morning.

NEGROES MOUNTING CANNON IN THE WORKS FOR THE ATTACK ON FORT SUMTER, 1861–MORRIS ISLAND (WILLIAM WAUD). LIBRARY OF CONGRESS.

During the conflagration, Gen Beauregard sent a boat to Major Anderson, with offers of assistance, the bearers being Colonels W. P. Miles, and Roger Peyor, of Virginia, and Lee. But before it reached him, a flag of truce bad been raised. Another boat then put off, containing Ex-Gov. Manning, Major D. R. Jones and Col. Charles Allston, to arrange the terms of surrender, which were the same as those offered on the 11th inst. These were official. They stated that all proper facilities would be afforded for the removal of Major Anderson and his command, together with the company arms and property, and all private property, to any post in the United States he might elect. The terms were not, therefore, unconditional.

Major Anderson stated that he surrendered his sword to Gen. Beauregard as the representitive of the Confederate Government. Gen. Beauregard said he would not receive it from so brave a man. He says Major Anderson made a staunch fight, and elevated himself in the estimation of every true Carolinian.

During the fire, when Major ANDERSON'S flagstaff was shot away, a boat put off from Morris Island, carrying another American flag for him to fight under – a noteworthy instance of the honor an chivalry of South Carolina Seceders, and their admiration for a brave man.

The scene in the city after the raising of the flag of truce and the surrender is indescribable; the people were perfectly wild. Men on horseback rode through the streets proclaiming the news, amid the greatest enthusiasm.

On the arrival of the officers from the fort they were marched through the streets, followed by an immense crowd, hurrahing, shouting, and yelling with excitement.

Several fire companies were immediately sent down to Fort Sumpter to put out the fire, and any amount of assistance was offered.

A regiment of eight hundred men has just arrived from the interior, and has been ordered to Morris Island, in view of as attack from the fleet which may be expected tonight.

Six vessels are reported off the bar, but the utmost indignation is expressed against them for not going to the assistance of Major Anderson when he made signals of distress.

The soldiers on Morris Island jumped on the guns every shot they received from Fort Sumpter while thus disabled, and gave three cheers for Major Anderson and groans for the fleet.

Col. Lucas, of the Governor's Staff, has just returned from Fort Sumpter, and says Major Anderson told him he had pleasanter recollections of Fort Moultrie than Fort Sumpter. Only five men were wounded, one seriously.

The flames have destroyed everything. Both officers and soldiers were obliged to lay on their faces in the casemates, to prevent suffocation.

The explosions heard in the city were from small piles of shell, which ignited from the heat.

The effect of the shot upon the fort was tremendous. The walls were battered in hundreds of places, but no breach was made.

Major Anderson expresses himself much pleased that no lives had been sacrificed, and says that to Providence alone is to be attributed the bloodless victory. He compliments the firing of the Carolinians, and the large number of exploded shells lying around attests their effectiveness.

The number of soldiers in the fort was about seventy, besides twenty-five workmen, who assisted at the guns. His stock of provisions was almost exhausted, however. He would have been starved out in two more days.

The entrance to the fort is mined, and the officers were told to be careful, even after the surrender, on account of the heat, lest it should explode.

A boat from the squadron, with a flag of truce, has arrived at Morris Island, bearing a request to be allowed to come and take Major Anderson and his forces. An answer will be given tomorrow at 9 o'clock.

The public feeling against the fleet is very strong, it being regarded as cowardly to make not even an attempt to aid a fellow officer.

Had the surrender not taken place Fort Sumpter would have been stormed tonight. The men are crazy for a fight.

The bells have been chiming all day, guns firing, ladies waving handkerchiefs, people cheering, and citizens making themselves generally demonstrative. It is regarded as the greatest day in the history of South Carolina.

What the Historians Say

Fort Sumter, which took place on April 12-14, 1861, in Charleston County, SC, was the sole operation in the Charleston Harbor campaign of April 1861. Major Robert Anderson of the U.S. Army surrendered the fort to Brig. Gen. G.F Beauregard of the Confederate Army. Fifty United States troops occupied the fort and 500 Confederates engaged it with no resulting casualties in the engagement.

On April 10, 1861, Brig. Gen. Beauregard, in command of the provisional Confederate forces at Charleston, South Carolina, demanded the surrender of the Union garrison of Fort Sumter in Charleston Harbor. Garrison commander Anderson refused. On April 12, Confederate batteries opened fire on the fort, which was unable to reply effectively. At 2:30 p.m., April 13, Major Anderson surrendered Fort Sumter, evacuating the garrison on the following day. The bombardment of Fort Sumter was the opening engagement of the American Civil War. Although there were no casualties during the bombardment, one Union artillerist was killed and three wounded (one mortally) when a cannon exploded prematurely while firing a salute during the evacuation on April 14.

This was a Confederate victory that had far reaching effects that would last four years.

2

First Manassas

First Pitched Battle of the War

Author's Commentary

July 21, 1861, was a difficult day for Henry J. Raymond, editor of *The New York Times*. Early Federal success at Bull Run spurred him to wire the *Times* that a Union victory was apparent.

As he returned to the battlefield alone for follow-up reportage, Raymond came face to face with the unbridled energy of a human force in wild retreat. The Federal army, intermixed with frightened Congressmen, disbelieving clergymen, and panic-stricken newspapermen, some careening wildly in carriages, others atop galloping horses, were in a wild race to get back to the safety of Washington.

In the panic, the incredible force of a huge, fast charging Army wagon swept up and crushed Raymond's horse-drawn carriage. Finding relief and transport with two fleeing Congressmen, he reached the capital at midnight. Because of earlier newspaper reports, Washington was largely under the impression of a victory. It had yet to receive news of the reversal.

Raymond's ordeal left him sunburned, filthy, and bereft of his distinguished demeanor. Hastily, he prepared to telegraph the *Times* of the disastrous turn of events. The censor promptly suppressed it. He was too late to countermand his earlier dispatch. Raymond caught the next train to New York, entered his office, and wrote the story headlined "Disaster To The National Army". The first battle of Manassas was the last battle Henry J. Raymond covered. He did visit General McClellan during the Peninsula Campaign, but his journalistic efforts were exercised at the editor's desk and the publisher's office during the remaining years of the Civil War.

July 18, 1861: From the *Charleston Mercury*

Manassas Junction, VA. Special to the *Charleston Mercury*. A battle has at last been fought and a great victory gained by the Confederate troops. Yesterday morning, our scouts having brought in the news that the Invaders were advancing in heavy columns towards Fairfax Court House, the Southern pickets at that place were withdrawn and fell back towards Bull Run, where a large body of the Confederate troops were concentrated and strongly entrenched.

At daybreak this morning, the enemy first appeared in force at Bull Run, where it crosses the road, about three miles northwest of Manassas Junction, and attempted to pass. Our troops immediately opened fire, which was replied to by the enemy, and the engagement soon became general.

On our side, Gen. BEAUREGARD commanded in person. It is not yet know what United States officer conducted the attack. The fighting extended along Bull Run for the distance of one mile.

The battle lasted, with intermissions, during the greater part of the day, the United States troops being three times repulsed, with heavy loss, and three times rallying again to the attack. At four oin the afternoon the battle reached its height. The enemy finally gave way and retreated in great confusion towards Alexandria. At five othe firing had ceased altogether.

The First and Seventeenth Regiments of Virginia Volunteers were conspicuous in the action, and behaved nobly. The Washington Artillery, of New Orleans, under Major WALTON, also occupied a prominent position, and worked their batteries with tremendous effect.

The loss on our side was but slight. WILLIAM SANGSTER, one of our riflemen, was killed. Capt. DULANY, of the Seventeenth Virginia Regiment, was wounded in the arm. Col. MOORE was also slightly wounded.

An United States officer of high rank was killed and his horse taken. Upon his person was found $700 in gold.

A shot passed through the kitchen of the house where Gen. BEAUREGARD was at dinner. The enemy, it is supposed, discovered his whereabouts. They also fired into our hospital, notwithstanding that they must have seen the yellow flag flying.

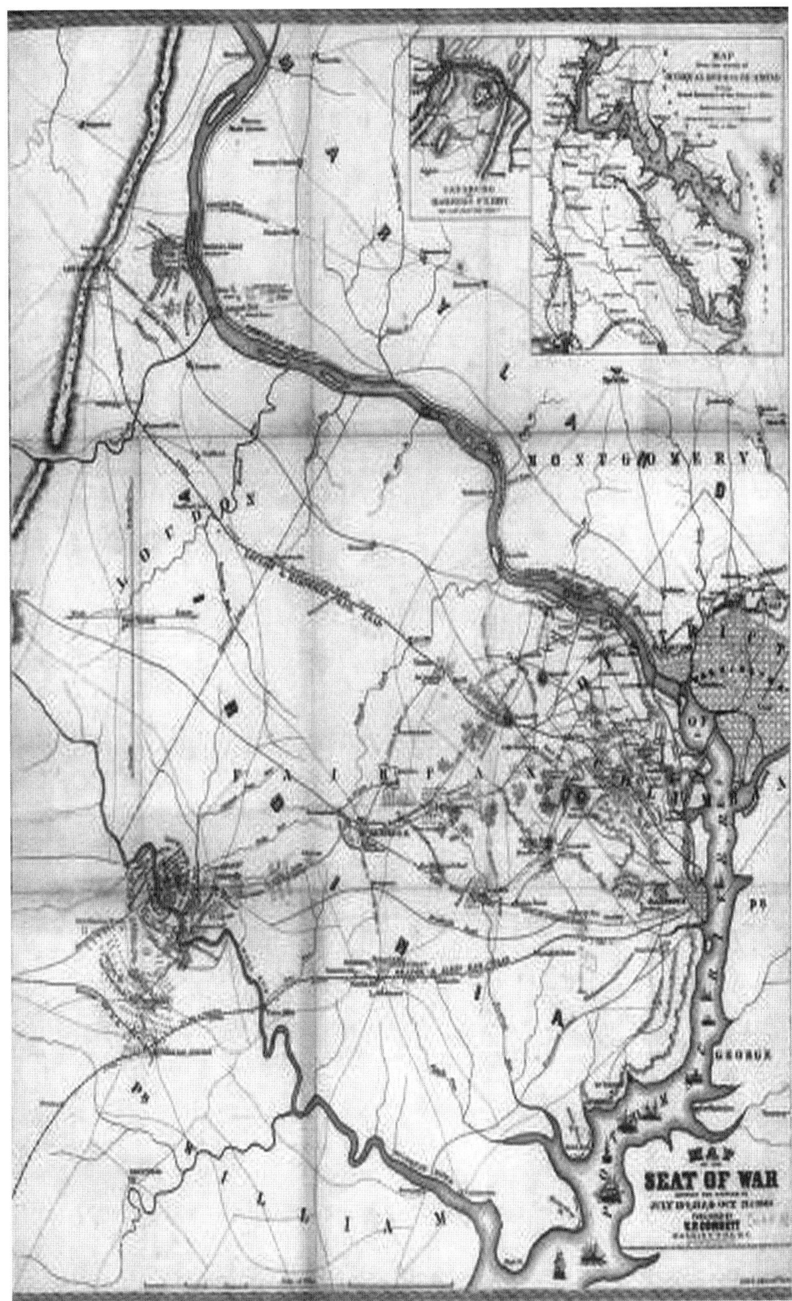

Battle of Bull Run: map of the seat of war, showing battles of July 18 & 21st, 1861 (Corbett, V.P.). Library of Congress.

We have no authentic information as yet concerning the number of the forces engaged or the amount of the loss of the enemy. It is, however, known to have been heavy. The impression prevails here that the battle will be renewed tomorrow.

Manassas Junction, Saturday Night, July 20 – During the greater part of yesterday afternoon the enemy was busy in burying the dead near Bull Run. We have, however, information that the Northern forces are concentrating against us in immense numbers. They are throwing up earthworks and planting batteries with great energy, as if to renew the attack. Our troops await the onset with the utmost confidence.

Gen. PATTERSON, with his entire force, has abandoned Martinsburg, and is now hastening to form a junction with McDOWELL. Troops are being thrown across the river in heavy bodies from Washington, and everything indicates that our positions will be attacked speedily by an overwhelming force.

Gen. BEAUREGARD yesterday afternoon issued an order that all civilians, women and children should leave Manassas Junction forthwith. He evidently anticipates a great battle here tomorrow.

The Battle

Manassas Junction, Sunday Night, July 21, 7 ½ o. – A great battle has been fought today at the Stone Bridge, on Bull Run, near this place. The Southern troops are again victorious. The slaughter on both sides was terrific.

Gen. JOHNSTON, who had been summoned from Winchester to come with all haste to the assistance of Gen. BEAUREGARD, arrived with his entire force in time to take part in the battle.

Gen. BEAUREGARD had his horse shot under him, while leading Hampton Legion into position.

Gen. JOHNSTON, during the thickest of the fight, seized the colors of a wavering regiment and rallied them in person, to the charge.

It is impossible at this moment to estimate the number of the dead and wounded. It is reported that the commander of the United States forces, Gen. McDOWELL, is mortally wounded.

FIRST AND SECOND RHOIDE ISLAND AND SEVENTY FIRST NEW YORK REGIMENTS, WITH THEIR ARTILLERY, ATTACHING REBEL BATTERIES (ALFRED WAUD) LIBRARY OF CONGRESS.

On our side, Col. FRANCIS S. BARTOW, of Georgia, who was acting Brigadier-General, was mortally wounded, and is since reported dead.

The battle began at 8 a. m., and lasted until 6 p. m.

The enemy is now in full retreat, and hotly pursued by our cavalry.

Second Despatch

Manassas Junction, July 21, 11½ op. m. – Amid the bustle and excitement here it is exceedingly difficult to get the correct particulars of the great battle of today. I have, however, obtained a few additional facts, which will be interesting to your readers.

The enemy opened their batteries of heavy artillery and small field pieces, at McLeanFord, about eight oin the morning. The engagement above the Stone Bridge, on Bull Run, began about ten o. The enemyforce, as near as can be ascertained, was at least 50,000. Our own force was but 20,000.

General N. G. EVANS, of South Carolina, led the Brigade first into action. Among the southern forces prominently engaged were Colonel SLOANFourth Regiment, Colonel KERSHAW Second Regiment and Colonel WADE HAMPTON-Legion, all of South Carolina Volunteers. Only three men were wounded in Col. KERSHAWRegiment. In Col. SLOAN-Regiment and HAMPTON Legion the loss of life was greater.

Adjutant THEODORE G. BARKER and Captain JAMES CONNER of the Washington Light Infantry, HAMPTONLegion, were slightly wounded. Lieut. Col. B. J. JOHNSON, of the Legion, was killed. Captains EARLE and ECHOLS were slightly wounded.Men never fought more desperately than did ours today. We have captured eighteen pieces of artillery, also from 300 to 400 prisoners. The number of killed and wounded cannot be ascertained with any accuracy until tomorrow. Our loss is estimated at two hundred killed and three hundred wounded, while the loss of the enemy could not have been less than several thousand. These figures, however, may be wide of the mark, for the lie of battle was extended, and it was almost dark when the enemy gave way.

The Washington Artillery of New Orleans was again in the foremost place, and did most effective work. Their fire fell upon the ranks of the foe with murderous effect.

The Oglethorpe Light Infantry, of Savannah, were cut to pieces. Colonel BARTOW'S fine Regiment of Georgians were nearly annihilated.

Gen. BARNARD E. BEE, of South Carolina was mortally wounded. Colonel WADE HAMPTON was slightly wounded.

Rebel Account of the First Fight

Louisville, Monday, June 22 – A special dispatch to the Nashville Union from Manassas, 18th. says that at the fight at Bull's Run Gen. Beauregard commanded in person. The enemy was repulsed three tines in great confusion and loss. The Washington Artillery of New Orleans, with seven guns, engaged Sherman's fifteen guns, and, after making the latter change position fifteen times, silenced and forced them to retire. Large quantities of arms were taken. Our loss was trifling. Maj. Harrison and two privates were killed. Capts. Dulany, Chittman and three privates were wounded. A National officer of high rank was killed. and $700 in gold taken from his body.

From *the New York Times*

Washington, Monday Morning, July 22, 1861: Special to *The New York Times* – I came in from Centreville last evening for the express purpose of sending you the latest intelligence of the great battle of yesterday. I left Centreville at half-past 5 and reached here at midnight. I sent a dispatch to the office, but, as it is to be subjected to the censorship of the Government, which gives no hint of what it refuses permission to pass, I have no means of knowing whether its contents reached you or not. I must therefore repeat its contents.

The battle yesterday was one of the most severe and sanguinary ever fought on the Continent and it ended in the failure of the Union troops to hold all the positions which they sought to carry, and which they actually did carry, and in their retreat to Centreville, where they have made a stand and where Gen. Mc Dowell believes that they are able to maintain themselves.

As I telegraphed you yesterday, the attack was made in three columns, two of which, however, were mainly feints, intended to amuse and occupy the enemy, while the substantial work was done by the third. It has been known for a long time that the range of hills which border the small, swampy stream known as Bull's Run, had been very thoroughly and extensively fortified by the rebels-that batteries had been planted at every available point, usually concealed in the woods and bushes which abound in that vicinity, and covering every way of approach to the region beyond. These are the advanced defenses of Manassas Junction, which is some three miles further off. Until these were carried, no approach could be made to that place; and after they should -be carried others of a similar character would have to be overcome at every point where they could be erected. The utmost that military skill and ingenuity could accomplish for the defense of this point was done. Gen. MCDOWELL was unwilling to make an attack directly in face of these batteries, as they would be of doubtful issue, and must inevitably result in a very serious loss of life. After an attack had been resolved upon, therefore, he endeavored to find some way of turning the position. His first intention was to do this on the Southern side-to throw a strong column into the place from that direction, while a feigned attack should be made in front. On Thursday, when the troops were advanced to Centreville, it was found that the roads on the south side of these positions were almost impracticable—that they were narrow, crooked and stony, and that it would be almost impossible to bring up enough artillery to be effective in the time required.

A CONFEDERATE BULL BATTERY PREVIOUS TO THE BATTLE OF BULL RUN (UNATTRIBUTED) LIBRARY OF CONGRESS.

This original plan was, therefore, abandoned; and Friday was devoted to an examination by the topographical engineers of the Northern side of the position. Maj. BARNARD and Capt. WHIPPLE reconnoitered the place for miles around and reported that the position could be entered by a path coming from the north, though it was somewhat long and circuitous. This was selected, therefore, as the mode and point of attack.

On Saturday the troops were all brought close-up to Centreville and all needful preparations were made for the attack which was intended for the :next day. Yesterday morning, therefore, the Army marched by two roads – Col. RICHARDSON with his command taking the Southern, which leads to Bull's Run, and Gen. Tyler the Northern–running parallel to it at a distance of about a mile and a half. The movement commenced at about 3 o'clock. I got up at a little before 4, and found the long line of troops extended far out on either road. I took the road by which Colonel Hunter with his command, and Gen. McDowell and staff, had gone, and pushed on directly for the front. After going out about two miles Colonel Hunter turned to the.right–marching obliquely towards the Run, which he was to cross some four miles higher up and then come down upon the entrenched positions of the enemy on the other side.

At half-past 11 we heard HUNTER'S guns on the opposite height, over a mile to the right. He was answered by batteries there, and then followed the sharp, rattling volleys of musketry, as their infantry became engaged. The firing was now incessant. Hunter had come upon them suddenly and formed his line of battle in an open field, at the right of the road. The enemy drew up to oppose him, but he speedily drove them to retreat and followed them up with the greatest vigor and rapidity.

Meantime, for some three hours previous, we had seen long lines of dense dust rising from the roads leading from Manassas, and, with the glass, we could very clearly perceive that they were raised by the constant and steady stream of reinforcements, which continued to pour in nearly the whole day. The Sixty-Ninth, Seventy-ninth, Second and Eighth, New-York-the First, Second and Third Connecticut, and the Second Wisconsin, were brought forward in advance of the wood and marched across the field to the right, to go to Col. HUNTER's support. They crossed the intervening stream and drew up in a small open field, separated from Col. HUNTER's column by a dense wood, which was filled with batteries and infantry. Our guns continued to play upon the woods which thus concealed the enemy, and aided materially in clearing them for the advance. Going down to the extreme front of the column, I could watch the progress of Col. HUNTER, marked by the constant roar of artillery and the roll of musketry, as he pushed the rebels back from point to point. At 1 o'clock he had driven them out of the woods and across the road which was the prolongation of that on which we stood. Here, by the side of their batteries, the rebels made a stand. They planted their flag directly in the road, and twice charged across it upon our men, but without moving them an inch. They were met by a destructive fire, and were compelled to fall still further back. Gradually the point of fire passed further away, until the dense clouds of smoke which marked the progress of the combat were at least half a mile to the left of what had been the central position of the rebels.

It was now 2 o'clock. I was at the advanced point of the front of our column, some hundred rods beyond the woods, in which the few troops then there were drawn up, when I decided to drive back to the town, for the purpose of sending you my dispatch. As I passed up the road the balls and shell from the enemy began to fall with more than usual rapidity. I did not see the point from which they came but meeting Capt. Ayres, he said he was about to bring up his battery, supported by the Ohio Brigade, under Gen. Schenck to repel a rumored attempt of cavalry to outflank this column. As I went forward he passed down. Gen, Schenck's Brigade was at once drawn up across the road, and Capt.ayres guns were planted in a knoll at the left, when a powerful body of rebels, with a heavy battery, came down from the direction of Bull's Run, and engaged this force with tremendous effect. I went to Centreville, sent off my dispatch, and started with all speed to return, intending to go with our troops upon what had been the hotly contested field, never doubting for a moment that it would remain in their hands.

I had gone but a quarter of a mile when we met a great number of fugitives, and our carriage soon became entangled in a mass of baggage-wagons, the officer in charge of which told me it was useless to go in that direction, as our troops wore retreating. Not crediting the story, which was utterly inconsistent with what I had seen but a little while before, I continued to push on. I soon met Quartermaster Stetson, of the Fire Zouaves, who told me, bursting into tears, that his Regiment had been utterly cut to pieces, that the Colonel and Lieutenant Colonel were both killed, and that our troops had actually been repulsed. I still tried to proceed, but the advancing columns rendered it impossible, and I turned about. Leaving my carriage, I went to a high point of ground and saw, by the dense cloud of dust which rose over each of the three roads by which the three columns of the Army had advanced, that they were all on the retreat. Sharp discharges of cannon in their rear indicated that they were being pursued. I waited half an hour or an. to observe the troops and batteries as they arrived and then started for Washington to send my dispatch and write this letter. As I came past the hill on which the Secessionists had their entrenchments less than a week ago, I saw our forces taking up positions for a defense if they should be assailed.

Such is a very rapid and general history of yesterday's engagement. I am unable to be precise or profuse in matters of detail, and must leave these to a future letter.

I hear nothing, on every side, but the warmest and heartiest commendation of our troops. They fought like veterans. The rebels did not, in a single instance, stand before them in a charge and were shaken by every volley of their musketry. I du not mean to praise any one at the expense of another. The Sixty-ninth fought with splendid and tenacious courage, They charged batteries two or three times, and would have taken and held them but for the reinforcements that were constantly and steadily pouring in. Indeed it was to this fact alone that the comparative success of the rebels is due. We had not over 20,000 men in action, the rest being held behind as reserves at Centreville; while the enemy must have numbered at least 60,000.

Washington Monday, July 22: Special to *The New York Times* – Stragglers from the Army create great but needless excitement, by stories that the rebels are coming to Washington. There is not the slightest cause for any such apprehension. The Army is falling back upon Arlington, and new regiments are constantly arriving from the North.

It is not easy to account fur the panic which occasioned the first movement of retreat, but the most probable account is, that it was caused by a charge of cavalry, which was repulsed by the regiment upon which it was made, but which threw another, upon which in turn, it fell into confusion.

The Army, in its retreat from Centreville, was protected in rear by Col. Milks' Reserve.

Some fifty or one hundred of the Fire Zouaves have just arrived here. The rumor is circulated that this is all that is left of the regiment, but this is not so. These are only those who have come on singly in advance.

Exaggerated statements about the losses of individual regiments increase the excitement and cause heedless grief. The official list will he published as speedily as possible. All access to the Army across the Potomac is impossible.

What the Historians Say

First Manassas, known also as First Bull Run, took place in Fairfax and Prince William counties in Virginia on July 21, 1861. It was the third and final engagement in the Manassas Campaign and the first large battle. The first two conflicts were at Hoke's Run and Blackburn's Ford and were repulsions of reconnaisance forces.

The principal commanders were Brig. Gen. Irvin McDowell of the Federal Army and Brigadier Generals Joseph E. Johnston and P.G.T. Beauregard of the Confederate Army. 28,450 men in the Union Army and 32, 230 Confederates clashed that day resulting in 2,950 and 1,750 casualties respectively.

This was the first major land battle of the armies in Virginia. On July 16, 1862, the untried Union army under Brig. Gen. Irvin McDowell marched from Washington against the Confederate army, which was drawn up behind Bull Run beyond Centreville. On the 21st, McDowell crossed at Sudley Ford and attacked the Confederate left flank on Matthews Hill. Fighting raged throughout the day as Confederate forces were driven back to Henry Hill. Late in the afternoon, Confederate reinforcements (one brigade arriving by rail from the Shenandoah Valley) extended and broke the Union right flank. The Federal retreat rapidly deteriorated into a rout. Although victorious, Confederate forces were too disorganized to pursue. Confederate Gen. Bee and Col. Bartow were killed. Thomas J. Jackson earned the nom de guerre "Stonewall." By July 22, the shattered Union army reached the safety of Washington. This battle convinced the Lincoln administration that the war would be a long and costly affair. McDowell was relieved of command of the Union army and replaced by Maj. Gen. George B. McClellan, who set about reorganizing and training the troops.

This was a major victory for the Confederate Army, and it had a decisive effect not only on the outcome of the Manassas Campaign but on the outcome of the war for it propelled the two sides of the conflict into a larger and much longer war than either side originally anticipated.

First Battle of Bull Run, Sunday Afternoon, July 21, 1861 (J. Brown) Library of Congress.

3

Fort Donelson

General Grant's First Important Victory

Author's Commentary

The capture of Fort Donelson was the first major Union success. The newspaper coverage from the battle site had been sparse because only a handful of northern reporters had been there, and it was not a pleasant four days for them. The weather was foul and rations were hard to come by. Some of the correspondents even took to firing arms at the Confederate garrison.

Franc Wilkie of *The New York Times* had tried it, too, but finding that his fire was being returned and seeing the splinters flying from the logs in front of him, deduced that his obligation to *The New York Times* came before his military instincts. He hastily retired from active combat.

When Fort Donelson had fallen, the news got out sparingly but enough to brighten Union hopes. Celebrations were held in cities from Chicago to New York and Washington. There was corresponding gloom in Richmond and the cities to the south.

Most newspapers got their information telegraphically by way of Captain Walke of the U.S. Navy, who was the commander of the *Carondelet*. When the ship arrived at Cairo, Illinois, the morning after the surrender, Walke announced the news to all dockside that Fort Donelson had been taken. The telegraph operator at Cairo, the nearest telegraph office to Fort Donelson, clicked his keys and sent the message to the world.

The *Charleston Mercury*, upon hearing the news, accepted it stoically but with resolve that further sacrifice would correct matters, while taking a swipe at the Yankees in the east as being an inferior lot to the hardy frontiersmen of the west who manged to take Fort Donelson.

Feb. 1862: From the *Charleston Mercury*

The crisis of the war is upon us. The fire with which our foes have so long threatened to surround us has been lighted at last, and whichever way we turn, we find the horrors of a brutal and relentless warfare pressing to our hearthstones. The events of the next fifteen days will, probably, have a controlling influence upon the duration of the war.

Nobly are our troops upon the banks of the Cumberland vindicating the reputation of Volunteer State. The men whom they have to face are not the dastard Yankees who fled in terror from the Plains of Manassas. The assailants of Fort Donelson are made of sterner stuff. They are the hardy frontiersmen of the Northwest, who are not wont to flinch in the day of danger. To drive back such men at the point of the bayonet is a task worthy of the prowess of our brave volunteers.

In North Carolina, the people of that sturdy old Commonwealth are rallying with one impulse: to beat back the invader from their shores. We shall have a sharp work there, ere long.

The ball will, ere long, open in our own neighborhood. Savannah is already a beleaguered city, and there are indications that Charleston, too, is to be attacked. Let our people, if they would avert desolation from their city, and destruction from whatever they hold most dear, range themselves, at once, in the ranks of the State defenders.

The *Charleston Mercury*

February 18, 1862

Fort Donelson

Our telegraphic columns bring us the intelligence that Fort Donelson has surrendered, that Nashville has been taken, and thirteen thousand of our troops have been captured. Making all due allowance for exaggeration and panic, it is reasonable to suppose that we have suffered a severe defeat in the West, and have lost our military position, together with a number of our troops. What then? No doubt it is a severe blow – well delivered and effective. But what then? It is only what we have foreshadowed for many months past in our journal, and only what was to be expected by reasonable men, who, unawed and calmly, would review the field of operations and all the circumstances of our position. We have said our say on the subject, and pronounced the defensive system of warfare adopted by our authorities, situated as we were with a coast of five thousand miles to defend, without a navy, with a limited supply of arms, and with our ports blockaded, as a monstrous absurdity, necessarily involving weakness and much unnecessary disaster and prolongation of the war. But others were wiser than ourselves. We were equally alarmists and precipitate.

The fruits of that policy are before us. They are disastrous enough, as we had feared. But our business now is not with the past. What is the burthen of the future? It has accumulated much during these last six months of inaction on our part; but it is far from insupportable, yet. There is power in the South, and there is nerve in the South to do much, and to endure much. We must pay for our inaction; but it brings with it a lesson to string every heart to redeem our errors. Let every man, who can strike a blow in defence of his household and his home, spring to his arms. Let us realize the work before us, and let us go forward into the breach, like men. Italy was overrun by the Carthaginians, under HANNIBAL, and Spain by NAPOLEON – perhaps the two greatest military leaders in ancient and modern times. Yet, both were defeated, and driven back from the soil they occupied. Prussia, likewise, was overrun by France, Russia and Austria; yet were they driven back by FREDERICK, after bloody defeats on his part, leaving twenty and thirty thousand dead men on the field. Our own revolution, in 1776, is strikingly illustrative of a similar lesson.

We must fight to retrieve the past – blood must be shed. We must fight like desperate men. But there is nothing before us to blench the hearts of resolute and earnest men. We must be up and doing, daring and achieving. The time for action is upon us – upon every one of us. Let us but act, act with bold decision and undertaking, and not stand still in passive abatement, and the time is not far distant when the Northern horde will learn the temerity of their aggressions.

FORT DONELSON, SHOWING CONFEDERATE EARTHWORKS BEFORE THE BATTLE OF FEBRUARY 1862. LIBRARY OF CONGRESS.

The *Charleston Mercury*

March 12, 1862

News by Telegraph from Richmond

Richmond, March 11

President DAVIS today sent a message to Congress stating that he had suspended Generals FLOYD and PILLOW from their respective commands, until they shall give more satisfactory accounts of their action at Fort Donelson. The President is not satisfied with their report. The President, in his message, says that neither the reports of FLOYD or PILLOW state that reinforcements were asked for. He further says that it is not shown that their position could not be evacuated, and the whole army saved, as well as a part of it; nor is it shown by what authority two senior Generals abandoned their responsibility, by transferring the command to a junior officer.

The official reports of the great naval battle in Hampton Roads have been received. Our entire squadron carried a total of only 21 guns, while the United States frigate *Cumberland* had 24, the *Congress* 50, the *St. Lawrence* 50, the *Minnesota* and *Roanoke* each 40, besides the land batteries at Newport News and the small United States gunboats, armed with heavy rifled guns. The action lasted three hours. The flag of the United States frigate *Congress*, and the sword of her commander, are now in our Navy Department. The casualties of the Confederates are: Capt. BUCHANAN, wounded in the thigh with a Minie ball, seriously; Lieut. MINOR wounded in the left side, not dangerously; two men killed and five wounded. Congress has passed a vote of thanks to Com. BUCHANAN, and the officers and men of the *Virginia* and other Confederate vessels, for their unsurpassed gallantry in the late action.

The House of Representatives has passed a resolution advising planters not to put in any cotton or tobacco this season, but to exert themselves to raise the largest possible amount of provisions, hogs, etc.

The Senate has passed a bill to organize the Supreme Court of the Confederate States.

From *The New York Times*

February 19, 1862

The following dispatch, giving a somewhat detailed account of occurrences at Fort Donelson – on Saturday and Sunday, with the correspondence between the commanding officers of the opposing forces preceding the surrender, and the names of some of the National killed and wounded – appeared in but a portion of our morning edition yesterday, owing to the late hour at which it was received:

Chicago, Monday, Feb. 17

A special from Fort Donelson says: The forces were about equal in numbers, but the rebels had all the advantage of position, being well fortified on two immense hills, with their fort near the river, on a lower piece of ground. From the foot of their intrenchments, rifle-pits and ahattis extended up the river, behind the town of Dover. Their fortifications on the land side, back from the river, were at least four miles in length. Their water battery, in the centre of the fortifications, where it came down to the river, mounted nine heavy guns.

The rebels were sure of success. In any other cause and against less brave troops, they could easily have held the position against a hundred thousand men.

The business of getting the different brigades in position for attaching the new arrivals to the different divisions took up the greater portion of Friday night.

At daylight Saturday, the enemy opened on the Eighteenth Illinois, when Col. OGLESBY'S Brigade was soon engaged, and was soon followed by WALLACE'S and MCARTHUR'S Brigades, the latter acting under McClernand as the position of the troops had been changed during the night, and Gen. Grant has been called away during the night to the gunboats.

The movements of all the troops, except those attached to MCCLERNAND'S division, were made without anything except general orders.

At suggestion from Gen. MCCLERNAND, Gen.WALLACE sent up four regiments to support his division, who were nearly out of ammunition.

From the commencement till near 10 o'clock the fighting was terrific. The troops on the right were disposed as follows: MCAUKEN'S Brigade, composed of the Ninth, Twelfth, Forty-first, Seventeenth, and Nineteenth Illinois Regiments; next Gen. OGLESBY'S Brigade, consisting of the Eighth, Thirteenth, Twenty-ninth, Thirtieth, and Thirty-first Illinois Regiments, SCHWARTZ'S and DRESSER'S batteries; next was Gen. WALLACE'S Brigade, of the Eleventh, Twentieth, Forty-fifth, and Forty-eighth Illinois Regiments. These three brigades composed Gen. MCCLERNAND'S Division, and bore the brunt of the battle.

It was found that the enemy was concentrating his main force to turn our right, which was done by our men getting out of ammunition, and in the confusion of getting up reinforcements, retreating about half a mile. As soon as the division, which had stood its ground manfully for three hours, retired, the enemy occupied the field, when Gen. GRANT ordered Gen. SMITH to move forward his division and storm the enemy's works on our left. This order was obeyed with great alacrity, and soon the cheers of our daring soldiery were heard, and the old flag displayed from within the enemy's intrenchments.

Gen. GRANT then sent word to Gen. MCCLERNAND that Gen. SMITH was within the enemy's intrenchments and ordering their forces to move forward and renew the attack on the right. One of Gen. WALLACE'S Brigades – the Eleventh Indiana, Eighth Missouri and some Ohio Regiments – was rapidly thrown into position and Company A, of the Chicago Light Artillery, was planted in the road; and as the rebels, supposing we were in retreat, came, yelling, out of their works into the road, the Chicago boys poured a hailstorm of grape and canister into their ranks, slaughtering dozens of them.

Simultaneously with this the infantry commenced firing at will, and the rebels went pell-mell back into their works, our men advancing and taking possession of the ground lost, and a hill besides. Fresh troops who had not been in the action were then thrown forward, and as the shades of night drew on were in a strong position to participate in a simultaneous attack to be made on Sunday morning.

Gens. OGLESBY, WALLACE AND McARTHUR'S brigades did the hardest fighting, and have suffered terribly. They would undoubtedly have held their first position but for the failure of their ammunition. The ammunition wagons were some distance off the hills preventing their being moved.

Some of our best officers and men have gone to their long homes.

Searching by torch-light for wounded soldiers after a Rebel assault on Schwartz's battery during the Union siege of Fort Donelson Tennessee (Harper's Weekly) Library of congress.

How the Surrender was Made

At daylight the advance was made, and when the full light of day broke forth, white flags were hung in many places on the enemy's works.

An officer at a convenient point was informed that they had stacked their arms and surrendered early in the morning, the following correspondence having passed between the commanders:

Gen. BRUCKNER to Gen. GRANT
Headquarters, Fort Donalson, Feb. 16

To Brig. Gen. U.S. GRANT, commanding United States forces near Fort Donelson.

Sir: In consideration of all the circumstances governing the present situation of affairs at this station, I propose to the commanding officer of the Federal forces the appointment of Commissioners to agree upon terms of capitulation of the forces at this post under my command. In that view, I suggest an armistice until 12 o'clock today.

I am, very respectfully, your obedient servant,
[L] B BUCKNER, Brig. Gen., C.S.A.

Gen. GRANT to Gen. BUCKNER
Headquartes on the Field
Fort Donelson, Feb. 16

To Gen. S. [H.] BUCKNER

Sir: Yours, of this date, proposing an armistice and the appointment of Commissioners to settle the terms of capitulation is just received. *No terms except unconditional surrender and immediate surrender can be accepted.* I propose to move immediately upon your works. I am very respectfully, your obedient servant,
U. S. GRANT, Brig. Gen, Com'd'g.

Gen. Buckner to Gen. Grant
HEADQUARTERS, DOVER, Tenn., Sunday, Feb
Brig. Gen. U. S. GRANT, U. S.A.

SIR – The distribution of the forces under my command incident to an *unexpected change of commanders* and the overwhelming force under your command compels me, *notwithstanding the brilliant Confederate arms,* to accept the ungenerous and unchivalrous terms which you propose.

I am, Sir, your servant

S. B. BUCKNER, *Brig. Gen.*, C. S.

Our force was soon in the enemy's works, when the rebel officers gave up their swords. The bulk of the rebels are chagrined as they knew of the surrender long before our men were apprised of it. PILLOW and FLOYD had planned and executed their escape during the night, taking with them Floyd's Brigade and a few favorites, occupying what few small steamer they had. The prisoners are loud in their denunciations of the runaways. Many of them acknowledged the hopelessness of their cause, and intimate a *willingness to take an oath of allegiance, and return to their homes.* To the question put to an officer, as to how many prisoners we had, he *replied "You have all out of twenty five thousand, who were not killed, or did not escape."*

What the Historians Say

The battle at Fort Donelson occurred on February 11-16, 1862, in Stewart County, Tennessee. It was the second battle in the Federal Penetration up the Cumberland and Tennessee Rivers Campaign of 1862. It followed the battle and Union victory at Fort Henry that occurred a week previously on February 6th.

The principal commanders were Brig. Gen. Ulysses S. Grant and Flag Officer A.H. Foote leading the United States forces. Commanding the Confederate forces were Brig. Gen. John B. Floyd, Brig. Gen. Gideon Pillow, and Brig. Gen. Simon B. Buckner.

The forces engaged consisted of the U.S. Army in the Field and the Confederate garrison in Fort Donelson. The estimated casualties were 2,331 and 15,067 respectively. After capturing Fort Henry on February 6, 1862, Brig. Gen. Ulysses S. Grant advanced cross-country to invest Fort Donelson. On February 16, 1862, after the failure of their all out attack aimed at breaking through Grant's investment lines, the fort's 12,000 man garrison surrendered unconditionally. This was a major victory for Brig. Gen. Ulysses S. Grant and a catastrophe for the South. It ensured that Kentucky would stay in the Union and opened up Tennessee for a Northern advance along the Tennessee and Cumberland Rivers. Grant received a promotion to Major General for his victory and attained stature in the Western Theater, earning the nom de guerre "Unconditional Surrender."

Fort Donelson was a major victory for the Union. It was its first significant victory and brought distinction to Grant.

4

Hampton Roads

The Battle That Changed the Nature of Naval Warfare

Author's Commentary

When, on April 17, 1861, Virginia seceded from the Union, the Confederate Navy took over the Gosport Naval Yard at Portsmouth. They raised several scuttled Federal ships, including the *Merrimac.*

On March 8, 1862, the *Merrimac*, now an armored Goliath of 275 feet and 3200 tons, complete with a brutish ramming device, sailed into Hampton Roads to tackle the wooden-hulled ships of the Blockading Squadron of the Union Navy. It headed straight for the *Cumberland*. On board the nearby *Minnesota*, a reporter for *The New York Times* saw the action up close. In a dispatch worthy of Stendhal, he described the scene:

"Now she nears the *Cumberland* sloop-of-war, silent and still, wierd [sic] and mysterious, like some devilish and superhuman monster, or the horrid creation of a nightmare. Now, but a biscuit toss from the ship, and from the sides of both pour out a living tide of fire and smoke, of solid shot and heavy shell. We see from the ship's scuppers running streams of crimson gore. Now the ram has taken her position bow on, and slowly she moves and horribly upon the doomed vessel. Like a rhinoceros she sinks down her head and frightful horn, and with a dead, soul-rendering crunch she pierces her on the starboard bow, lifting her up as a man does a toy."

On the following day, Goliath met David. The *Monitor*, a fraction of the size of the *Merrimac*, neutralized the larger ship with a four-hour display of maneuverability, speed, and firepower from its revolving gun turret.The *Monitor's* gun turret, which changed naval warfare the world over, is considered one of the most important innovations in warship design.

Mar. 13, 1862: From the *Charleston Mercury*

THE GREAT NAVAL VICTORY—The Virginia papers teem with additional details of the recent Southern naval victory in Hampton Roads. We collate from various sources the more interesting portions of these accounts. The following graphic narrative of the battle on Sunday (written by an eye-witness), is taken from the *Norfolk Day Book* of Tuesday.

The Battle on Sunday

On Sunday morning faint cannonading was heard below. When the thick vapors that overhung Hampton Roads lifted, Lieutenant Commanding C.A.P.R. Jones got under weigh, and began his attack upon the enemy. At 10 o the steamer Harmony shoved off from the Dock Yard and shot down the harbor. After threading our way through the barriers, and passing the forts, dark, as on the previous day with masses of soldiers of all arms, we saw a strange picture—a picture at once novel and beautiful. The gunboats were lying in line of battle under SewellPoint, with the thick masses of smoke floating lazily above them, firing now and then a shot, while the Virginia, looking grim and mysterious as before, steamed in pursuit of a wonderful looking thing that was justly compared to a prodigious box on a plank, and box being of a Plutonian blackness.

THE NAVAL ENGAGEMENT BETWEEN THE MERRIMAC AND THE MONITOR AT HAMPTON ROADS ON THE 9TH OF MARCH 1862 (E. SACHSE) LIBRARY OF CONGRESS.

The Fight with the Ericsson Battery

At first we could see the great puffs of white smoke jetting out, now from the Virginia, now from the Minnesota, and at long intervals from the black box.But these white wreathes of smoke blew off to seaward without a sound reaching us, for the wind had now risen, and the warm calm of early morning was succeeded by a piercing Northeaster. Away we went across Craney Island flats, and presently we could hear the guns, louder and louder. But the strange looking battery, with its black, revolving cupola, fled before the Virginia. It was, as somebody said, fighting a ghost. Now she ran down towards Old Point, now back towards Newport News, now approached to fire, and then ran away to load, but evidently fighting shy, and afraid of being put 'chancery,' as the pugilists call it, by her powerful pursuer. The projectiles from her great piece of ordnance, a 10 inch solid shot gun, came dancing across the water with a series of short, sharp pops, which made a music more exciting than melodious. Now she overshot the Virginia, and the spray flew more than 30 feet high. Now she shot to this side, now to that. Now she steamed close up, and hit her fairly. In one of these encounters we thought her iron castle had been shot away, but when the smoke cleared away, there it was and the long, plank-like hull in shore again, driving along like the 'Flying Dutchman.'

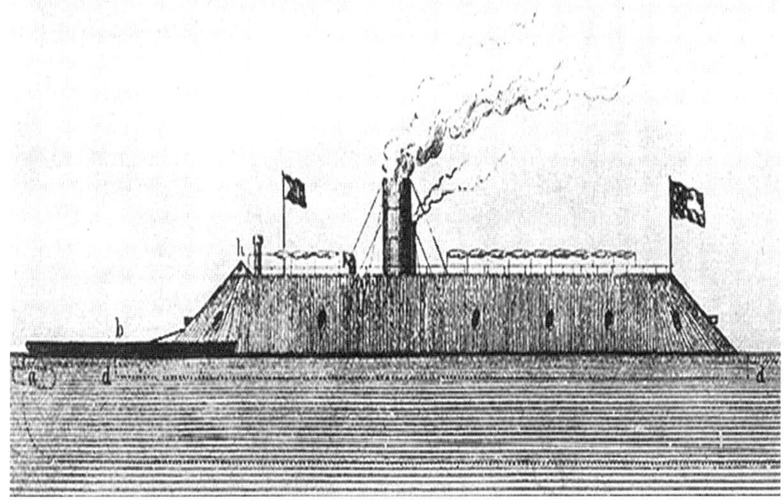

SKETCH PLAN OF THE CSS VIRGINIA (LT. B.L. BLACKFORD, MARCH, 1862) NAVAL HISTORICAL CENTER.

The Virginia Aground

Meanwhile the Virginia crept up towards the Minnesota, crept up and paused in that mysterious silence which fell upon her at all times—a silence awfully impressive to us aboard the tug. Was she aground? One thought yes. Another could make out that she was moving. A third discovered that it was our forging ahead which imparted to her the apparent motion we had a moment before congratulated ourselves upon. The minutes seemed like hours as we stood watching the noble ship, against which the combined batteries of the Minnesota and Ericsson were now directed. The shot fell like hail, the shells flew like rain drops, and slowly, steadily she returned the fire. There lay the Minnesota with two tugs alongside. Here, there, and everywhere, was the black box. There lay the Virginia, evidently aground, but still firing with the same deliberate regularity as before. Presently a great white column of smoke shot up above the Minnesota, higher and higher, fuller and fuller in its volume, and beyond doubt, carried death all along her decks, for the red tugboiler had been exploded by a shot, and that great white cloud canopy was the steam thus liberated—more terrible than the giant who grew out of the vapor unsealed by the fisherman in the fable.

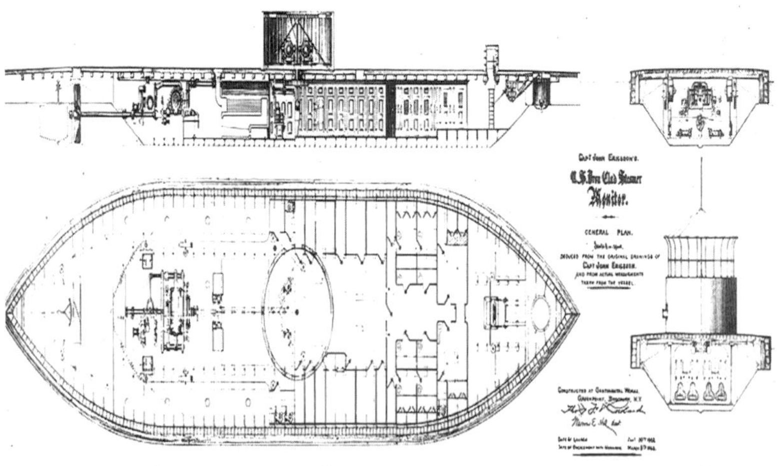

Sketch inboard plans of the USS Monitor, Naval Historical Center.

The Virginia Gain Afloat

And now the Virginia moves again. There can be no error this time, for we see her actually moving through the water, and can mark the foam at her prow. And, strange to say, these long, painful hours, measuring time by our emotions, are condensed by the unsympathetic hands of our watches into fifteen minutes! At 12 m. she was steaming down for Sewell, while the strange looking battery bore away for the frigate ashore. We steamed down to meet her, mustered all hands, and running close alongside, gave her three cheers—three cheers which came from the bottom of our hearts—which were expressive of praise and thankfulness—of benediction and delight. Her company was mustered on the grating and returned our cheers. We ran in closer, and there was her Commander, Catesby A. P. R. Jones, looking as calm and modest as any gentleman within the jurisdiction of Virginia. The Commodore hailed the ship, heard the reply, complimented the quiet, thoughtful looking man who had managed and fought her from the time Flag Officer Buchanan was wounded up to that moment, and then, with cordially spoken eulogies upon the gallant men on board, we shot ahead.

The same scene was enacted and re-enacted as she passed each vessel, and, with Flag Officer Forrest in the van, the squadron steamed cautiously along towards the barricades. As the ships grouped against the soft, hazy sky, followed the Virginia, the picture was one never to be forgotten, the emotions excited such as can never be described.

From *The New York Times*

March 11, 1862

The Battle in Hampton Roads
Special Dispatch from Washington

Washington, Monday, March 10 – A gentleman who witnessed the naval engagement in Hampton Roads, on Saturday and Sunday, says that only one man was killed by the shelling of Newport's News. The fire of our ships had no effect on the *Merrimac* until the arrival of the *Monitor.* The *Merrimac* can do no damage to a vessel or fort, unless within a half mile, on account of the lowness of her guns, which are barely above the level of the water. In a gale she would be powerless.

NAVAL ENGAGEMENT IN HAMPTON ROADS: THE CONFEDERATE IRON-PLATED STEAMER MERRIMAC (OR VIRGINIA) RAMMING INTO THE FEDERAL SLOOP CUMBERLAND (T. NAST). LIBRARY OF CONGRESS.

The report of the *Monitor*'s guns was much heavier than those of the *Merrimac*'s. Not a man was to be seen on either ship—all being housed.

One informant says the *Merrimac* is a "devil," but the *Monitor* a little more so—and that unless a gun explodes on the Monitor, she would have the advantages over her adversary.

The *Monitor* has the advantage of being all the time broadside on, and able to deliver her fire from any position. Her guns being so arranged that she can rake her own decks, if necessary.

The Merrimac was struck seventy-five times, but no perceptible effect was produced, though she hauled off and returned to Norfolk. The Monitor was wholly uninjured.

Washington, Monday. March 10 – P. M. – The Government has no uneasiness about the *Merrimac*. The *Monitor* is considered by naval men to have clearly established her superiority in the conflict of Sunday. The *Merrimac* cannot escape.

Lieut. WORDEN, who handled the Monitor so splendidly, and who was the only man wounded in the engagement, arrived in Washington to-day, and reported to the Navy Department in person. WORDEN is injured about the eyes, which are closely bandaged, and he has to be led from place to place. He gives many interesting incidents of the fight, and is quite sure that three of his heavy shot penetrated the *Merrimac*.

When the news was received in Washington of the *Merrimac's* advance, and the havoc she was committing among our war-vessels, there was a burst of indignation against the Navy Department for not having been prepared to meet her.

It was for the moment forgotten that Congress had made noappropriation to enable Secretary WELLES to build iron-plated ships, although he had urged it three months ago, and, if Congress had acted, the iron-plated ships might now be in service.

Editorial and Historians

A Panic on a Small Scale – We hope the recent news from Hampton Roads has somewhat reassured the timid souls who were certain, on Sunday night, that the *Merrirnac* would speedily visit this harbor and lay New York in ashes. Their magnificent project of sinking stone-boats in the channel, for the purpose of keeping her out, may safely be postponed for a few weeks. Naturally enough the exploits of the *Merrimac* excited some consternation. Her movements were bold and brilliant and if she had met nothing more formidable than the ordinary wooden frigates of our navy, it is not easy to limit the amount of mischief she might have done. But it was absurd to suppose that under any circumstances, she might have been tempted to visit New York. In the first place, it is very doubtful whether she could possibly stand the sea voyage. In the next, there is scarcely one chance in three that she could pass the forts that guard the entrance to the harbor. And in the third place, even if she could get in, it is not easy to see how she could possibly get out. In any event, she is not likely to embark upon such an adventure as a hostile visit to this port; and it is not worth while to destroy the harbor by way of protecting the City just yet.

What the Historians Say

The naval battle at Hampton Roads, known also as the Monitor vs. Virginia (Merrimac) and the Battle of the Ironclads, took place on March 8-9, 1862, at Hampton Roads, Virginia, and was the beginning of the Peninsula campaign of March-September, 1862. The Principal Commanders were Lt. John Worden of the U.S. Navy commanding the Monitor and Capt. Franklin Buchanan and Lt. Catesby R. Jones of the Confederate Navy. The estimated casualties were 409 Union and 24 Confederate sailors respectively.

On March 8, 1862, from her berth at Norfolk, the Confederate ironclad Virginia steamed into Hampton Roads where she met and sank the U.S.S. *Cumberland* and ran the U.S.S. *Congress* aground. On March 9, the Union ironclad Monitor arrived to do battle and initiated the first engagement of ironclads in history. The two ships fought each other to a standstill, but the Virginia retired. The results were inconclusive. The neutralizing of the Virginia had an important effect on the continuation of the Peninsula campaign.

USS Monitor in action against the CSS Virginia, March 9, 1862 (J.O. Davidson) Naval Historical Center.

5

Shiloh

The First Union Victory in a Large Land War

Author's Commentary

Neither *The New York Times* nor the *Charleston Mercury* had correspondents at the great battle in the West. Only ten correspondents happened to be there. Franc Wilkie, the *Times*' reliable correspondent, had been covering the important Army-Navy joint operation at Island Number Ten. Wilkie was in Cairo, Illinois, when he first heard of the battle from a correspondent for *The Cincinnati Gazette.*

The New York Times' first reportage, however, came from a less direct source, a reprint from another Cincinnati paper, the *Cincinnati Daily Times*. A reporter for that newspaper, along with one from the *New York Herald*, a newspaper some considered to be of unscrupulous repute and *The New York Times*' biggest competitor, had been at the battle. The morning after, under the pretext of being on General Grant's staff, both men entered the Army's telegraph service and got their stories out to their newspapers, virtually scooping all other reporters who had been at the battle.

Information of the battle to southern newspapers was much slower and less certain. The *Charleston Mercury*, perhaps spoiled by early Confederate victories in the East, proclaimed it a southern victory before less certain news filtered in. Hermes, the *Mercury's* columnist, facetiously claimed in the April 21st edition that they hoped to receive an official report of the battle, which occurred on April 6th and 7th, by the fourth of July.

pr.18, 1862: **From the *Charleston Mercury***
News by Telegraph
The Great Battle of Shiloh
Full and Interesting Accounts
Death of Gen. A. S. JOHNSTON
General BEAUREGARD'S Despatch
Richmond, April 7
The following official despatch was received at the War Department this morning:

Battlefield of Shiloh

April 6

To S. Cooper, Adjutant and Inspector-General:

We this morning attacked the enemy in a strong position in front of Pittsburg, and, after a severe battle of ten hours, thanks be to the Almighty, gained a complete victory, driving the enemy from every position.

The loss on both sides was heavy, including the loss of the Commander-in-Chief, Gen. A. S. JOHNSTON, who fell, gallantly leading his troops in the thickest of the fight.

Signed
G.T. BEAUREGARD, General Commanding.

The *Charleston Mercury*

April 11, 1862

News by Telegraph
The Latest from the West
Further details of the Victory at Shiloh

Chattanooga, April 9
By passengers on the train this morning from Corinth, we learn that on Monday Gen. BUELL, with an overwhelming force – composed partly of fresh troops and partly of those who had fled in dismay and disorder from before our troops on Sunday, and which he had succeeded in rallying – attacked Gen. BEAUREGARD in his new lines, in advance of

the battleground of Sunday. The two armies fought desperately with heavy loss on both sides, yesterday and today, with short intervals of rest.

Gen. BEAUREGARD, pressed by vastly superior numbers, finally fell back, in masterly style and in good order, to his former position, which is naturally strong and well fortified. Gen. BUELL was expected to renew the attack today, at the head of all the forces under his command.

General HINDMAN'S leg was shot off. General BRECKINRIDGE won immortal honors. His clothes were shot off and two horses were killed under him. Cols. WILLIAMS and HATTEN, of Arkansas, were killed. Lieut. J. J. JACOBUS, of the Washington Artillery of Augusta, Ga., was killed. Gen. JNO. K. JACKSON, of Georgia, and his staff, are safe.

The remains of Gen. A. S. JOHNSTON will be brought for temporary interment to Atlanta, where his sister and one or more nieces are sojourning. His wife is in California, and thither, at some future day, his body may be carried for permanent interment.

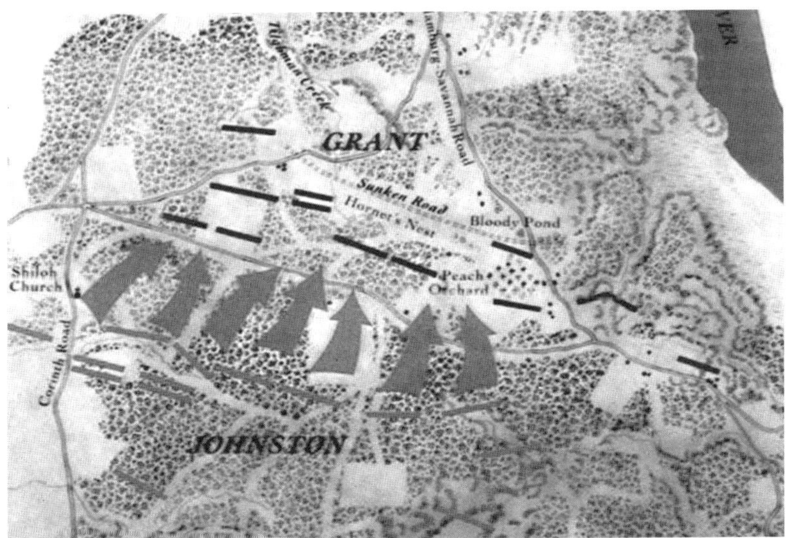

PLACE OF PEACE, THE BIBLICAL MEANING OF "SHILOH," WAS ANYTHING BUT PEACEFUL ON THE MORNING OF APRIL 6, 1862. IN THE BLOODIEST BATTLE OF THE WAR, CONFEDERATE GENERAL ALBERT SIDNEY JOHNSON ATTACKED THE UNION ARMY, COMMANDED BY U.S. GRANT, AT PITTSBURG LANDING, TENNESSEE. LIBRARY OF CONGRESS.

The Latest
Mobile, April 10. The latest intelligence from Corinth says that the enemy are badly whipped. Our loss in killed and wounded is less than 1,000. We took nearly 3,000 prisoners. Their gunboats prevented our troops from making the victory complete. A despatch, dated last night, says that 500 of our cavalry had attacked the enemy, killing many and capturing 48 prisoners. Advices received by the train this morning give positive information that BUELL has been killed. We have also the intelligence that under a flag of truce an armistice of two days had been agreed upon to bury the dead. The enemy only attacked us when they were reinforced; and every time they were beaten back under cover of their gunboats. General PRENTISS told BEAUREGARD that he had 65,000 of the flower of the Federal army, but could not whip 125,000 Confederates. BEAUREGARD replied that he had only 38,000 in the field, and could whip the Federals three to one on a fair field. The 21st Alabama Regiment covered itself with glory; but all behaved nobly. The charges of our troops were irresistible.

Many uncertain rumors are in circulation. I send only reliable reports.

The *Charleston Mercury*

April 18, 1862

The Death of General Gladden – It is with a proud yet heartfelt sorrow that the people of this State will have learned the death of their gallant countryman, Gen. GLADDEN, from a wound received on the battle field of Shiloh. Had Gen. GLADDEN done nothing else, his distinguished services to the State during the Mexican war, as leader of the Palmetto Regiment after the fall of BUTLER and DICKINSON – a regiment that shed glory upon our arms – would have entitled him to the gratitude of our people no less than their admiration. Few remain of that noble band, and now its only surviving field officer is gone – but he has fallen as a brave man and a true soldier would fall, stricken at the head of his troops, and in the arms of glorious victory.

Distinguished in Mexico, on the bloody fields of Contreras and Cherubusco, he received honorable wounds. Having become a citizen of Louisiana, and selected to command a noble brigade, he has again accumulated honor upon this, his native State, illustrated its martial fame, served her no less than Louisiana with his life, and sealed the great cause with his best blood.

Energetic and thorough in what he undertook, he had the simplicity, frankness and manly bearing of a dashing and daring soldier – and, withal, the amiability, and kindness and courtesy of a true heart. Inspiring confidence, he led troops to victory. Let us all remember his name, in order to emulate his deeds.

The *Charleston Mercury*

April 21, 1862
Richmond News and Gossip
From Our Own Correspondents

RICHMOND, Wednesday, April 16 – As usual, we are indebted to the Yankees for the first account of the battle of Shiloh, or Shiloah, as it is now spelled. Our own official report may be confidently looked for about the 4th of next July. To thank the Lord for a loss of 20,000 killed, wounded and missing, and to reverse the facts in regard to the captured guns and generals, is a proceeding truly Yankeefied and very wonderful, if it had not occurred so uniformly. We may always gauge the enemyloss by his report of our own. Confessing to 20,000 at Shiloh, they put down the rebel loss at 35,000 to 40,000; we may rest satisfied, therefore, with this last statement as an accurate account of the damage they received. Verily, Johnston and Beauregard hit them a heavy blow. Another funny feature in the Yankee news of this morning is the assertion that the object of the *Merrimac* was to engage the *Monitor* while the *Patrick Henry* and the *Jamestown* ran the blockade; and yet the *Merrimac* affects the stock market unfavorably, although she is match for the *Monitor*.

Conjecture busies itself about the visit of the French Minister to this city. Wags say that he comes to look after his compatriot who was captured in the balloon the other day, or else to lay in a summer supply of the peculiar and high flavored frogs which grow only on the banks of the James River and Kanawha Canal – a luxury of which he has long been deprived. Reasonable folks say that he comes to look after the tobacco owned by the Emperor, which is stored in our warehouses, and is in danger of being burned in the face by McClellan as he advances to the capture of rebel Capital, rebel President, and rebel Congress. It is certain that our Secretary of State did not look as smiling this morning as the bright weather warranted; and the determination of Congress to tracks on Monday next reminds one of the Pennsylvania regiments who marched from the field of Manassas to the sound of the enemy cannon.

Floydaccount of the defences at Donelson will increase the admiration of the country for the devoted and heroic men who sacrificed themselves for the cause in that wretched man trap. He tells us that the fort mounted only thirteen guns, of which but three were of any use whatever against iron gunboats, and that the entrenchments and rifle pits were hastily thrown up, in the face of the enemy, after the fight had commenced. Yet the telegraph reported Donelson as, and I well recollect the phrase, 'lines are entrenched all around; Donelson can be taken.' The Whig is hardly too severe when it characterizes the concoctors of such dispatches as or knaves.

Infantry and cavalry in large numbers passed through this morning. The men were mostly Virginians, not at all showy or imposing in their dress and physique, but serviceable for all that. I believe the Virginians have fought well wherever they have been tried. A large body of artillery have also passed through.

HERMES

The *Charleston Mercury*

May 2, 1862

HOW THE REBELS WERE INSTRUCTED TO ACT IN THE BATTLE OF SHILOH – A New York paper says that the following order of Gen. BEAUREGARD was picked up on the battlefield of Shiloh:

(General Order No. 14.)
HEADQUARTERS ARMY OF THE MISSISSIPPI,
JACKSON, Tenn., March 14, 1862.

1. Field and company officers are especially enjoined to instruct their men, under all circumstances, to fire with deliberation at the feet of the enemy. They will thus avoid over-shooting, and, besides, wounded men give more trouble to our adversary than dead, as they have to be taken from the field.

2. Officers in command must be cool and collected; hold their men in hand in action, and caution them against useless, aimless firing. The men must be instructed and required each one to single out his mark. It was the deliberate sharpshooting of our forefathers in the Revolution of 1776, and New Orleans, in 1815, which made them so formidable against the odds with which they were engaged.

3. In the beginning of a battle, except by troops deployed as skirmishers, the fire of file will be avoided. It excites the men and renders their subsequent control difficult. Fire by wing or company should be resorted to instead. During the battle, the officers and non-commissioned officers must keep their men in the ranks, enforce obedience, and encourage and stimulate them if necessary.

4. Soldiers must not be permitted to leave the ranks even to assist in removing our own dead, unless by special permission, which shall only be given when the action has been decided. The surest way to protect the wounded is to drive the enemy from the field. The most pressing, highest duty is to win the victory.

THE BATTLE OF SHILOH (EHRGOTT). LIBRARY OF CONGRESS.

5. Before the battle, the Quartermaster of the division will make all necessary arrangements for the immediate transportation of the wounded from the field. After consultation with the medical officers, he will establish the ambulance depot in the rear, and give his assistants the necessary instructions for the efficient service of the wagons and other means of transportation.

6. The ambulance depot to which the wounded are to be carried for immediate treatment should be established at the most convenient building nearest the field of battle. A red flag marks the place to it.

The active ambulances follow the troops, to succor the wounded and remove them to the depot. Before the engagement, about five men – the least effective under arms to the company – will be detailed to assist the ambulance conductors in removing wounded, providing water, and otherwise assisting the wounded. These men will not loiter about the depots, but must always return to the field of battle as soon as practicable.

Before and immediately after the battle, the roll of each company will be called, and absentees must be strictly accounted for. To quit their standard on the battlefield under fire, under pretence of removing or aiding the wounded, will not be permitted. Any one persisting in it will be shot on the spot, and whoever shall be found to have quit the field, or his regiment, or his company, without authority, will be regarded and proclaimed as a coward, and dealt with accordingly. By command of Gen. BEARURGARD

THOS. JORDAN, Acting Adj. Gen.

From *The New York Times*

April 10, 1862

Pittsburg *via* Fort Henry
Wednesday, April 9 – 3:20 A. M.
The greatest battle of the war has just closed, resulting in the complete rout of the enemy, who attacked us at daybreak Sunday morning. The battle lasted without intermission during the entire day, and was again renewed on Monday morning, and continued undecided until 4 o'clock in the afternoon, when the enemy commenced their retreat and are still flying toward Corinth, pursued by a large force of our cavalry. The slaughter on both sides is immense.

The fight was brought on by a body of three hundred of the Twenty-fifth Missouri Regiment, of Gen. Prentiss' Division, attacking the advance guard of the rebels, which were supposed to be the pickets of the enemy in front of our camps. The rebels immediately advanced on Gen. Prentiss' division on the left wing, pouring volley after volley of musketry, and riddling our camps with grape, cannister and shell. Our forces soon formed into line and returned their fire vigorously, and by the time we were prepared to receive them, had turned their heaviest fire on the left centre of Sherman's Division and drove our men back from their camps, and bringing up a fresh force, opened fire on our left wing, under Gen. McClernand. This fire was returned with terrible effect and determined spirit by both infantry and artillery, along the whole line for a distance of over four miles.

Gen. Hubleburt's Division was thrown forward to support the centre, when a desperate conflict ensued. The rebels were driven back with terrible slaughter, but soon rallied and drove back our men in turn. From about 9 o'clock, until night closed on the bloody scene, there was no determination of the result of the struggle. The enemy exhibited remarkably good generalship. At times engaging the left with apparently their whole strength, they would suddenly open a terrible and destructive fire on the right or centre. Even our heaviest and most destructive fire upon the enemy did not appear to discourage their solid column. The fire of Maj. Taylor's Chicago Artillery raked them down in scores, but the smoke would no sooner be dispersed than the breach would again be filled.

The most desperate fighting took place late in the afternoon. The rebels knew that if they did not succeed in whipping us then, that their chances for success would be extremely doubtful, as a portion of Gen. Buell's forces had by this time arrived on the opposite stide of the river, and another portion was coming up the river from Savannah. They became aware that we were being reinforced, as they could see Gen. Buell's troops from the river bank, to which point they had forced their way.

At five o'clock the rebels had forced our left wing back so as to occupy fully two-thirds of our camp, and were fighting their way forward with a desperate degree of confidence in their efforts to drive us into the river, and at the same time heavily engaged our right

Up to this time we had received no reinforcements, Gen. Lew. Wallace failing to come to our support until the day was over, having taken the wrong road from Crump's Landing, and being without other transports than those used for Quartermaster's and Commissary stores, which were too heavily laden to ferry any considerable number of Gen. Buell's forces across the river, those that were here having been sent to bring up the troops from Savanna. We were, therefore, contesting against fearful odds, our forces not exceeding thirty-eight thousand men, while that of the enemy was upwards of sixty thousand.

Our condition at this moment was extremely critical. Large numbers of men had straggled toward the river and could not be rallied. Gen. Grant and staff, who had been recklessly riding along the lines during the entire day, amid the unceasing storm of bullets, grape and shell, now rode from right to left, inciting the men to stand firm unil our reinforcements could cross the river.

Col. Webster, Chief of Staff, immediately got into position the heaviest pieces of artillery, pointing on the enemy's right, while a large number of the batteries were planted along the entire line, from the river bank northwest to our extreme right, some two and a half miles distant. About an hour before dusk a general cannonading was opened upon the enemy from along our whole line, with a perpetual crack of musketry. For a short time the rebels replied with vigor and effect, but their return shots grew less frequent and destructive, while ours grew more rapid.

The gunboats *Lexington* and *Tyler*. which lay a short distance off, kept raining shell on the rebel hordes. This last effort was too much for the enemy, and ere dusk had set in the firing had nearly ceased, when, night coming on, all the combatants rested from their awful work of blood.

Our men rested on their arms in the position they had at the close of the night, until the forces under Major General Wallace arrived and took position on the right, and General Buell's forces from the opposite side and Savannah were now being conveyed to the battle-ground. The entire right of Gen. Nelson's Division was ordered to form on the right, and the forces under Gen. Critenden were ordered to his support early in the morning.

The Second Day's Battle

Gen. Buell arrived on Sunday evening. In the morning the battle was opened at daylight simultaneously by Gen. Nelson's Division on the left and Major Gen. Wallace's Division on the right. Gen. Nelson's force opened up a most galling fire on the rebels, and advanced rapidly as they fell back. The fire soon became general along the whole line and began to tell with terrible effect on the enemy. Generals

McClernand, Sherman and Hurlburt's men, though terribly jaded from the previous day's fighting, still maintained their honors won at Donelson; but the resistance of the rebels at all points of the attack was worthy a better cause.

But they were not enough for our undaunted bravery, and the dreadful desolation produced by our artillery, which was sweeping them away like chaff before the wind. But knowing that a defeat here would be the death blow to their hopes, and that their all depended upon this great struggle, their Generals still urged them on in the face of destruction, hoping by flanking us on the right to turn the tide of battle. Their success was again for a time cheering, as they began to gain ground on us, appearing to have been reinforced; but our left, under Gen. Nelson, was driving them, and by eleven o'clock Gen. Buell's forces had succeeded in flanking them and capturing their batteries of artillery.

They however again rallied on the left, and recrossed, and the right forced themselves forward in another desperate effort. But reinforcements from General Wood and Gen. Thomas were coming in, regiment after regiment, which were sent to Gen. Buell, who had again commenced to drive the enemy.

About three o'clock in the afternoon Gen. Grant rode to the left, where the fresh regiments had been ordered, and finding the rebels wavering, sent a portion of his body-guard to the head of each of five regiments, and then ordered a charge across the field, himself leading, as he brandished his sword and waved them on to the crowning victory, while cannon balls were falling like hail around him.

The men followed with a shout that sounded above the roar and din of the artillery, and the rebels fled in dismay, as from a destroying avalanche, and never made another stand.

Gen. Buell followed the retreating rebels, driving them in splendid style, and by 5'½ o'clock the whole rebel army was in full retreat to Corinth, with our cavalry in hot pursuit, with what further results not known, they not having returned up to this hour.

We have taken a large amount of their artillery and also a number of prisoners. We lost a number of our forces taken prisoner yesterday, among whom is Gen. Prentiss. The number of our force taken has not peen ascertained yet. It is reported at several hundred. Gen. Prentiss was also reported as being wounded. Among the killed on the rebel side was their General-in-Chief, A. Sydney Johnston, who was struck by a cannon ball on the afternoon of Sunday. It is further reported that Gen. Beauregard had his arm shot off.

This afternoon Gens. Bragg, Breckinridge, and Jackson were commanding the rebel forces.

What the Historians Say

The battle at Shiloh, known also as Pittsburg Landing, occurred on April 6-7, 1862, in Hardin County, Tennessee. It was the fourth battle of the Federal penetration up the Cumberland and Tennessee Rivers Campaign of 1862.

The principal commanders were Maj. Gen. Ulysses S. Grant and Maj. Gen. Don Carlos Buell of the U.S. Forces and and Gen. Albert Sidney Johnston and Gen. P.G.T Beauregard of the Confederate Army. The forces engaged were the United States Army of the Tennessee and Army of the Ohio consisting of 65,085 men facing the Confederate Army of the Mississippi consisting of 44,968 troops. The estimated casualties were 13,047 and 10,699 respectively.

As a result of the fall of Forts Henry and Donelson, Confederate Gen. Albert Sidney Johnston, the commander in the area, was forced to fall back, giving up Kentucky and much of West and Middle Tennessee. He chose Corinth, Mississippi, a major transportation center, as the staging area for an offensive against Maj. Gen. Ulysses S. Grant and his Army of the Tennessee before the Army of the Ohio, under Maj. Gen. Don Carlos Buell, could join it. The Confederate retrenchment was a surprise, although a pleasant one, to the Union forces, and it took Grant, with about 40,000 men, some time to mount a southern offensive along the Tennessee River toward Pittsburg Landing. Grant received orders to await Buell's Army of the Ohio at Pittsburg Landing. Grant did not choose to fortify his position; rather, he set about drilling his men many of which were raw recruits. Johnston originally planned to attack Grant on April

4, but delays postponed it until the 6th. Attacking the Union troops on the morning of the 6th, the Confederates surprised them, routing many. Some Federals made determined stands and, by afternoon, they had established a battle line at the sunken road, known as the 'Hornets Nest.' Repeated Rebel attacks failed to carry the Hornets Nest, but massed artillery helped to turn the tide as Confederates surrounded the Union troops and captured, killed, or wounded most. Johnston had been mortally wounded earlier and his second in command, Gen. PG.T Beauregard, took over.

The Union troops established another line covering Pittsburg Landing, anchored with artillery and augmented by Buell's men who began to arrive and take up positions. Fighting continued until after dark, but the Federals held. By the next morning, the combined Federal forces numbered about 40,000, outnumbering Beauregard's army of less than 30,000. Beauregard was unaware of the arrival of Buell's army and launched a counterattack response to a two-mile advance by William Nelson's division of Buell's army at 6:00 a.m., which was, at first successful.

Union troops stiffened and began forcing the Confederates back. Beauregard ordered a counterattack, which stopped the Union advance but did not break its battle line. At this point, Beauregard realized that he could not win and, having suffered too many casualties, he retired from the field and headed back to Corinth.

On the 8th, Grant sent Brig. Gen. William T. Sherman, with two brigades and Brig. Gen. Thomas J. Wood with his division, in pursuit of Beauregard. They ran into the Rebel rearguard, commanded by Col. Nathan Bedford Forrest, at Fallen Timbers. Forrest's aggressive tactics, although eventually contained, influenced the Union troops to return to Pittsburg Landing. Grant's mastery of the Confederate forces continued; he had beaten them once again. The Confederates continued to fall back until launching their mid-August offensive.

It was a very significant Union victory and had a decisive effect on the direction of the war.

6

Williamsburg

First Land Battle in the Peninsula Campaign

AUTHOR'S COMMENTARY

It was a new time for the American press.Standards for war coverage were far from set, and each one reporting the war took what liberties he felt might not only get the job done but help his side as well. The *Charleston Mercury's* correspondent, Hermes, the pseudonym used by George William Bagby, was in peaceful times a doctor and a man of letters. His description of the Williamsburg battle, written from Richmond, captures the imagination of the reader in a manner worthy of a novelist describing the Napoleonic Wars.

In the North, newspapers were fabricating stories of Union soldiers' bravado and General McClellan's Napoleon-like greatness. L.L. Crounse of *The New York Times*, who reported from Williamsburg, was an unlikely candidate for writing such stories, at least about McClellan. Returning from the field to the home of the Whitaker family, who had made quarters available to Crounse and several of his newspaper colleagues, he discovered that the house had been taken over by General McClellan for his headquarters and that Crounse and his colleagues would be quartered in the cellar. That night, as McClellan slept well in bed, Crounse and a fellow correspondent had to stretch out on a table for a nocturnal experience far less comfortable than the one being enjoyed by the young "Napoleon."

May 8, 1862: From the *Charleston Mercury*

Special to the *Charleston Mercury*, May 12, 1862. The fight at Williamsburg, which JOHNSTON characterizes as an affair, must have been a battle of some magnitude, as LONGSTREET'S troops and STUART'S brigade of cavalry, were engaged against an equal, if not a superior, force of the enemy. Our infantry used the bayonet freely, and with brilliant success. The fighting of our cavalry is described by a French officer, who witnessed it, as more brilliant and daring than anything he ever witnessed in Europe. It was hand to hand combat with Federal cavalry of the regular army, whose practice with the sword could not overcome the pluck and superior horsemanship of our troops. The old tricks of raising a flag of truce, trailing arms, and open professions of friendship, were resorted to by the Yankees, and, strange to say, succeeded. Corsi regiment from Alexandria was thus fired into at a distance of thirty yards, with fearful effect. The volley was returned, and our boys rushed in with the bayonet. No quarter should have been given. As to the casualties, reports vary greatly. One account says 300, another 1000, in killed and wounded. Enemy loss rated very high. I hear from a good source that probably as many as 20 pieces of cannon were captured by us, but all were left behind, owing to the mud and lack of horses. Many of our sick and wounded fell into the enemy hands, and I fear prisoners too – those of the enemy amounting to 600 or more. Our citizens are called upon today to go down and receive our wounded, and also to prepare food for them.

With regard to the fight at Barhamsville, we are completely in the dark. The courier who brought General Johnston despatch, which (as published) says there has been no fight, and no prospect of one, declares that fighting had been going on from early in the morning till 12 0, the hour at which he left. From this courier or other sources, the papers get the names of Generals killed and wounded at Barhamsville. Johnston is calling for reinforcement, and the impression is that our position is critical. But this is kept back from the public.

Still nothing from Corinth. A despatch on business from Beauregard was received on Monday. Apprehensions of a flank movement are entertained. Reports are current of a movement of Yankees upon the Virginia and Tennessee Railroad, and of a naval engagement in James River, but I can get no particulars of the latter. The withdrawal of Border

States members from the Yankee Congress, intimated as probable in the latest Northern news, is a delusion. Where would the creatures go? They couldncome to us; they may kick up a little, but they have eaten the red pottage and decided their fate. Johnston has sent several thousand well soldiers here for fear of their catching the measles. So the soldiers say. Weather cool, clear and bright.
HERMES

Embalming the Dead

A Washington correspondent gives the following account of the process of embalming adopted there:

The body is placed on an inclined platform; the mouth, ears, nose, etc., are stopped with cotton; if wounded, cotton is put in the wound, and a plaster is put on; an incision is made in the wrist, the attachment is made from an air pump, and fluid ejected into the arteries. The wound is then sewed up and the body is hoisted up to dry. To save the eyes from sinking in, wax is put under the eyelids. The hair I found to come out very easy, but after the embalming it could not be removed. The bodies take on an average about seven quarts, but Gen. Lander took seventeen quarts. There were some eight bodies on hand; some had been there thirty days. The operators say in four months the body will become solidified like marble, but no chance has yet been had to prove it. Col. Baker's body, on arriving at San Francisco, was in an advanced state of decomposition. Dr. Holmes, late of Williamsburg, Long Island, is the oldest in the business here, and I am informed he has made thirty thousand dollars.

Messrs. Brown and Alexander are trying to get a bill through Congress for the exclusive right to embalm bodies, and to have Congress authorize a corps of embalmers for each division. The charges are $50 for an officer and $25 for a private, and I must say the bodies look as life-like as if they were asleep.

The Charge of the South Carolina Troopers At Williamsburg

Special to the *Charleston Mercury*, May 23, 1862 – The accounts of the parts taken by the different corps in the late actions near Williamsburg have been very imperfect, and, of course, somewhat partial, in the absence of any official report as yet of the engagement. The *Richmond Examiner* learned the following incidents of the brilliant charge of the cavalry of the Hampton Legion, and gives them as an interesting portion of the history of the late remarkable action or series of battles in the neighborhood of Williamsburg:

It appears that on the 14th instant, the cavalry of the Hampton Legion, consisting of the Brooks Troop, Capt. Lanneau, Beaufort District Troop, Capt. Sevier, Congaree Troop, Capt. McFie, and the Edgefield Hussars, under command of Lieut. P. M. Butler, Capt. Clark being absent on account of sickness, under the command of Major M. C. Butler, were pro-tecting the rear of our army on its retirement from Yorktown, in conjunction with the cavalry of Col. Davis and Lieut. Col. Wickham a few miles before the army reached Williamsburg.

The enemy made their appearance, hurrying up our rear guard. The cavalry were in position to meet their advance, when a courier arrived, announcing that General Johnston had sent for the cavalry to meet that of the enemy. Major Butler, with his squadron, immediately responded to the order at a gallop, and reported to Gen. Johnston, who ordered him to report to General McLaws, who was in Fort Magruder, who did so. General McLaws pointed to the enemy cavalry across the ravine and ordered him to disperse them, which he accomplished in the most gallant and successful manner.

THE ARMY OF THE POTOMAC ARRIVING AT YORKTOWN FROM WILLIAMSBURG (A. WAUD. AS PUBLISHED IN HARPER'S WEEKLY). LIBRARY OF CONGRESS.

KEARNY (SIC) AT THE BATTLE OF WILLIAMSBURG (ALFRED WAUD). LIBRARY OF CONGRESS.

The fight soon became a hand to hand one, the enemy making a stout resistance; but they had to yield to the superior courage of the cavaliers of South Carolina, although the enemy outnumbered them. Captain Lannauu, at the first blow, severed the head of a Hessian. Captain Sevier, Captain McFie and Lieutenant Butler, all were conspicuous in the charge for their coolness and gallantry. In fact, all of the officers acquitted themselves with spirit. In the charge we lost two killed: privates B. W. Boggs and Stephen Boynton, who fell in the front ranks. Among the wounded were Sergeant Low, Privates McGinnis, Fowles, Richard Flanigan, who received severe sabre cuts, and Gillespie Thornwell, a beardless boy, son of Rev. J. H. Thornwell, who was wounded four times by their sabres, and, when surrounded, declared he would die before he would surrender. In the fight the squadron captured fourteen prisoners; killed fifteen or twenty; took ten horses, saddles, bridles, and a number of Coltrepeaters and sabres. In this desperate charge not a man faltered, but followed boldly their gallant leader, who was in front, whilst he threw his irresistible column upon them. The Hessians could not stand the shock and gave away in disorder.

Gen. Johnston has exhibited his appreciation of this charge in a complimentary general order, and has said that its success saved Gen. Stuartentire's command, who were, for a time, cut off. Well did the squadron sustain the hard-earned and lasting honors of the Hampton Legion, and Major Butler the prestige of his name.

From *The New York Times*

Williamsburg VA, May 7, 1862 – Now that the smoke of the battle has somewhat cleared away, I am able to give you a more connected account of the engagement, on Monday, between our advance guard and a large force of rebels who opposed our entrance into this town. The position from which the rebels assailed our forces was an exceedingly strong one, being along the line of defenses established by them just below Williamsburgh, last Spring, previous to their fortification of Yorktown and Warwick Creek. Near the centre of a broad plain, at the upper side of which stands Williamsburgh, and right across the turnpike road leading to the city, they erected a substantial bastion, large enough to accommodate six or seven thousand men, and commanding the place in every direction, so that a force approaching it from any point must be exposed to a raking fire for three-quarters of a mile or more. Well supplied with artillery, and defended with determination by a force of 5000 men, this bastion would give a world of trouble to an army of five times that number. It was supported by five smaller flanking works of the same pattern, on the right, two on the left, each of them having platforms for two guns. The large work being fitted for five guns.

THE C. DE PARIS RIDING INTO YORKTOWN WITH THE FIRST CLEAR ACCOUNT OF AFFAIRS AT WILLIAMSBURG (WAUD). LIBRARY OF CONGRESS.

The approach to the plain thus defended from the direction of Yorktown was by two roads, the one on the left, taken by Hooker's Division and its supports, being a straight path through the wends. That on the right, along which Hancock advanced, led over a brook or creek, which had been dammed at this point, where the road crossed it through a defile in such a way as to convert the defile into a deep pond, passed at the lower side by a narrow causeway, commanded by an earthwork looking down upon it at a height of fifty feet, and from a bold bluff on the other side. Over this causeway troops would be compelled to march four abreast for a distance of more than one-eighth of a mile, exposed to the fire of a fort above the reach of their artillery. For some reason, however, this position has never been occupied. Probably it was intended to mount artillery there, as the occasion demanded. The fact that this work, and the flanking works about Fort Magruder, were none of them occupied on Monday, shows plainly that the rebels had not proposed to make any decided stand against us here. Indeed, the command of the York River, secured to us by the evacuation of Yorktown, made their position at this point of the Peninsula untenable, as we could easily throw a force above them to take them in the rear.

The rebels had, to fact, pushed on several miles beyond Williamsburgh with their main body, before our advance approached on Sunday night, retaining a small force only at the forts in their rear. But leaving everything behind them, our troops pushed on so rapidly after the rebels, struggling through the mud with their heavy wagons, that they found it absolutely necessary, to hold us in check long enough to secure their retreat. Accordingly, on Monday morning, troops were hurried back to the support of their rear guard, occupying Fort Magruder. They continued to come in all through the day, supplying fresh troops to oppose our men. Commencing with a small force, each party continued to swell its numbers with reinforcements, until the rebels had finally fifteen or twenty thousand men on the ground, and we about the same number. The rebels had the advantage of hurrying their troops along more rapidly, so that some of our men were compelled to stand their ground for hours against a much superior force opposing them.

What the Historians Say

The battle at Williamsburg, known also as the battle at Fort Magruder, in York and Williamsburg Counties, occurred on May 5, 1862. In the first pitched battle of the Peninsula Campaign, Gen. George McClellan and his 40,768 Federal troops went up against Maj. General James Longstreet and his 31,823 Confederate troops resulting in 2,283 and 1,560 casualties respectively.

Following up the Confederate retreat from Yorktown, Gen. Hooker's Union division encountered the Confederate rearguard near Williamsburg. Hooker then assaulted Fort Magruder, an earthen fortification alongside the Williamsburg Road, but was repulsed. Confederate counterattacks, directed by Maj. Gen. Longstreet, threatened to overwhelm the Union left flank, until Gen. Phillip Kearny's division arrived to stabilize the Federal position. Gen. W.S. Hancock's brigade then moved to threaten the Confederate left flank, occupying two abandoned redoubts. The Confederates counterattacked unsuccessfully, but Hancock's localized success was not exploited. The failure of the Union troops to press the advantage resulted in an inconclusive conflict. The foundation of indecisiveness was being established by McClellan, which allowed the Confederates to eventually press the advantage.

Soldiers Accompany Wagon Train Passing Through Williamsburg on Duke of Gloucester Street (William McIlvane). Library of Congress.

7

Second Manassas

Return to Hallowed Ground

Author's Commentary

The telegraph lines to the south hummed with news of the Confederate victory. The *Charleston Mercury* reported directly from the battlefield. Not so *The New York Times*. Due to several newspapers early reportage of McClellan's movements on the Peninsula, General Halleck reportedly sent word to General Pope to dismiss war correspondents from the field. In his article published by *Harper's Magazine* in October 1863, L.L. Crounse, who covered the Army of the Potomac for *The New York Times*, stated that all but two newspapers were expelled from the field. The resultant coverage of the *Times*, an expelled paper, consisted of General Pope's dispatches, private sources, and the reportage lifted from the *Washington Star*, presumably one of the two papers allowed coverage.

The closest field coverage for *The New York Times* in proximity to the battlefield was established at U.S. Army Headquarters between Alexandria and Bristor Station on the line of the Orange and Alexandria Railroad on August 28 and nearby Fairfax Court House on August 29.

Sept. 1, 1862: From the *Charleston Mercury*

Progress of the War

Highly Important Rumors of Our Progress Beyond the Rappahannock

The *Richmond Dispatch* of Friday says:

The news from the line of the Rappahannock, though not so full and complete as we could desire, is, nevertheless, interesting and important. It is understood as perfectly reliable that the advance of our forces have reached Manassas Junction, where they captured some eight or ten heavy guns and an immense quantity of valuable stores.

The portion of the Yankee army under Pope was at Warrenton on Wednesday, and it is stated that its retreat in the direction of Alexandria is entirely intercepted. The only route by which he could reach that point is by way of the Junction, which is now in possession of our forces. It is not probable that he will succeed in forcing his way back to the Potomac by taking that route. If this statement be correct – and we have no reason to question its authenticity – the only road for his escape would seem to be by way of the Plains to Middleburg, and from thence to Leesburg, in Loudoun county.

We have not intelligence of any heavy fighting, and it is somewhat surprising that our troops have met with so few obstructions in their advance. In government circles there seems to be not the slightest apprehension for the safety of our army. Indeed, we have reason to believe that the most lively hopes are entertained of a triumph which will eclipse any that has been vouchsafed to our arms since the war commenced. The intelligence that the enemy has been reinforced has created no uneasiness, and not the remotest idea of a reverse is entertained.

To sum up the whole, we are warranted in the conclusion that the enemyforces are so situated that a further retreat would be decidedly more disastrous than the acceptance of battle, and that in either event he is inevitably subjected to a reverse from which it will be no easy matter to recover.

The Richmond papers of Saturday contain nothing additional from the seat of war. The *Examiner* says:

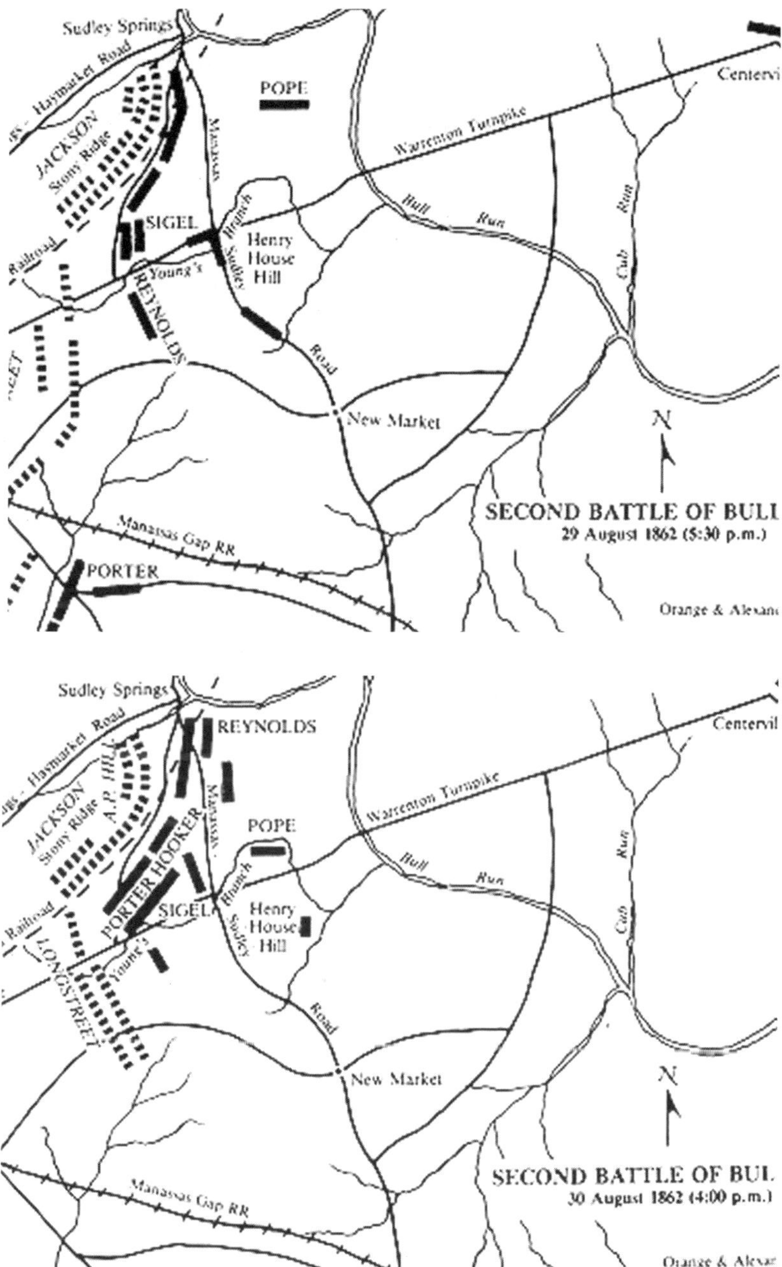

Second Manassas, also known as The Second Battle of Bull Run, was fought primarily around the Virginia towns of Groveton, Centerville, Gainsville, and Bristow Station before concluding on the third day on the Plains of Manassas.

We are unable to obtain any information of the enemy position or numbers not already known. Popearmy lies between Warrenton and the railroad junction of that name on the Orange and Alexandria railroad. Pope is said to have been reinforced by two divisions, who landed on the Potomac near the mouth of the Occoquan. Gen. Trimble of Ewelldivision is said to occupy Manassas in Poperear. As to the whereabouts of Jackson there are not even any conjectures ventured.

The *Charleston Mercury*

September 2, 1862

A Great Battle – the last, we hope, that is to purple the soil of the Old Dominion – has been fought and won. The news is direct, official and satisfactory. General LEE is no braggart. He announces to the President that the valor of our troops has again prevailed upon the Plains of Manassas. On the memorable field McCLELLAN and POPE had marshalled their united hosts to meet our advancing columns. On Thursday, the 28th, and Friday, the 29th of August, the conflict was opened by the enemy. Our right and left wings commanded respectively by Stonewall JACKSON and LONGSTREET, were successively assailed; but, in both instances, the attack was repulsed. On Saturday, the 30th of August, our whole army became engaged with the combined forces of the enemy, and achieved signal victory. This is the sum of our information. It is enough to indicate that the fight is likely to prove, in its fruits, the most important success, this far, of the war.

The country will join with General Lee, in grateful acknowledgment to the Lord of Hosts, who has thus smiled once more upon our cause. But vain indeed, and costly would be our triumph, if we should fail to grasp the advantages which it offers. We trust and believe that there will be no such failure.

The beaten and demoralized masses of the Yankee army can scarcely be rallied for another struggle south of the Potomac. The road lies open, to the gates of the Yankee Capital. Let our Generals but unleash their victorious legions, and Washington is ours. Maryland will arise and cast aside her fetters; and in thirty days the seat of war will be transferred to the outer boundaries of the Confederacy.

We await with impatience the next tidings from the Potomac. For we believe that there can be no more delays upon the sod which covers the dead heros of Manassas.

The *Charleston Mercury*
September 3, 1862

The community yesterday was jubilant and sanguine at the news from Manassas. Flags were streaming all day long from the public places, and the discussions at the bulletin boards turned chiefly upon the precise distance from Manassas to Washington, which, as all the world knows, the first 'Grand Army' of the Yankees ran in a single night.

Progress of the War from the Seat of the War in Virginia
The extraordinary reticence of the Government throws back all the Virginia papers upon the resources of their old and indefatigable friend 'The Reliable Gentleman.' The following account of the events immediately preceding the second great Battle of Manassas is taken from Mondayissue of the *Richmond Dispatch*.

It is asserted, on what ought to be regarded as reliable authority, that our forces, in large numbers, have gained the rear of the enemy, and that on Saturday, and perhaps yesterday, a bloody struggle was in progress on Bull Run, in the immediate vicinity of the battle field of the 21st July, 1861. Coupled with this statement is another, to the effect that other divisions of our army were pressing the enemy from this side, and forcing him on in the direction of our forces that have already been thrown between him and Washington. These statements we believe to be entitled to fuller consideration than should be given to mere street rumors, but we do not claim for them the sanction of unquestionable authority. We give them because we think them not at all improbable.

There are also reports of a heavy battle on Friday, near BristowStation, four miles south of Manassas, between the division of Gen. Ewell and the forces of the enemy, in which it is said that our forces were twice driven from their position, with severe loss, but receiving reinforcements, finally drove the enemy back, capturing several batteries and some five thousand prisoners. Reports conflict as to the precise locality of this engagement, one representing it at Bristow Station, and the other near the Plains, on the Manassas Gap road. If such a fight really took place, we think it more than likely the latter location is correct. It is also stated by some that the divisions of Jackson, A. P. Hill, and Ewell, were all in the battle, and others that it was fought by Ewell division alone.

Another report, which was brought to the city by passengers on Saturday, and again yesterday, represent that General Stuart has taken HarperFerry, and holds possession of the Baltimore and Ohio Railroad Bridge at that point. No particulars of the capture of this place are furnished, but those familiar with Stuartdashing exploits are generally ready to believe any report with reference to his daring feats. The latest information from HarperFerry placed the Federal forces there at four regiments. This force may have been withdrawn, or it may have been increased. The Federals have for some time boasted that the town was strongly fortified and prepared to resist the attack of a vastly superior force. How much truth there was in these boasts will be shown by a confirmation or contradiction of the report of its capture. If it has fallen into our hands it has been captured by a cavalry force, unsupported by infantry or artillery.

A member of Congress, who came down on the Central train yesterday afternoon, says that the *Baltimore Sun*, of Thursday, had been received in the Valley, in which it was stated that our forces had captured at Manassas, on Wednesday, five trains of cars loaded with provisions, and that later on the same day five other trains, on board of which were some two thousand Yankee troops. This affair was commented upon by the Yankee press as very discreditable to their commander, and some harsh reflections as to his fitness for his position indulged.

Our own account of this affair reports that a portion of our cavalry had advanced on the Orange and Alexandria Railroad to Bull Run bridge, about five miles beyond Manassas, and having burned the bridge, continued their advance to Dye Station, where they concealed themselves, and arrested the approach of a number of trains of which they had previously received information. After the trains had passed the concealed portion of the cavalry the track was torn up behind them. When they reached the bridge, the officers on board finding that something was wrong, determined to return to Alexandria, but before backing far they found the track torn up, and their retreat effectually intercepted.

The cavalry then approached in superior numbers, and the enemy surrendered without firing a gun. The number of prisoners reported captured agrees with the statement of the *Sun*, being estimated at 2,000, together with all the officers, regimental and company, and a quantity of arms and ammunition, which were being conveyed to General Pope. After this brilliant affair, this cavalry returned to Manassas, without sustaining the loss of a single man.

Some fifteen hundred to two thousand Yankee prisoners were yesterday between Rapidan Station and Gordonsville, and may be expected in this city today. It is supposed that these are the prisoners captured at DyeStation by our cavalry.

The *Charleston Mercury*
September 5, 1862

The News from Richmond
(Correspondence of the *Mercury*)

Richmond, Tuesday, September 2.
The plains of Manassas have been again dyed in blood, perhaps more deeply than before, and this time there has been no rain to swell the Potomac, no lack of transportation, no army of PATTERSON to come from HarperFerry to defend Washington; and now, shall we cross the Rubicon? The master of Arlington Heights must answer this question.

All we know, up to the present moment, is that McClellan and Pope have been routed, and that our boys are pursuing the fragments of the two armies towards the Occoquan – it is believed – for all seem to agree that McClellan landed there. A part of McCarmy (five or six thousand men) had not left Fortress Monroe on Saturday, the day of the decisive battle; and we hear nothing of Burnside, who has been at Fredericksburg, and is now, doubtless, en route to McClellan. Hence we see that there are still some veteran troops to encounter, in addition to the raw recruits now at Washington. Still, we ought to be able to advance.

We look anxiously for the train this evening, to hear what losses we have sustained. They have been heavy, unquestionably. Pope admits a loss of 8,000 in Thursday fight, which Lee speaks of as an affair of small moment.

There is wailing in all New England,
And by Schuylkill banks a knell,
Yes, and there is sorrow enough in all the South.

Gen. Lee will probably head the army of invasion, or, at least, of deliverance to Maryland. That he has been meditating work in and beyond his present vicinity, was inferred weeks ago from an expression of impatience which escaped him at hearing that some of our guerillas had again broken up the Baltimore and Ohio Railroad. 'It will be invaluable to us,' said he.

Much dissatisfaction is expressed against the course pursued by Congress in regard to extending the Conscript Law and making adequate preparation for the new Yankee levies. But Job is in Congress as well as in the Chair of the Executive, and Job is timid and afraid to look a coming danger in the face. De Quincy, considering murder as a Fine Art, says that a man who begins with murder may gradually rise to the high crime of procrastination. In our case, just at the present time, procrastination is not paradoxically worse than murder–it is murder of the direct proportion–national murder.

The *Examiner,* always urgent in its appeals to the people and the Government to make timely preparation, came out yesterday morning in a lengthy leader in behalf of the Conscript extension. The article is said to have been dictated by Jno. M. Daniel himself, whose wound has been well, or nearly so, for some weeks. But his arm and hand will be of no use to him for many months to come.

Congress appears timid in the matter of retaliation. Why, Popelate backdown ought to encourage them. By the way, I am glad to hear from a friend, just from the departments, that we have captured Gens. Blenker and Thomas, of Popearmy. The common sense of the country long since called for retaliation, and the success which has attended even its semblance, as given in General Order No. 54, ought to induce our legislators to put more trust in the sense of their fellow countrymen.

I hear that Gen. Beauregard has been assigned to the command of the Atlantic coast, with his headquarters at Charleston. Gen. J. E. Johnston takes charge of the Trans-Mississippi Department, with Gens. Price, Magruder and Holmes under him. Gen. G. W. Smith retains command here, and has taken a house not far from the President.

The Army of the Potomac marching over the Second Bull Run battleground near Groveton (Forbes). Library of Congress.

Frank Vizitelly, a well known artist of the *London Illustrated News*, has been at the Spotswood for some weeks, having a gay time with a number of young bloods of the army and navy. Vizitelly had to run the underground railroad to get to our side; after being with the Yankee army of the Potomac for a year, no wonder they refused him a pass to our lines. He has made a number of sketches of scenes in and around Richmond.

The weather has been singularly cool today.

HERMES.

The *Charleston Mercury*

September 5, 1862

News by Telegraph
The Latest from the Seat of War
Particulars of the Battle of Saturday – the Casualties

Manassas, August 30 (via RAPIDAN, September 4) – The second Battle of Manassas has been fought on precisely the same spot as that of 21st of July, 1861, with the difference that our forces occupied many of the positions which were held by the enemy at that time, and that the enemy fought upon the ground that had been held by us. Several of our regiments entered the field just where McDOWELL'S divisions did a year ago. The fight began about three o in the afternoon, near Groveton, on the Warrenton turnpike. LONGSTREET was on the right and JACKSON on the left, their line being in the form of a broad V, with the enemy within. The enemy made their first advance by endeavoring to turn JACKSON'S flank, but were repulsed in great confusion–a battery of twenty pieces of artillery, commanded by Col. STEPHEN D. LEE, of South Carolina, mowing them down by scores. LONGSTREET at once threw forward HOODS'S and BRYSON'S brigades, and advanced his whole line, which was in a short time separately engaged. JACKSON now gave battle, and the enemy was attacked on every side. The fight was fiercely contested until after dark, when the Yankees gave way and were driven in disorder for a distance of three miles. Their forces consisted of McDOWELL'S, SEIGEL'S, BANKS', MORELL'S, SICKLES', MILROY'S, McCLELLAN'S, and POPE'S divisions. The loss of the enemy exceeds that of the Confederates in the ratio of five to one. Their dead literally cover the field. Our men captured a number of batteries, numerous regimental colors, thousands of prisoners, and from six to ten thousand stand of arms. We might have taken more of these last; but the men could not be burdened with them. One Yankee Brigadier General is now lying dead at the negro Robinsonhouse, where the Yankee bodies are so thickly strewn that it is difficult to pass without stepping on them. Generals EWELL, JENKINS, MAHONE and TRIMBLE, are wounded. Colonels MEANS, MARSHALL and GADBERRY, of South Carolina, are killed. Colonels BENBOW, MOORE and McGOWAN, of the same State, are wounded. Major D. C. KEMPER is severely wounded in the shoulder; Captain TABB and Captain MITCHEL, of the First Virginia (the latter a son of JOHN MITCHELL, the Irish patriot), are wounded. Adjutant TOMPKINS, of the Hampton Legion, and Adjutant CAMERON, of the Twenty-Fourth Virginia, were both wounded. About fifty Yankee of Washington, who had come out to witness the show, have been bagged by our forces.

Richmond, September 3
No official despatches have been received from the seat of war in Northern Virginia today. The reports brought by passengers all indicate that our victory over the Yankees was complete, and that our troops are in pursuit of the routed enemy.

The Casualties at Manassas

The *Columbia Carolinian*, of yesterday, gives a telegraphic report from Richmond, that Gen. JENKINS and Col. BENBOW, of this State, are mortally wounded. The Federal Generals POPE and McDOWELL are also mortally wounded, and Gen. SICKLES killed.

The *Charleston Mercury*

September 6, 1862

Manassas

Slowly the smoke is clearing away from the famous field of Manassas, and, while we can learn but little of the later movements of the opposing forces, it is easy to see that the struggle of Saturday was, indeed, for us, signal victory. Already the sounds of wailing and lamentation come echoing from the North. Thousands upon thousands of the invading host have gone down before the valor of our veteran troops; the third Grand Army which had been marshalled upon Virginia soil for the subjugation of that noble State, is beaten, and has fled utter rout; Maryland, from her eastern shore to the Blue Ridge, is throbbing with the hope of an early deliverance, and sits uneasy in her chains; while Washington, the centre of official falsehood and corruption, is quaking at the approach of the very army that the Yankee leaders were lately so confident of crushing and driving the wall.

But new blows must be struck and new victories won before the enemy can be brought to his senses. The army of KIRBY SMITH must press forward from Lexington until the tramp of its brigades shall startle the people who dwell beyond the Ohio. Our victorious troops in Virginia, reduced though they be in numbers, and shattered in organization, must be led promptly into Maryland, before the enemy can rally the masses of recruits whom he is rapidly and steadily gathering together. When the Government of the North shall have fled into Pennsylvania, when the public buildings in Washington shall have been razed to the ground, so as to forbid the hope of their ever again becoming the nest of Yankee despotism, then, at last, may we expect to see the hope of success vanish from the Northern mind, and reap the fruit of our bloody and long continued trials.

The *Charleston Mercury*

September 8, 1862

Proclamation by the President
To the People of the Confederate States

Once more upon the plains of Manassas have our armies been blessed by the Lord of Hosts with a triumph over our enemies. It is my privilege to invite you once more to His footstool, not now in the garb of fasting and sorrow, but with joy and gladness, to render thanks for the great mercies received at His hands. A few months since, and our enemies poured forth their invading legions upon our soil. They laid waste our fields, polluted our altars, and violated the sanctity of our homes. Around our capital they gathered their forces, and with boastful threats claimed it as already their prize. The brave troops which rallied to its defence have extinguished these vain hopes, and under the guidance of the same Almighty hand, have scattered our enemies and driven them back in dismay. Uniting these defeated forces and the various armies which had been ravaging our coasts with the army of invasion in Northern Virginia, our enemies have renewed their attempt to subjugate us at the very place where their first effort was defeated, and the vengeance of retributive justice has overtaken the entire host, in a second and complete overthrow.

To this signal success accorded to our arms in the East, has been graciously added another equally brilliant in the West. On the very day on which our forces were led to victory on the plains of Manassas in Virginia, the same Almighty arm assisted us to overcome our enemies at Richmond, in Kentucky. Thus at one and the same time, have the two great hostile armies been stricken down, and the wicked designs of our enemies set at nought.

In such circumstances, it is meet and right that, as a people, we should bow down in adoring thankfulness to that gracious God who has been our bulwark and defence, and to offer unto Him the tribute of thanksgiving and praise. In His hand are the issues of all events, and to Him should we, in an especial manner, ascribe the honor of this great deliverance.

Now, therefore, I, JEFFERSON DAVIS, President of the Confederate States, do issue this my proclamation, setting apart THURSDAY, the 18th day of September, instant, as a day of prayer and thanksgiving to Almighty God, for the great mercies vouchsafed to our people, and more especially for the triumph of our arms at Richmond and Manassas; and I do hereby invite the people of the Confederate States to meet on that day at their respective places of public worship, and to unite in rendering thanks and praise to God for these great mercies, and to implore Him to conduct our country safely through the perils which surround us, to the final attainment of the blessings of peace and security.

Given under my hand, and the seal of the
Confederate States, at Richmond, this fourth day of
September, A.D. 1862.
JEFFERSON DAVIS.

By the President:
J.P. BENJAMIN, Secretary of State.

The *Charleston Mercury*
September 8, 1862

The Casualties in the Late Battles at Manassas – The lists of casualties in the recent battles in Northern Virginia, owing, doubtless, to the distance intervening between the scene of hostilities and the nearest telegraph station, come in very slowly. We gather, however, from private sources the following details:

Gen. JENKINS has telegraphed that he will be home in ten days. We are induced to hope, therefore, that his wound is not serious.

Capt. JOHN WITHERSPOON, of Col. MEANS' regiment, received a severe wound in the thigh, breaking it. He is at Warrenton.

Mr. RUDOLPH SEIGLING, of the German Artillery (Charleston), was killed.

THE BATTLE OF GROVETON (FORBES). LIBRARY OF CONGRESS.

Lieut. P.A. AVEILHE, of Capt. MURDEN'S company, 23d S.C.V., and private L. SIDNEY AVEILHE, of the W. L. I. Volunteers, were slightly wounded. Also, private THADDEUS L. CAT, of the W. L. I. Volunteers.

A private letter from the Quartermaster Sergeant of the 17th S. C. V., dated Rappahannock river, August 25, contains the following in regard to the battle of the 23d ult.: 'Our regiment lost one man killed, and three wounded. The Holcombe Legion lost sixteen wounded and their color bearer killed. He fell just as they were mounting a Yankee redoubt, with the colors (Mrs. PICKENS' gift) in his hand. He was brought in and buried close to our camp. I saw our friend Lieut. MUNRO brought in badly wounded.'

Lieut. WM. ALLEN, of the Chicora Rifles, was killed. The *Columbia Guardian* of yesterday publishes the following private despatches:

CHARLOTTESVILLE, VA., September 5. – The following is a list of the casualties in the Johnston Riflemen, Company K, Captain Meetz, 13th Regiment S.C.V.: Killed – J.F.M. Lucas, James W. Esenger, J.B. Clamp. Wounded – severely – Sergeant W.H. Counts, J.F. Harman, Colorbearer J.C. Drafts,

Calvin Pearce, J.E. Rowe, J.J. Hooper, J.J. Lawn, J.R. Miller, Wilson Taylor, William Holman; slightly, J.P. LaPorte, H.N. Gorley, J.P. Hornell, H.J. Boatwright, Capt. Meetz, hurt by a fall after the battle.

The *Charleston Mercury*

September 13, 1862

The South Carolina Zouaves at Manassas

We have been favored with the following extract from a private letter of a member of the South Carolina Zouaves, dated Manassas Plains, August 30:

Thank God! my life is spared after a terrific engagement. On the 29th July our company joined the Legion, near Richmond, where we remained one week. We have since marched two hundred miles, and, on the 29th of August, one month after our arrival, we were marched through the woods on to a hill, perfectly clear of timber, where we formed in line and prepared for a charge. All were cool and self-possessed. In our front was a regiment, which all thought friends (it being after 7, p.m., we could not distinguish), when they fired on us. Three men, Lockwood, Hutto and Felder, dropped wounded, each in the leg; nothing serious though. Being still under the impression that the men in front were the 18th Georgia Regiment, we held back our fire and advanced. On arriving at the foot of the hill we asked who was there, and the scoundrels answered 'Friends, and 5th Texas!' Just then a United States flag was observed, and then they said: 'New York and 76th Pennsylvania!' In a flash we opened and charged, completely routing the regiment. We followed, and fired again; but our main chance was lost. We killed about twenty and wounded a great many. We occupied the field. Volunteers being called for to go in advance and see if the enemy were near, Gelling and I jumped out. We discovered several wounded and took some prisoners, and captured their flag. During the night we retired to our former position in the woods. But that was childplay. All the following day we remained in concealment till about 5 p.m., yesterday, when we were marched out again. Crossing a piece of woods, a tremendous volley was poured into us. I had not fired, but felt sharp pain in my left ankle, and knew I was shot. Deliberately raising my rifle, I fired into a clump of bushes, where some of the foe were concealed, with what success I could not learn. My wound prevented my going on, so I turned to help some worse hurt than myself. Our fellows routed them and they retired. Soon after commenced an awful shelling; bullets fell thick and fast, but steadily forward moved our men. Back they drove the foe! Such volleys, such firing, I never heard; it was frightful. But I cannot go on, not having time. In the fight the Captain was wounded in the head, ankle and thigh; Lieut. Palmer in the left breast, and Clarke in the thigh; Oliver Gregory was hurt in four places – only one painful wound in the leg – nothing serious; George Gelling, by a spent ball, in the thigh; Cook, Brown and Dewane, killed; and, all told, 13 wounded that we know of. My ankle feels stiff, but I can easily walk. Geo. Gelling is with us, and Oliver Gregory in the hospital. I think 20 will cover our whole loss.

I have seen a battle field, and never desire to see another. Lieut. Allen is killed; I saw him this morning. We now occupy the battle field of Manassas Plains.

The *Charleston Mercury*

September 16, 1862

A Cavalry Charge

During the last battle of Manassas, about four o, p.m., as the columns of the enemy began to give way, Gen. Beverly Robinson was ordered by Gen. Longstreet to charge the flying masses with his brigade of cavalry. The brigade, numbering a thousand men, composed of Munford, Myer, Harman and Flournoyregiments, was immediately put in motion, but before reaching the infantry General Robinson discovered a brigade of the enemy fifteen hundred strong drawn up on the crest of a hill directly in his front. Leaving one of his companies in reserve, he charged with the other three full at the enemyranks. As our men drew near, the whole of the Yankee line fired at them a volley from their carbines, most of the bullets, however, whistling harmlessly over their heads. In another instant the enemy received the terrific shock of our squadrons. There was a pause, a hand-to- hand fight for a moment, and the enemy broke and fled in total rout. All organization was destroyed, and every man trusted for his safety only in the heels of his horses. Our cavalry followed them close, cutting them down and taking prisoners at every step. Before reaching Centreville we had slain at least three hundred, and captured five hundred prisoners. The rest made good their escape by flight. It is said they did not draw a rein nor slacken their pace until they reached Alexandria. Two of their captains and several other commissioned officers were left dead on the field. The Yankee papers report the death of their commander, Gen. Buford, but if killed his body was carried off by his men.

We have received this account from a participant in the engagement. Our informant, from his position as a cavalry officer, had fine opportunities of judging of the condition of the Yankee troops during the retreat. He describes them as utterly demoralized and disorganized. They hurried along in great droves like frightened cattle, officers and men being mingled indiscriminately and inextricably. Our men followed them up and slaughtered them at leisure. Had the rout taken place two hours earlier, the entire army would have been destroyed or taken prisoners. *Richmond Examiner.*

From *The New York Times*

Defeat of the Rebels on the Old Bull Run Battle-Ground. DISPATCH FROM GEN. POPE. A Terrific Battle on Friday, Lasting All Day. The Combined Forces of the Enemy Engaged. The Rebels Driven from the Field. Our Losses Not Less than Eight Thousand Killed and Wounded. The Rebel Losses Probably Double. Important Capture Made by our Forces. Retreat of the Rebels Toward the Mountains on Friday Morning. PROMPT PURSUIT BY GEN. POPE.

ANOTHER GREAT BATTLE YESTERDAY. OFFICIAL DISPATCH FROM GEN. POPE.

HEADQUARTERS FIELD OF BATTLE. GROVETON NEAR GAINESVILLE, AUG. 30, 1862.
To Major-Gen. Halleck, General-in-Chief, Washington, D. C:
We fought a terrific battle here yesterday, with the combined forces of the enemy, which lasted with continuous fury from daylight until after dark, by which time the enemy was driven from the field, which we now occupy.

Our troops are too much exhausted to push matters, but I shall do so in the course of the morning, as soon as FITZ-JOHN PORTER'S corps come up from Manassas. The enemy is still in our front, but badly used up.

We have lost not less than eight thousand men killed and wounded, and from the appearance of the field, the enemy have lost at least two to our one. He stood strictly on the defensive, and every assault was made by ourselves.

Our troops have behaved splendidly.

The Battle was fought on the identical battle-field of Bull Run which greatly increased the enthusiasm of our men.

The news just reached me from the front that the enemy is retreating toward the mountains. I go forward at once to see.

We have made great captures, but I am not able yet to form an idea of their extent.

JOHN POPE, MAJOR-GENERAL COMMANDING

The Second Bull Run Battle

Washington, Saturday, Aug. 30

To-day's *Evening Star*, speaking of the battle of yesterday says:
"The battle was continued by the army corps of Generals HEINTZELMAN, MCDOWELL and SIGEL against a [rebel force] believed to number near fifty to sixty thousand strong that is against the army corps of JAMES LONGSTREET. We defeated a portion of the rest of LEE'S army that has succeeded in making its way down from White Plains through Thorough-fare Gap.

The location of the battle of the day was in the vicinity of Haymarket, and from Haymarket off in the direction of Sudley Church, or, in other words but a few miles northwest of the scene of the never-to-be-forgotten battle of Bull Run.

HEINTZELMAN'S Corps, if we are correctly informed, came up with the enemy's rear about 10 A.M., seven miles from Centreville, which point he left at daybreak. He found STONEWALL JACKSON fighting with MCDOWELL or SIGEL, or both, on the right, in the direction of Haymarket, the position they took by going north from Gainsville, to command the entrance to and exit from Thorough-fare Gap.

Our own informant, who left Centreville at 4 o'clock in the afternoon, a cool and clear-headed man, says that up to that hour, the impression prevailed there that nothing had definitely resulted from the day's fighting, which, though continuous, had not been a very bloody battle.

Persons subsequently arriving, who were on the field of action themselves until 4 P.M., however, represent that the tide of success was decidedly with the Union army, which pushed the rebels successfully on both sides.

OFFICERS AND SOLDIERS ON THE BATTLEFIELD OF SECOND BULL RUN, RECOGNIZING THE REMAINS OF THEIR COMRADES (EDWIN FORBES). LIBRARY OF CONGRESS.

An impression prevails that the reserve of LEE'S army, supposed to be from twenty to forty thousand strong, might suddenly appear near the field, and we know that the heavy corps under FITZ-JOHN PORTER was so posted that it could instantly move upon LEE with equal ease, whether attacking McDOWELL, SIGEL or HEINTZELMAN.

The railroad, we are happy to say, has already been repaired quite up to Bull Run, and supplies, etc., are now being transported over it to that point.

By midnight we have every reason to believe that the Bull Run bridge will again be passable, when the trains can run again to Manassas.

Ere evacuating Manassas, the rebels paroled the 700 Union prisoners they had taken since the commencement of the movement for which they are paying so dearly.

The rebels realized that prisoners in their present strait were an elephant in their hands, and wisely thus got rid of them.

These 700 prisoners covered all the stragglers they had taken, as well as the 500 of TAYLOR'S Brigade.

Washington, Saturday, Aug. 30

The following is gathered from private sources:

On Wednesday morning, or rather on Tuesday night, a report reached Warrenton Junction that JACKSON was again in our rear, and that, instead of making an attack and retiring, as his cavalry did on Friday night last, at Catlett's Station, he had taken up a position on the railroad near Bristor, four miles south of Manassas; had burned two railroad trains, torn up the railroad tracks, cut the telegraph, and took prisoners all the guards along the road.

These reports prove to have been true, and the events of Wednesday showed his determination not to be easily driven from the neighborhood.

It seems from what can be learned from the rebel wounded in our hands, that JACKSON and EWELL started from the vicinity of Warrenton Springs on Sunday, with three divisions, crossed the Rappahancock some six miles south of Blue Ridge, and proceeded by way of Orleans and Salem to Bristor, making the distance in about two and a half days.

On reaching this point their first object of attack was the house of MR. LIPSCOMBE, where ten officers were stopping, and who were on the back porch at the time, smoking. The house was attacked both front and rear, and the bullet holes in the wood and plaster, with the fact that none of the party were wounded, showed what poor marksmen these rebel cavalry were. The entire party, however, with the exception of Capt. 0. A. TILDENMORE, were taken prisoners.

The next attack of the rebels was upon a company of the One Hundred and Fifth Pennsylvania Infantry and some dozen of Pennsylvania Cavalry, left to guard the road, two or three of whom were killed, and the remainder are supposed to be captured.

A train of empty cars then came along from Warrenton, and was fired into by a regiment of infantry and one of cavalry, but escaped without serious injury.

Orders were then issued by JACKSON to tear up the railroad tracks, which was done, and a second train coming along, ran off the track, and was fired into.

A third train following ran into the second and was also fired into, and some persons on board were taken prisoners.

A fourth train made its appearance, but the Engineer suspected something wrong, stopped at a distance and blew a whistle, and being answered by one of the others, backed and returned toward Warrenton.

Two trains were then fired, under the direction of JACKSON, and entirely consumed, excepting the iron-work.

The rebels then proceeded a mile down the tracks, burned the bridge of Cattle Run, tore up some thirty feet of the track, and cut the telegraph.

They also burned the bridge across Broad Run, at Bristor.

On Wednesday morning, EWELL's Rebel Division were placed in position on each side of the railroad, having three batteries, one on the right, one on the left, and the other near the railroad, with infantry and cavalry between, the entire force being concealed behind bush-woods and the artillery with an open field in front.

The result of this action was that the enemy was beaten and driven from the field, sustaining a loss about equal to our own.

Our loss was about fifty killed and over two hundred wounded, a complete list of which was collected, but stolen.

The Second New-York regiment lost about ten officers and some ninety or one hundred killed and wounded.

The Excelsior Brigade suffered severely.

The physicians on the ground (Dr. MORROW of the Second New Hampshire being the only named I can now recollect) exerted themselves to relieve the wounded; and although the accommodations to operate were very poor, they succeeded during the afternoon and night in attending to all.

Gen. POPE arrived on the ground in the evening and proceeded towards the scene of action, but the fighting was then over and the enemy in full retreat.

JACKSON had left for Manassas during the day with his division, where he pillaged the place, capturing a large number of prisoners, and burning every building, except the telegraph building and a few shanties, after taking off their own old rags, and putting on our good clothing, and helping themselves to food of all kinds, arms, equipments, and whatever else they could carry away out of the cars, about a hundred of which were at that place, for the greater part loaded with supplies for our army.

The rebels then set fire to all the cars, and they now present a mass of bleached ruins.

On their arrival, they found a portion of two New-Jersey Regiments of Infantry, which had arrived there during the forenoon. They immediately attacked them, our troops defending themselves for some time, but finding the number of the enemy so great, and that they were being flanked, they retreated towards Centreville, and got away with the loss of some forty wounded and about twelve killed. The rebels captured six hundred and twenty-five of them, but they were paroled yesterday morning just before the battle commenced.

The pursuit was continued towards Centreville on Thursday afternoon, and a squadron of the Second Pennsylvania Cavalry, with Gen. BIRNEY, was in the advance, and stopped at Centreville to inquire the route taken by the enemy. While there a woman waved a flag from the back window, at which signal a force of rebel cavalry, about 2,000 strong, under Gen. LEE, emerged from the woods. Our men had scarcely time to mount their horses and escape, coming down the road at full speed, the enemy in swift pursuit. They were followed until they came to where our infantry were drawn in line of battle on each side of the road, at which point, the rebels received a volley which caused them to retreat at more than a double-quick.

Our troops took up the line of march, and followed the rebels during the night on the Gainesville or Warrenton road, and soon came in sight of the old Bull Run battleground in strong position.

The action commenced about 9 o'clock, our batteries having been placed in position, and MILROY'S Brigade having the advance, was ordered to charge the rebels through the woods, and to cross toward the railroad switch, when the enemy poured into our troops a perfect storm of grape and canister.

This caused them to fall back, but they soon rallied, and paid the enemy with interest.

The rebels here rose en masse behind the railroad track, and again caused our men to fall back, which they did behind HAMPTON'S Pittsburgh Battery, which opened upon the rebels terrifically. The enemy were at the time only about thirty yards distant, and the effect of the fire destroyed at least 600 of them. In this action, however, HAMPTON lost one of his guns. He had to change his position to the left, as he was unable to maintain himself under the fire which the rebels poured into him.

The battle in other quarters raged furiously, the general result of which has already been stated from other sources.

The position of the forces on Thursday night remained about the same as it was at the commencement of the action.

The loss on both sides is heavy.

Gen. DURYEE, when engaged in making a reconnaissance to-day, was wounded in the hand.

The fighting up to 12 o'clock to-day was of a desultory character.

We occupy the ground where the rebels had buried their dead.

Fighting Stopped at Noon Yesterday

Philadelphia, Saturday, Aug. 30

The *Washington Star* says:
"At 121/2 o'clock this afternoon, the fighting that has been heard all day stopped, as we learn from parties just down from Fairfax County. We trust this fact means the surrender of the rebels, and we don't see how it can mean aught else."

The *Star* also contains some severe statements on the slow movements of Gen. FRANKLIN'S Division which were open to criticism in Washington to-day. According to the accounts of those last from the battle-field, the belief there was that Jackson was aiming to get off from POPE in the direction of Aldie. The *Star* doubts this.

A dispatch is published from Capt. MASSER, late Commissary in charge of Centreville, announcing his arrival there with 624 paroled prisoners.

The *Star* contains an urgent call for nurses, for whom prompt railroad transmission has been ordered by the War Department.

Previous News in Washington From the *Washington Star* on Friday Evening

Philadelphia, Saturday, Aug. 30

We have information that satisfies us that the rebel force that suddenly appeared between the position of the army of

Gen. POPE, and at Bristor and Manassas, on Tuesday night last, was the army corps of JACKSON, and STUART'S independent cavalry corps. They consisted of infantry and artillery, and marched about thirty thousand strong from near Waterloo, on the head waters of the Rappahannock, around by White Plains to Manassas, about forty miles in two days, without wagons, tents, blankets, or even knapsacks, thus leaving their baggage of every description to be transported by wagons, with the other army corps of LEE'S following behind them.

Instead of fighting merely a portion of STUART'S Cavalry at Manassas, on the day before yesterday, TAYLOR'S brigade were actually confronted by a greater portion of Jackson's corps d'armee, Maj. Gens. JACKSON, EWELL, TALIAFERRO, A. P. HILL, and STUART, and the General and Chief, Robert LEE, and his son, Brig. Gen. FITZHUGH LEE, being present at Manassas during the battle.

Yesterday, at 1 o'clock P.M. JACKSON'S advance of cavalry had collected their own wounded of the action of the day before with TAYLOR, if not their wounded of the engagement on the same day with HOOKER, and also the prisoners they took from TAYLOR.

In the afternoon, about 800 of this cavalry force under STUART in person, moved down from Fairfax Court-house to Vienna.

HOOKER'S battle, of the day before yesterday, was with EWELL'S division, and was a gratifying success.

Maj. Gen. POPE, by 91/2 o'clock yesterday morning, had concentrated his very large army, so as to badly interfere with the calculations upon which the rebel Generals must have ventured their bold and extraordinary movement.

At 4 P.M. yesterday an engagement commenced between POPE and JACKSON'S rear or LONGSTREET'S advance, somewhere about Manassas. If with the former, then HEINTZELMAN'S corps d'armee, or a portion of it, were engaged on our side. If with the latter, then McDOWELL'S or SIGEL, or both, commenced it. It continued through the balance of the afternoon.

We had gotten McDOWELL'S force, including SIGEL's probably, between JACKSON'S rear and LONGSTREET'S front, and had also all the rest of his army well up within supporting distance. Thus it continued through the balance of the afternoon.

Facts within our knowledge lead to the impression that in twenty-four hours direct communication will have been established between Washington and Maj. Gen. POPE'S army; more especially as there are signs that JACKSON'S army corps is endeavoring to proceed northwardly, as though making for the experiment of opposing the reestablishment of such communications with his immediate front, with Pope's army practically between him and the other rebel corps d'armee.

We may add that Gen. MCCLELLAN is disposing of his heavy Union force around Washington and Alexandria, and the fortifications, so as to make it play an important part in the eventful drama of the hour.

In the battle of yesterday, the attack certainly came from our side.

Our Correspondence from the Field

The Guerrilla Raid upon the Orange and Alexandria Railroad
The Attack Near White Plains
Capture of a New York Battery at Manassas
The Fight at Bull Run
Headquarters in the Field Between Alexandria and Bristor Station, Thursday, P.M., Aug. 28, 1862

I have fortunately been able to obtain some reliable and interesting details of the transactions during Tuesday night and a portion of yesterday (Wednesday) on the line of the Orange and Alexandria Railroad and vicinity. Tuesday evening, between 5 and 8 o'clock, five trains of empty cars were captured and mostly destroyed by a rebel cavalry force on the road between Bristor Station and Manassas Junction, and on the same evening the enemy destroyed a bridge across Broad River, and subsequently the bridges across other small creeks on the railroad. There were stationed at Manassas Junction, Tuesday, the Twelfth Pennsylvania Cavalry, numbering between 500 and 600 men, Col. WHITE, and the First New-York Battery-10 pieces—with about 300 men to serve them. At 6 o'clock, a dispatch was received by telegraph from Warrenton Junction, directing the cavalry to proceed immediately to White Plains, (15 miles) on the Manassas road, and keep a sharp look out for the enemy, who, it was understood, had crossed the Rappahannock in force on Sunday, and by the way of Jeffersonton and Little Washington, was making his way for some point on the line of the Orange and Alexandria Railroad, with a view, no doubt, to divide our forces and isolate the command of Gen. POPE—a position which the commander of the Union forces desired him to take, and a fatal one to the enemy it is certainly believed to be. The Pennsylvania cavalry left for the point directed, but finding none of the enemy at White Plains, at a late hour the corps started to return to the Junction. When within eight or nine miles of the latter place, they found a corps of about 1,000 cavalry, supposed to be commanded by FITZHUGH LEE, drawn up to dispute their further progress. A brisk skirmish took place, when our cavalry cut their way through the rebel ranks, losing a number in killed, wounded and prisoners. There was a kind of running fight kept up until the Junction was reached, at about 1 o'clock A.M. of Wednesday, when the rebels apparently retired satisfied. The cavalry fell back to a position one mile north of the Junction, know as BEAUREGARD'S Headquarters, were under arms all night, without knowing what had transpired at the Junction during their absence at White Plains. In this interval the rebels had fallen upon the F. New-York Artillery by surprise—the officer in command supposing the approac force to be our own cavalry until too late—and captured eight of their guns. This not done, however until after a test of sanguinary resistance, resulting in the killing and wounding of many men on both sides. A member of the Pennsylvania Cavalry, not knowing that the Junction was in the hands of the rebels, walked very deliberately to the camp and finding himself in a trap, coolly asked the first re he met "how things were going," and in reply the rebel soldier said, "All right—have had lots of fun and plunder." Our soldier then attempted to set loose a number of Government horses tied in a stable, when an officer said, "That is not one of our men—shoot him." At about this time the two guns saved from the New-York Batte commenced throwing shell, and this soldier escaped and reached his own command. It was now 7 o'clock Wednesday morning. The rebels occupied the earthworks in the Junction, but after a time advanced from their position and made an unsuccessful attempt to take the remaining guns of the New-York Battery. A running fight was kept up along the line of the railroad, our troops gradually falling back until near mid-day, when at a point one mile south of Fairfax Station, they were met by a force of infantry and artillery under the command of Brig. Gen. TAYLOR, of New Jersey and the rebels were driven back to Manassas Junction forthwith. A fact especially worthy of notice in this connection is, that upon the person of a prisoner captured was found a copy of the identical dispatch sent by telegraph from Warrenton Junction, between 4 and 5 o' clock P.M. of Tuesday, directing the cavalry at Manassas Junction to leave for White Plains, so that they were enabled to attack the place when the least resistance could be offered. It is believed by many that this dispatch could not have been obtained in any other way than through the agency of some employee of the Government.

Of the fight that took place Wednesday afternoon with Gen. TAYLOR'S force, on the road between Manassas Junction and Bull Run, and at the latter place, but little reliable information can be obtained at this time. The engagement was a sharp and deadly one—the rebels holding their position at night; but those who ought to know what occurred this morning look very good-natured, and hence we, who are in the dark, draw the inference that the rebels got their dessert this morning. The rebel force in action at Bull Run, Wednesday evening, is believed to have been about

5,000 men, principally cavalry and artillery. Our force consisted of ten regiments of infantry, and ten guns. Gen. TAYLOR was so badly wounded in one of his legs, by the explosion of a shell, that the leg was amputated to-day. The Eleventh and Twelfth Ohio Regiments, it is said, suffered the most—the latter having, according to a statement of a member, eighty wounded and twelve killed. The wildest rumor was circulated in Alexandria to-day about the result of the fight yesterday and this morning, but there is no occasion for any alarm. A force of men, left the vicinity of Alexandria early this morning for the scene of action—a force which, with that under Gen. POPE'S immediate command, is sufficient to crush a very respectable force of the enemy. I shall send forth additional details as soon as anything reliable can be obtained. The excitement was somewhat intensified in Alexandria last night, by the 12th Virginia Cavalry rushing into the city in a panic; and the excitement was again renewed this morning by the return of a train of cars that started for Manassas Junction. The train was fired upon when fifteen miles out and returned.

I escaped from the Rappahannock just at the right moment. Had I been 20 minutes later on Tuesday night, I should have been captured by the rebels. The train that kept us company all the way up was nabbed. It is supposed that JACKSON had nearly his whole force near White Plains. If so there is no escape for them as far as I can see. POPE must have 200,000 well-disciplined troops south of JACKSON. There are 75,000 fresh troops encamped about Washington, and then there is an immense force of tried men—say 50,000 men—between this point and JACKSON'S position. Gen. MCCLELLAN reached Alexandria Wednesday morning, and was at the telegraph office writing dispatches—orders—nearly all night. He can write with facility with either hand. To-day he is confined to his room by reason of slight indisposition. The rebels captured a saddle of mine at Manassas Junction, and a small bundle of papers and clothing. They were placed on the train just behind the one in which I took passage, by mistake. I hope that HALLECK's infamous order about correspondents will be modified soon. It is very unsatisfactory to be compelled to obtain information as we do now. The Tenth New-York Cavalry, 750 men (new corps), is now passing to the front. They are the finest set of men, and best mounted, in the service. They elicit the admiration of every one.

New regiments are rolling in upon us here almost every hour in the day—quite as fast as they can be accommodated. Three hundred paroled prisoners, I suppose, left Washington yesterday for Dixie, and Fortress Monroe. But these matters you get by telegraph.

The report in the *Tribune* of the fighting on the Rappahannock are, for the most part, grossly erroneous.

The Operations of Gen. Taylor's Brigade at Bull Run and Vicinity

Wednesday, Aug. 27
Jackson Completely Cut Off on Thursday
By General Hooker and Kearny

Fairfax Court House, Friday, Aug. 29, 1862

In my last I gave you a correct and somewhat detailed account of the operations of the Twentieth Pennsylvania Cavalry, and First New-York Battery at Manassas Junction and vicinity, on Wednesday, the 27th, down to the time when they were relieved by reinforcements. To continue in order as the events occurred, Brig. Gen. TAYLOR, in command of the New Jersey Brigade, 1,600 strong—all infantry—left Alexandria early on Wednesday morning, to reinforce the command Manassas Junction. When one mile north of Bull Run Bridge, they found the track obstructed by the debris of a destroyed train of cars, and, disembarking, proceeded on foot toward Manassas Junction. Upon arriving in sight of the latter place, they saw the Stars and Stripes flying, and heard the roar of cannon; as the flag was there and no shots were directed toward Gen. TAYLOR'S column, that officer concluded that our forces were firing upon a force of the enemy beyond, and consequently pressed forward at a double-quick. Too late the discovery was made that the troops at the Junction were rebels, and that the raising of the Stars and Stripes, and the aiming of their guns in an opposite direction was a ruse of the enemy. When within half gunshot distance, the rebels opened upon Gen. TAYLOR'S command, right, left, and front, with the eight 32-pound cannon which they had captured a few hours before from the New-York Battery. Their cavalry immediately fired a volley and charged at the same time, which for a moment created a panic in our ranks. Gen. TAYLOR speedily obtained order, and gradually fell back to Bull Run Bridge, he having no artillery or cavalry to use against the rebels. At the latter place Gen. TAYLOR was reinforced by the arrival of the Eleventh and Twelfth Ohio Volunteers—the latter a cavalry corps—and quite a brisk fight took place, when the rebels were finally repulsed. Gen. TAYLOR was wounded in the leg while gallantly rallying his men against a superior force of the enemy, composed of cavalry and artillery. Late at night, the commander of our forces, learning that the rebels had received large re-inforcements, fell back to Fairfax Station, and at 11 o'clock at night moved on to this place, as the advance of a large force which left Alexandria on Thursday morning. The rebels had disappeared.

It is alleged that the Twelfth Pennsylvania Cavalry acted in the most scandalous manner at Bull Run, and the bulk of the regiment made a rapid retreat toward Alexandria. To the truth of this, however, I cannot vouch.

Jackson Cut Off

The movements on Thursday, the 28th, were more important than any that have taken place during the present conflict. Gens. HOOKER and KEARNY with their commands advance upon the rear of JACKSON and have forced him to where he is completely cut off, and must, with his whole force, be captured and destroyed unless some stupendous error is made on our side. JACKSON will probably get into

Washington somewhat sooner than he expected, and in a manner less agreeable than he anticipated.

There is heavy firing northwest of this place this morning, and it is supposed that our force has compelled Jackson to face about and fight.

What the Historians Say

The second battle at Manassas—known also as Manassas, Second Bull Run, Manassas Plains, Groveton, Gainesville and Brawner's Farm—occurred on August 28-30, 1862, In Prince William County, Virginia. It was the fifth and largest of the six battles in the Northern Virginia Campaign, which took place from June through September, 1862.

The principal commanders were Maj. Gen. John Pope commanding the Union Army forces and Generals Robert E. Lee and Thomas (Stonewall) Jackson commanding the Confederate Army. The estimated casualties were 13, 830 and 8,350 respectively.

In order to draw Pope's army into battle, Jackson ordered an attack on a Federal column that was passing across his front on the Warrenton Turnpike on August 28. The fighting at Brawner's Farm lasted several hours and resulted in a stalemate. Pope became convinced that he had trapped Jackson and concentrated the bulk of his army against him. On August 29, Pope launched a series of assaults against Jackson's position along an unfinished railroad grade. The attacks were repulsed with heavy casualties on both sides. At noon, Longstreet arrived on the field from Thoroughfare Gap and took position on Jackson's right flank. On August 30, Pope renewed his attacks, seemingly unaware that Longstreet was on the field. When massed Confederate artillery devastated a Union assault by Fitz John Porter's command, Longstreet's wing of 28,000 men counterattacked in the largest, simultaneous mass assault of the war. The Union left flank was crushed and the army driven back to Bull Run. Only an effective Union rearguard action prevented a replay of the First Manassas disaster. Pope's retreat to Centreville was precipitous, nonetheless. The next day, Lee ordered his army in pursuit. This was the decisive battle of the Northern Virginia Campaign and was of major significance in the intensification of the war.

Retreat of the Army of the Rappahannock, commanded by General Pope, through the town of Centreville after the battle of Second Bull Run (Forbes). Library of Congress.

Antietam

The Great Battle that Encouraged Abraham Lincoln to issue the Emancipation Proclamation

Author's Commentary

Ridicule was a weapon the press on both sides of the war used particularly well. Truthfulness would suffer as a result. *The New York Times* took aim at Stonewall Jackson and his men just prior to the battle at Antietam, describing Jackson and his men entering Harpers Ferry, which they had just taken: "(He was) dressed in the coarsest kind of homespun, seedy and dirty at that, uniform, wearing an old hat which any Northern begger would consider an insult to have offered him. In his general appearance, he was in no respect to be distinguished from the mongrel, barefooted crew who followed his fortunes." Hardly an objective analysis of what was then a conquering army.

A week later, the *Charleston Mercury* put a northern general in its sights. Focusing on George McClellan, it took aim at his claim of victory at Antietam as a geneological flaw. George Bagby, a pre-war physician who certainly knew better and the paper's Richmond correspondent, writing under the pseudonym, Hermes, wrote that McClellan's father, also a physician, was "a braggart and fibber" for having claimed that he had extirpated the parotid gland. "Drs. Gibson and Physick proved by repeated dissections of the dead body that the extirpation of this gland was an utter impossibility: but old Dr. McClellan stuck to his fib until death. General George has long ago announced the morality of lying in war."

It is obvious that "Hermes" took liberty with the truth. The parotid gland was first successfully extirpated by a McClellan other than George McClellan's father. Dr. John McClellan of Greencastle, Pennsylvania, performed the operation in 1805–fifty-seven years before Antietam.

Sept. 1862: From the *Charleston Mercury*

From Our Army in Maryland

The Battle of Sharpsburg and Fall of Harper's Ferry

The Richmond papers bring us some further and interesting accounts of the recent brilliant operations of our army on the Upper Potomac and in Maryland. The following is a brief resume of the various accounts of these important movements, concerning which the telegraphic news hitherto received has been so vague and unsatisfactory. Our army in Maryland is divided into three corps, commanded by Generals JACKSON, LONGSTREET and D.H. HILL. Of these corps JACKSON'S was engaged in the siege of HarperFerry, and the other two covered his operations. Conceiving it to be of great importance to raise the siege and to relieve the beleaguered forces, which amounted in numbers almost to a corps d, McCLELLAN resolved to make a powerful effort. He left Washington, it is said, with a force of 80,000 men. From the correspondents of the Yankee papers we heard of him at Rockville and other places on the National road, some time last week, from which we conclude that his army marched upon that road in the direction of Frederick. Whether he passed through Frederick we know not; but the first we hear of him is at Sharpsburg, some twenty miles west of Frederick, and about ten miles northwest of HarperFerry. At this place, on Sunday, he fell with his whole enormous force (80,000 men) upon the corps of Gen. D.H. HILL, which was the rear guard of the army. The battle was long, furious and bloody; but Gen. HILL, although attacked by vastly superior forces, stood his ground without yielding an inch. In the night Gen. LONGSTREET'S corps arrived, and on Monday the two combined attacked McCLELLAN and defeated him, driving his forces before them for five miles. But for the intervention of night, it is said the route would have been complete. At ten o, while the battle was still raging at Boonesborough, General MILES, with his whole army, variously estimated at eight, ten, and twelve thousand men, surrendered to Gen. JACKSON. Vast quantities of stores, 12,000 small arms, fifty pieces of artillery, and at least 1,000 negros (some say 2,500) were captured. Having disposed of MILES and his army, Gen. JACKSON was marching rapidly down the Potomac, with the intention of crossing below and getting in the rear of McCLELLAN, thus cutting him off effectually from Washington.

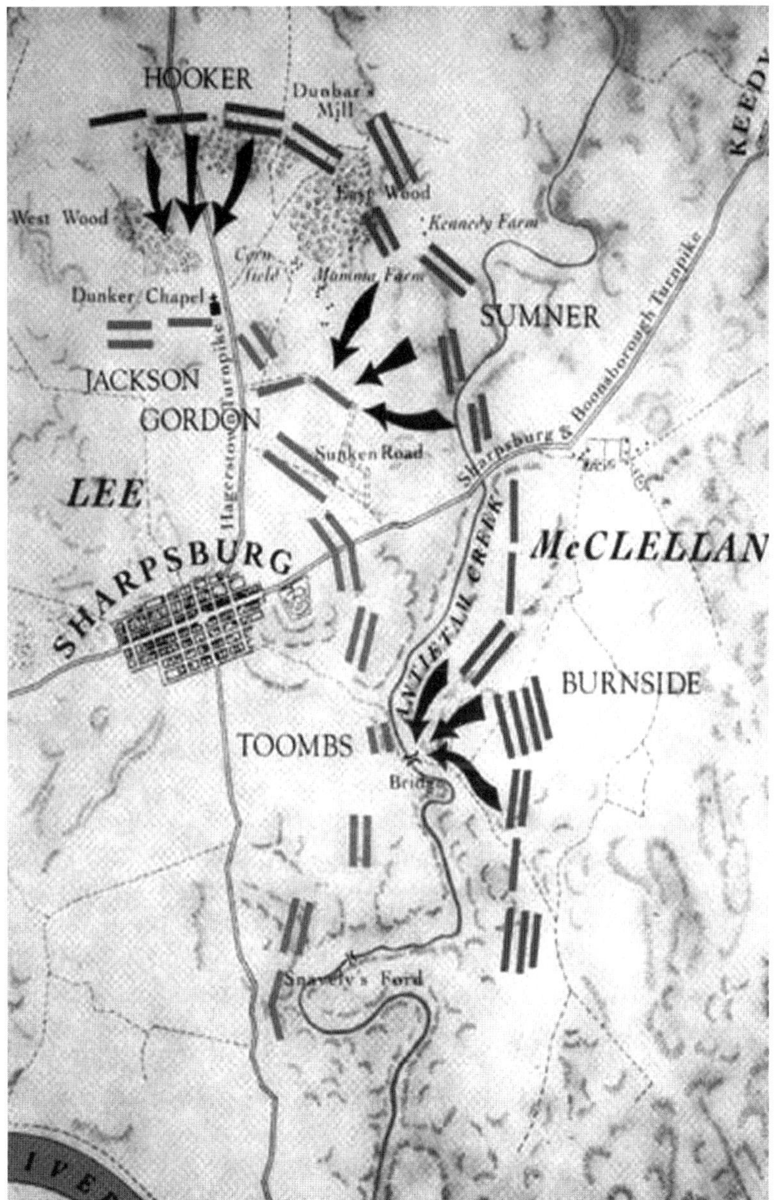

THE BATTLE OF ANTIETAM: THE BLOODIEST SINGLE DAY OF THE WAR BEGAN JUST OUTSIDE SHARPSBURG EARLY ON THE MORNING OF SEPTEMBER 17, 1862, WHEN UNION TROOPS UNDER GENERAL JOSEPH HOOKER ATTACKED THE CONFEDERATES NEAR THE DUNKER CHAPEL. LATER, THE FIGHTING WOULD MOVE TO THE SUNKEN ROAD, AND THEN TO A BRIDGE OVER ANTIETAM CREEK, ACROSS WHICH TROOPS UNDER GENERAL AMBROSE BURNSIDE MANAGED TO FIGHT THEIR WAY ONLY TO BE WITHDRAWN AGAIN WHEN REBEL REINFORCEMENTS ARRIVED AT THE END OF THE DAY. LIBRARY OF CONGRESS.

It should be mentioned that several days previous to the battle at Sharpsburg, a despatch from McCLELLAN to Col. MILES, commanding at HarperFerry, urging him to hold the position, promising reinforcements, was intercepted by Gen. LEE, who, accordingly, posted Gen. D.H. HILL'S Division near Boonesboro to check the reinforcing column, and made such disposition of the remaining forces as would ensure the discomfiture of the Yankee hosts.

The *Charleston Mercury*

Tuesday, September 23, 1862

News by Telegraph
Latest from the Potomac
The Great Battle of Sharpsburg
Movements of Lee

Richmond, September 21–The *Enquirer* has received a despatch dated Warrenton, September 20, announcing that a terrific battle took place at Sharpsburg, Md., on Wednesday last, in which we had decidedly the advantage. The loss was very heavy on both sides. Generals STARK, MANNING and BRANCH were killed, and Gens. RIPLEY, D.R. JONES, R.R. JONES and LAWTON were wounded. The whole strength of both armies was engaged. Report says that the battle was renewed on Thursday, and that the enemy was routed and driven back nine miles.

(The Latest)
Monday, September 22. The accounts that reach us of the battle at Sharpsburg, are meagre and somewhat contradictory, but all agree in representing it to have been the most bloody and desperately contested engagement of the war. The Confederate army, though opposed by largely superior numbers, again illustrated its valor and invincibility by successfully repelling the repeated onsets of the enemy.

Officers have arrived here, who state that they went over the battlefield on Thursday, and they assert that the advantage remained on our side, the enemy having fallen back.

The city papers this morning report, on the authority of passengers who arrived last night, that Gen. LEE has recrossed the Potomac on Friday, at Shepardstown, which is near Sharpstown, and several miles above HarperFerry.

The *New York Herald*, of the 18th, has been received. It claims that the fight at Sharpsburg on Sunday was a Yankee victory. Its despatches in regard to the fight are contradictory, but concur in stating that the Confederates were defeated.

Letters from Louisville claim that the Yankee forces in Kentucky had gained a victory over DUNCAN'S and SCOTT'S commands at Munfordsville, Kentucky.

A Bermuda correspondent of the *New York Herald* says that five steamers are now lying at the port of St. George, awaiting an opportunity to run the blockade.

The United States Arsenal at Pittsburg was accidentally blown up on Wednesday. Between seventy-five or eighty boys and girls were killed.

In New York, on Wednesday last, gold opened at 116 7/8, but subsequently advanced to 117 3/4.

The *Charleston Mercury*

September 25, 1862

The Great Battle of Sharpsburg

The *Enquirer* professes to have obtained from the most reliable sources, the following details of the great battle of Wednesday:

On the afternoon of Tuesday, the 16th, the enemy opened a light artillery fire on our line. Early the next morning it was renewed more vigorously and large masses of the Federals, who had crossed the Antietam above our position, assembled on our left. They advanced in three compact lines. The divisions of Generals McLaws, R.H. Anderson, A.P. Hill and Walker, who were expected to have joined General Lee on the previous night, had not come up. Generals Jackson and Ewel ldivisions were thrown to the left of Generals Hill and Longstreet. The enemy advanced between the Antietam and the Sharpsburg and Hagerstown turnpike, and was met by General D.H. Hilland the left of General Longstreet divisions, where the conflict raged, extending to our entire left. The enemy was repulsed and held in check; but prior to the arrival of the divisions of McLaws, Anderson and Walker, who had been advanced to support the left wing and centre, as soon as they had crossed the Potomac on the morning of the 17th, that portion of our line was forced back by superior numbers. As soon, however, as these forces could be brought into action a severe conflict ensued. The enemy was driven back, our line was restored, and our position maintained during the rest of the day.

In the afternoon the enemy advanced on our right, where General Jones' division was posted, and he handsomely maintained his position. The bridge over the Antietam Creek was guarded by General Toombs' brigade, which gallantly resisted the approach of the enemy; but their superior numbers enabling them to extend their left, they crossed below the bridge and forced our line back in some confusion. Just at this time, between 3 and 4 p.m., General A. P. Hill, with five of his brigades, having reached the scene of action, drove the enemy immediately back from the position they had taken, and continued the contest until dark, restoring our right and maintaining our ground.

When the battle closed, after having raged furiously during the entire day, we retained possession of the field, and the enemy retired to his former position. The conduct of many of our officers is reported by General Lee to have exhibited the most conspicuous and brilliant courage. Our loss was considerable, and we have to deplore the fall of Generals Branch and Starke, who died as soldiers love to die – in defence of their country.

Previous to the battle of Antietam, Rebels crossing the Potomac River. Union scouts are in the foreground (Waud). Library of Congress.

SKIRMISH BETWEEN THE BROOKLYN 14TH AND 300 REBEL CAVALRY (WAUD). LIBRARY OF CONGRESS.

Gens. R. H. Anderson, Lawton, Ripley, Armistead, Gregg and Wright, are reported to have been wounded—none of them, however, dangerously. In addition to the above, we learn from persons who have arrived from the field, that on the followin gday Gen. Lee, who remained in possession of the field, took measures to renew the engagement; but the enemy had disappeared from his front; and it is further reported that after the removal of his wounded and the burial of the dead, Gen. Lee determined to cross the Potomac, and had established his headquarters at or near Shepherdstown.

Another account says:

On Wednesday (17th) the fight was terrific, with tremendous losses on both sides, though the advantage was decidedly in our favor—we holding the battlefield. Yesterday there was a suspension of hostilities. Our loss in general officers is particularly severe, and is as follows:

Major General R. H. Anderson, severely wounded in hip.

Brigadier General Starke, killed, shot in four places.

Brigadier General Wright, in breast and leg, flesh wounds.

Brigadier General Branch, killed.

Brigadier General Lawton, wounded in leg, not dangerously.

Brigadier General Armistead, wounded in foot.

Brigadier General Ripley, wounded in neck.

Brigadier General Ransom, slightly wounded.

Col. Alfred Cummings (commanding Wilcoxbrigade) woundedslightly.

It is also reported that Col. Lee (son of the General) is killed, but it is only a rumor, and, I sincerely hope, incorrect.

It was far the most terrific battle of the war, and it is impossible to approximate to the killed of the Yankees. They lie in vast heaps on the field, and are counted by thousands.

The *Charleston Mercury*

September 27, 1862

News by Telegraph Late and Highly Important from the North

Richmond, September 26 – Northern dates of the 23d inst.have been received.

ABRAHAM LINCOLN has issued a proclamation declaring the slaves of rebel masters free, from and after the 1st of January next.

Tremendous excitement prevails at Louisville. A despatch from Jeffersonville, Ind., dated September 22d, says that the rebel Generals BRAGG and KIRBY SMITH have divided their forces. SMITH is to hold BUELL (who is marching towards Louisville) in check, while BRAGG advances on the city. BRAGG had summoned General BULL NELSON, who commands the army for the defence of Louisville, to surrender. NELSON refused, and ordered all the women and children to leave the city at one hour notice. Thousands of citizens were crossing the river into Indiana. BRAGG was some distance from the city, but was rapidly advancing.

The *New York Herald* acknowledges a heavy loss in the fight at Sheperdstown, Va., on Saturday. It says that the rebels were dressed like Union soldiers, and displayed a flag of truce to induce the Federal forces to cross the river. Gen. SUMNER'S corps d alone lost 5,203 in killed, wounded and missing at the battle of Sharpsburg. A Yankee correspondent, writing from the battlefield on the 22d, says that the Federal troops were still bringing in their dead at the rate of about one thousand per diem, but that they expected to get through the day. General HOOKER was shot through the foot by a rifle ball, and will not for a long time be fit for duty. Gen. CRAWFORD'S wound is more serious than was expected. Lieut. Colonel DWIGHT, of the 2d Massachusetts, was killed; Lieut. Colonel HINKS, of the 19th Massachusetts, was badly wounded; Gen. RICHARDSON was wounded in the shoulder and heart, and will die; Gen. DANA, in the knee. In the 38th Massachusetts, Col. WILD lost an arm at the shoulder joint; the Lieutenant Colonel, the Adjutant and eight Captains are wounded. The correspondent of *The New York Times* says that the slaughter was awful, particularly among the officers.

In New York on the 23d Exchange was firm at 129 1/2; gold, 117 3/8. Cotton, 54 cts.

The *Charleston Mercury*
October 1, 1862

The News from Richmond (Correspondence of the *Mercury*)

Richmond, Saturday, September 27 – LINCOLN'S negro-freeing proclamation does not tally well with McCLELLAN'S at Sharpsburg. It is ABE'S last card, which he has been holding in terrorem over us for a longtime, and it being played is a good sign for us. It is good also for the Abolitionists, who now have the upper hand in any event. If the South is conquered, there will be no slaveholding rebel party to coalesce with the Union as-it-was Democrats in ousting them from power. On the other hand, if disunion is accomplished, the party holding the sword and purse will take care to keep them, and Dr. Olds, of Ohio, who blood at the polls next Fall, will prove to be a prophet. There will be no more free suffrage at the North. We shall see now what the Seymour Richardson – Vallandigham party will do to circumvent the Republicans.

The Yankees confess to a loss of 5,203 in a single corps at Sharpsburg. They have there six corps and one division. It is fair, then, to put down their total loss there and at Boteler

Mills at 25,000. Add 11,500 prisoners at HarperFerry, and 500 for killed and wounded; also, 5000 at Boonesboro—a lowestimate—and the weekwork foots up a loss to McClellan of 42,000 men. Pope campaign of two months could not have cost him less than 40,000. During this time Kirby Smith used up 8000 at Richmond, Bragg captured 5000 at Munfordsville, 1800 at Cave City, and 3000 at Green River Bridge—total 17,800; whilst Loring operations will swell to at least 20,000. Thus, in the space of three months, we have placed hors du combat 102,000 Yankees—if those captured observe their parole.

At last, the conscript extension has passed. Mr. Boteler's mpassioned appeals, inspired by actual vision of our army sufferings and needs, hastened this desirable consummation. It is to be hoped the country will respond promptly to the bill, but past experience gives us pause.

Many have wondered that Stuart has done nothing brilliant of late. The fact is, the cavalry was much broken up before it entered Maryland—men and horses being alike exhausted. Hence the impossibility of dashing circuits and forays; but frequentand desperate charges have been made in battle, and scores of troopers have fallen. Charges, not raids, are the business of cavalry.

McClellan extraordinary mendacity is explained by the fact, that his father before him was a great braggart and fibber. Dr. McClellan held himself up to the admiration and envy of the surgical world by proclaiming that he had extirpated the parotid gland. Drs. Gibson and Physick proved,by repeated dissections on the dead body, that the extirpation of this gland was an utter impossibility; but old Dr. McClellan stuck to his fib until death. General George has long ago announced the morality of lying in war.

Several hundred of our wounded soldiers, who, after marching 60 miles, had been lying for nearly a week at Culpeper on the bare ground, with little food, without shelter, with undressed wounds, reached here last night at 11 o. The government officials, paid to attend to these suffering patriots, could no where be found. The members of the Citizens' Relief Committee were roused from their beds, and, on repairing to the depot, found no ambulances, no provisions whatever for the reception of the wounded; the hospitals were all closed, and so they were compelled to bring the poor fellows into the capitol square and place them on the benches, the stone steps, the gravelled walks, the dewy grass. The night was quite cold. The soldiers were literally in a state of starvation. It was pitiable to see them devour dry bread brought from the bakers. All this occurred at the seat of government, with an immense and costly system of hospitals, presided over by a set of men who have just been beautifully white washed by a so called Examining Committee of Congress.

The new moon, last evening, was what weather prophets call a wet moon—the wettest sort of a moon. Sure enough, the clouds already cover the whole sky and are thickening. HERMES.

From *The New York Times*

September 20, 1862

BATTLE OF ANTIETAM CREEK
Full Particulars from Special Correspondent
The Most Stupendous Struggle of Modern Times
Battle-Field of Antietam Creek

Thursday, Sept. 18, 1862
Another giant battle has been fought, and the cause of the Union has once more been vindicated upon one of the most bloody and well-contested fields known to ancient or modern times. Wednesday, Sept 17, 1862, will, we predict, hereafter be looked upon as an epoch in the history of the rebellion, from which will date the inaugeration of its downfall. On that day about one hundred and sixty thousand men met in deadly strife upon the field of Antietam—a name which will occupy a leading position in the history of the war—and there, marshaled by brave and able men, fought with a desperation and courage never before excelled, and rarely, if ever equaled, for twelve hours, leaving the Union army in possession of the contested ground. This victory was not gained, however, without the sacrifice of many valuable lives, and the maiming of thousands of individuals.

Preceding Events
Before attempting to present even a glance at this battle, let us first prepare the reader for a correct undersanding of it by relating – in continuation of my last letter – the events

immediately preceding the great contest. My last brought Gen. McClellan's advance into Maryland up to midday on Tuesday, Sept. 16, at which time the army occupied a position in close proximity to the road leading from Boonesville to Sharpsburgh, and upon and near the left bank of the little creek known by the name of Antietam, which rises in Central Pennsylvania, and, after running in a southerly direction, its waters are mingled with the turgid waters of the Potomac, about five miles above Harper's Ferry.

The enemy occupied a position on the right bank of the Antietam, favorably located for both offensive and defensive operations, and in this respect had the advantage. To circumvent the enemy, and secure an equally favorable position, was the first object to be obtained. That this required the genius of a great leader needed no military man to elucidate, for the whole position of affairs could be taken in at a glance. How well and successfully this object was accomplished, the success of our arms is abundant evidence. Of some of the details of the movement to this end we shall give in the proper place. Just across the creek, in plain view from the eastern bank, the enemy's skirmishers could be distinctly seen, and from elevated positions massed forces of infantry and cavalry could be discovered in every little valley and ravine for miles on either hand. Two hundred thousand men was what the. enemy pretended to have within the scope of the eye, and from repeated personal inspection, aided by an excellent glass, while standing in a favorable position, I should judge the figure named not an exaggerated one.

Between 12 and 2 o'clock P. M. all was silent along the lines. The German Battery of sixteen 20-pound Parrott guns, upon the eminence overlooking the river's bank, were silent. Major Asndt had fallen, and the infantry battalions were quietly resting upon the ground under the hill, upon the tops of which were planted our artillery. This quietness was like the quietness that precedes the storm. The Commanding General had arrived upon the ground at an early hour the day before, and had made himself familiar with the position, and at the time of which we write was busily engaged in giving the necessary instructions to the Commanders of Corps, so as to render our success in the impending conflict as much a matter of certainty as possible.

THE BATTLE OF ANTIETAM. THE BURNING OF MUMMA'S HOUSE AND BARNS (A. WAUD). LIBRARY OF CONGRESS.

Preparations for a Movement

The Movement

Soon after 2 o'clock P. M. the Parrott guns, to which allusion has been made before, were opened upon the enemy and worked with great rapidity, and nearly every shell thrown, as I afterward ascertained, did fearful execution in the massed columns of the enemy. In a brief space after this terrible fire had been opened, there was a movement of the troops inexplicable to the uninitiated at the moment, but the object of which was soon revealed to the careful observer. The Antietam was to be crossed! Gen. Hooker's Corps, by a flank movement, gained a point to the north of between two and three miles, and changing direction to the left reached the river at Kelly's Ford. A portion of the Pennsylvania Reserve under command of Brig. Gen. Meade were thrown across the river and were deployed as skirmishers, and under their cover and the support of the German New York Battery, Gen. Hooker's column very speedily gained a foothold upon the opposite bank. Our skirmishers were met with a galling fire, poured in by the skirmishers of the enemy and the fire from a battery of four or six pieces, so located as to give a raking fire to the advancing column. Fortunately this battery was not well managed and most of the missiles were thrown too high, hence our losses at this point were comparatively trifling. The battery was speedily silenced and the mood, and the rapid movements of Gen. Hooker's column, soon placed it in jeopardy; but the enemy, always on the alert, managed to get their pieces out of the way before a battery could be thrown across to sustain the Infantry column in its local movements. The enemy's skirmishers were forced back step by step by the Reserves to their main body, by which time the whole of the advancing column was in position, and ready for more decisive offensive operations. The enemy rushed forward seemingly bent upon annihilating the comparatively small force sent against them, and several times there was some wavering under the terrible and impetuous resistance; but the troops quickly rallied, and, under the lead of ther able commander, secured a much coveted and necessary position to secure success. This movement across the river was one for which Gen. Hooker was peculiarly qualified, and he executed in a manner highly creditable to his skill as a General. Here the bottle of Antietam commenced in earnest. Until nightfall set in Gen. Hooker pressed the enemy back, and every step was gained by hard fighting.

The Battle of Antietam

On Wednesday morning, Sept. 17, the sun rose in a cloudless sky, and all nature seemed to smile as if the world were filled with the elect of God. But its splendors were soon dimmed with the smoke rising from the battle-field.

To enable the reader to understand the events of this day, he should look at a map which has laid out the principal roads throughout the State of Maryland. With a pencil, follow the road or " pike" from Boonsboro direct to Sharpsburgh, which is nearly three mlies west of the river, at the point where the road crosses it; the battle-field is on both sides of that road-between the river and Sharpsburgh—the bulk of it being north of the Boonsboro road, and in the triangle formed by the roads connecting Bakersville and Middletown and Bakersville and Sharnsburgh. The surface is interspersed with hill and vale, and covered with cornfields and grass land, and skirting and stretching toward the centre from different points are thin belts of forest trees—all of which gives advantage to the enemy acting on the defensive, he having an opportunity to select his position for defensive operations, and when forced from one position he has only to fall back a short distance to find a position naturallv as strong as the first. The engagement was opened early Wednesday morning with the advance of a strong line of our skirmishers. They were met by a similar movement on the part of the enemy. The latter were forced back until the right of our line (Gen. Hooker's) came into action with the enemy's left, commanded by Gen. Hill, who commands a portion of Longstreet's corps. Bank's corps was. within a half an hour, at work, and was followed soon after by Gen. Patterson's command. The first fire was at about 5 o'clock and at 6 o'clock the infantry arm entered upon its work. The line thus formed.

The Enemy's left was forced back for nearly three miles from the ford where the bulk of our troops crossed the creek before 9 o'clock, when they were relieved by Gen. Sedgwick's coming to the front. Just previous to this, Morris' Brigade, of Hooker's command, had advanced from a belt of timber across a plowed field into a piece of woods, where the enemy, massed in great force, were repulsed, and the troops fell back to the belt of timber in some disorder, but soon rallied again, and regained the field in front. It was at this time that Gen. Mansfield, in command of Gen. Banks' corps, was mortally wounded, carried from the field and died soon afterward. Gen. Williams succeeded to the command of the corps, and Gen. Crawford took command of Williams' Division, until he was wounded and taken from the field. The repulse of Morris' Brigade was accomplished by an old and contemptible trick of the enemy. As the corps advanced to the woods across the plowed field, the rebels unfurled the Stars and Stripes, and waving them, cried out, " What the h--l are you doing ? Don't fire upon your friends!" Our troops, deceived by this ruse, ceased firing, when the rebels opened upon them a murderous volley of musketry and cross fire, and creating a temporary panic. They rallied and drove the rebels back, but it was done at a great sacrifice of life.

These troops were relieved by GEN. SEDGWICK'S COMMAND coming up on their left. The enemy, who had gained a point of timber extending some distance in front of our line, at the left of Gen. Banks' corps, were driven out. and across a plowed field in front, to the timber beyond, with great slaughter – Ayers battery opening upon them with great effect, strewing the ground with the dead. At one point, just on the brow of a little roll of the ground that the infantry, emerging suddenly upon the open field, supposed that it was a rebel force in waning for them, and the dead rebels got an entire volley. This corps came into action bt brigades between 8 and 9 o'clock—Gorman's, Dana's and Howard's. While preparing for action, the enemy appeared from an unexpected quarter and opened a terrific fire with a view of breaking the line by a sudden attack with musketry and artillery, he believing that it was composed of raw troops. But they soon discovered that mistake, these veterans, notwithstanding the sudden attack, though their lines were broken for a moment, were not disconcerted, but received it with cheers. While under this galling fire, the Fifteenth Regiment Massachusetts made a dash forward and seized the battle-flag of one of Gen. HILL's regiments, and now have it to show to their friends as a trophy of the day. In this connection it should be mentioned that Capt. Hows and Lieut. Whittier, of Gen.Sedgwick's Staff, distinguished themselves in the action by rallying the left of Gen. Sedgwick's division, and on several occasions, by their example, they encouraged the men in discharging their duties faithfully. Gen. Sedgwick's horse was killed, and he was wounded twice, but remained on the field until he was ordered to the rear with his command.

French's Division

The division under Gen. French occupied a position to the left of Sedgwick's and was fairly engaged by 10½ o'clock. The fighting on the extreme right at this time was confined mostly to artillery, while the tide of infantry fighting swept along toward the left of our line. The left of this division gave way and fell back from the superior force they had to contend against—the rebel hordes making pell mell after them. The left fell back in pretty good order, and upon a walk, under as galling a fire of musketry as is often experienced. This movement was evidently no fault of the men. The rebels advanced as they ventured a little to the rear of our line. At that point Col. Burke (acting Brigadier-General in Gen. Richardson's Division,) changed his front, and poured in several volleys upon their flank strewing the ground with dead. The balance, hastened somewhat by a cross fire from Ayer's battery, fled in utter dismay. The left of French's Division advanced again, and fought like heroes until ordered to the rear.

THE CHARGE ACROSS THE BURNSIDE BRIDGE (FORBES). LIBRARY OF CONGRESS.

Richardson's Division

Three Brigades of this Division, commanded by Gen. Meagher, Gen. Caldwell, and Col.Burke's Tenth Pennsylvania, did not cross the creek until Wednesday morning, when Gen. Richardson was ordered to form on the left of French's Division. The Division crossed the river and moved up with alacrity near the line of battle, ready for action. Having filed through the valleys to avoid letting the enemy know of the movement, the Division laid down under the brow of a hill, just in rear of the line of battle, until wanted. It was now about 9 o'clock.

The Irish Brigade

In less than half an hour after taking this position Gen. Meagher was ordered to enter the line with the Irish Brigade. They marched up to the brow of the bill, cheering as they went, led by Gen. Meagher in person, and were welcomed with cheers by French's Brigade. The musketry fighting at the point was the severest and most deadly ever witnessed before—so acknowledged by veterans in the service. Men on both sides fell in large numbers every moment, and those who were eye-witnesses of the struggle did not suppose it possible for a single man to escape. The enemy here, at first, were concealed behind a knoll, so that only their heads were exposed. The brigade advanced up the slope with a cheer, when a most deadly fire was poured in by a second line of the enemy concealed in the Sharpsburgh road, which at this place is several feet lower than the surrounding surface, forming a complete rifle-pit, and also from a force partially concealed still further to the rear.

At this time the color-bearer in the right wing advanced several paces to the front, and defiantly waved his flag in the faces of the enemy; as if by a miracle he escaped without serious injury.

The line of the brigade, in its advance up the hill, was broken in the centre temporarily by an obstruction, the right wing having advanced to keep up with the colors, and fell back a short distance, when Gen. Meagher directed that a rail fence which the enemy a few minutes before had been fighting behind should he torn down. His men, in face of a galling fire, obeyed the order when the whole brigade advanced to the brow of the hill cheering as they went and causing the enemy to fall back to their second line – the Strasburgh road, which is some three feet lower than the surroundings face. In this road were massed a large force of infantry, and here was the most hotly contested point of the day. Each brigade of this Division was in turn brought into action at this point and the struggle was truly terrific for more than four hours – the enemy finally, however, were forced from their position. In this work the New York German Battery, stationed on the hill across the Creek, rendered efficient service by pouring in upon their massed forces a constant stream of 20-pound shells.

Gen. Cauldwell's Brigade was next ordered into action by Gen. Richardson in person. They two advanced in good order and were received with cheers by the Irish Brigade. It was at about this time that the left of French's Division, commanded by Gen. Brooks of the Tenth Pennsylvania, was directed by Gen. Richardson to wheel to the right, and a murderous flanking fire was poured into the flank of an advancing division of the enemy, causing him to recoil, and fall back in disorder.

This division was actively engaged for nearly five hours, and lost nearly half of the men taken into action.

THE BATTLE OF ANTIETAM – CHARGE OF BURNSIDE'S 9TH CORPS ON THE RIGHT FLANK OF THE CONFEDERATE ARMY (FORBES). LIBRARY OF CONGRESS.

What the Historians Say

The battle at Antietam in Washington County, Maryland, occurred on September 16-18, 1862. Known also as the battle at Sharpsburg, it was the key battle in Robert E. Lee's Maryland Campaign in which his Army of Northern Virginia confronted the Army of the Potomac. The great battle resulted in 23,100 casualties.

On September 16, Maj. Gen. George B. McClellan confronted Lee's Army of Northern Virginia. At dawn September 17, Hooker's corps mounted a powerful assault on Lee's left flank that began the single bloodiest day in American military history. Attacks and counterattacks swept across Miller's cornfield and fighting swirled around the Dunker Church. Union assaults against the Sunken Road eventually pierced the Confederate center, but the Federal advantage was not followed up. Late in the day, Burnside's corps finally got into action, crossing the stonebridge over Antietam Creek and rolling up the Confederate right. At a crucial moment, A.P. Hill's division arrived from Harper's Ferry and counterattacked, driving back Burnside and saving the day. Although outnumbered two-to-one, Lee committed his entire force, while McClellan sent in less than three-quarters of his army, enabling Lee to fight the Federals to a standstill. During the night, both armies consolidated their lines. In spite of crippling casualties, Lee continued to skirmish with McClellan throughout the 18th, while removing his wounded south of the river. McClellan did not renew the assaults. After dark, Lee ordered the battered Army of Northern Virginia to withdraw across the Potomac into the Shenandoah Valley.

The battle was decisive in affecting Lee's campaign because he was forced to return to Virginia. Tactically the battle was inconclusive but proved to be a strategic victory for the Union because it gave President Lincoln cause to issue the Emancipation Proclamation.

9

Fredericksburg

A Great Federal Embarrassment

Author's Commentary

The telegraph service played an important role during the War both for correspondents relaying their stories to their papers and for military dispatches to Washington and official areas. Strict censorship was a constant practice as were frequent misinterpretations. Sometimes one would follow another. News of the Union disaster at Fredericksburg was censored by General Burnside and again at Washington. News of the disaster did not get out for forty eight hours. Two weeks later, the *Times* pontifically chided Washington officials for preventing the news from getting out. Two weeks following that in mid-January, *Times* Editor Henry J. Raymond received a telegram from the Times Washington office advising him that a telegram from a Col. Swain had arrived advising him that the corpse of his brother, a Union soldier who had been ill, was at Belle Plain and he should come immediately. A boat was leaving shortly. Upon arrival at Belle Plain, Raymond, searching for his brother's corpse, found him to be quite alive. The telegraph operator inadvertently used the word "corpse" when conveying that Raymond's brothers Army Corps was in Belle Plain.

Dec. 20, 1862: **From the *Charleston Merury***

BURNSIDE doubtless has under command an immense and admirably equipped army. Say he has lost ten, fifteen or twenty thousand men in the battle of Fredericksburg. This would be but a small proportion of the forces in hand, and, barring the demoralization produced by so signal a failure as this attempted advance, and the extraordinary disproportion of the slain, there is no reason why BURNSIDE should not try it again forthwith, at some other point along the Rappahannock. This repulse, however bloody, would hardly deter a great General, bent upon striking at Richmond. There is a strong pressure on the Yankee commander to proceed. His reputation, his opportunity, his future, are staked upon the success or non-success of the move. He has a howl at his back to drive him on. But, notwithstanding all this, his course is by no means clear. If he delays, and hesitates, it will take probably more time than the Northern mob will allow him, and the military baton will be transferred by the LINCOLN dynasty to a new chief, HOOKER or some other. If, therefore, BURNSIDE withdraws from the Rappahannock, the transfer will occupy some time; and meanwhile active military operations will cease in Eastern Virginia.

In Tennessee we have little idea that ROSECRANS will come out of his works around Nashville to fight Gen. JOHNSTON. He is more likely either to evacuate the place, as the despatch today would indicate, or he will attempt to garrison and hold it against a siege, trusting to relief so soon as the Cumberland River rises.

Indications now point to the State of Mississippi, and particularly the works at Vicksburg, as the next scene of large and earnest operations. Gen. McCLERNAND'S expedition, soon to descend from Cairo, is of formidable proportions of itself. GRANT is already there advancing with numerous forces. And if, as has been stated, reinforcements are further concentrated upon Mississippi, from Missouri, Arkansas and West Tennessee, it will require excellent generalship and the utmost promptitude and exertion on our part to foil the enemy, and drive him back from the accomplishment of his object.

THE BATTLE OF FREDERICKSBURG: ALMOST THREE MONTHS AFTER ROBERT E. LEE BEGAN HIS WITHDRAWAL FROM SHARPSBURG, MARYLAND, MCCLELLAN'S SUCCESSOR, AMBROSE BURNSIDE, MANAGED TO BRING HIM TO BATTLE AGAIN IN VIRGINIA. LIBRARY OF CONGRESS.

We, therefore, look with anxiety to Mississippi, and trust that every effort will be made to save Vicksburg, and redeem that State. Officers, men and arms should be supplied on the spot to the extent of the capacity of the Government, for the indications are of danger.

The *Charleston Mercury*

December 22, 1862

Incidents of the Battle

From the accounts contained in the Richmond papers, several of which came to hand yesterday, we glean the following incidents of the battle:

The behavior of our troops is said to have been admirable, full of zeal and courage. It is said that such an eagerness for fight was never before manifested by soldiers of the Confederacy; and we are assured that on the day of the action not one thousand stragglers could be counted in our whole army.

The Yankees are said to have exhibited more than their ordinary cowardice on the field, and to have fought with but little display of zeal or energy. Several hundred prisoners were captured in one lot, who excused their surrender by the circumstance that all their officers had run away.

The portion of our force actively engaged is said not to have exceeded eight to ten thousand men, while that of the enemy could not have been less than thirty thousand. The enemy occupied a low flat, partly wooded, and was not in a position to use his artillery with any effect. From our semicircular line of battle on the crown of the Massaponax hills a deadly fire was poured into the enemy ranks. There was no hand-to-hand encounter during the day, the fight being conducted with artillery and distant musketry. We did not lose a single piece of artillery nor any prisoners, but a few stragglers who may have fallen into the enemy hands.

On the left, where the fighting was intensely severe, the brigade of South Carolinians, commanded by General Kershaw, suffered heavily. The 3d Regiment of S.C.V. was badly cut up. In the early part of the engagement, their Colonel, Nance, Lieut. Colonel, and Major were all wounded, and the command devolved upon the senior Captain, who was killed in fifteen minutes after assuming the command. His place was supplied by the second senior Captain, and he, too, fell mortally wounded in a very short time.

At several points on our line the enemy made repeated charges, which in every instance were repulsed. At one point, just outside of the town of Fredericksburg, our troops were sheltered behind a stone wall. It is said that three different attempts were made by the enemy to take this position, without success. The third time, as their column of assault was broken, our troops rushed from their cover and pursued the enemy, our men loading and firing as they ran after the mass of fugitives until they had got to the cover of their batteries.

One of the most conspicuous spectacles of the action is said to have been the figure and behavior of Gen. Jackson; this commander, who has the reputation of being rather seedy in his dress, having donned, for the first time, for the particular occasion, a splendid new uniform, which attracted all eyes, and might naturally be supposed to make him a mark for the enemy fire. In his unusual and magnificent attire, General Jackson is said to have ridden along the line of battle, his appearance alone being sufficient to give to the men whom he commanded inspiration of fresh and invincible courage.

Siegel corps has come up to the Rappahannock. The importance of this event, however, is not considerable. This command is formidable neither in number or material, as according to the best accounts, it does not exceed fifteen thousand men, and is composed entirely of raw troops raised by the recent levies. A report from Gordonsville says that Siegel went to Washington, thence down the Potomac on the Maryland side to Budd Ferry, and crossed over at Evansport to join Burnside.

Building pontoon bridge at Fredricksburg (Waud). Library of Congress.

The enemy shamefully violated the flag of truce under which he had sought permission to bury his dead. His ambulance trains had no sooner come upon the battle field than they fell to work removing the wounded, who were properly prisoners within our lines. This system of recaptures was indignantly protested against by Gen. Jackson, in consequence of which the permission given to the enemy was withdrawn, and his dead and wounded left alike in our hands.

Telegraphic News
Latest from the North
Comments of the Yankee Press on Burnside's Defeat
RICHMOND, December 19 – The *Washington Chronicle*, of the17th, LINCOLN'S organ, has the following article, based on BURNSIDE'S despatch that he had re-crossed the Rappahannock: 'At this writing, we have nothing but the simple telegraphic announcement yesterday morning, from Falmouth, that our troops are all this side of the river, and that the pontoons are up. If they retired back to Falmouth without loss of men and material in the operation, as it is reported they did, it indicates skill and good fortune on the part of our Generals, or inattention or over caution on the part of the rebels, or all these things together. Our army, if unable to face the enemy works, was in a most dangerous position on the south side of the Rappahannock, and the rebels, in permitting the escape, have lost an opportunity such as they have not had since they neglected to take Washington, after the first battle of Bull Run. The failure at Fredericksburg has taken the public, especially our military authorities, so much by surprise, that opinions are hardly yet formed as to what ought either now be done, or what is likely to be done. For ourselves. we hope that as a few weeks will terminate the winter of this latitude, the army designed for the defence of Washington will go at once into winter quarters.'

The *Star* says: 'The failure to bag the rebels has stricken the whole country with feelings of painful surprise.' It adds, sarcastically, that perhaps the army was not gotten up, after all, to annihilate the rebels, but to guard Washington, and advises that it go into quarters for the remaining winter months.

Intelligence from Norfolk states that a desperate affray occurred in that town on Monday night, between a large number of soldiers and the forces of the Provost Marshal. Someone in the Theatre proposed three cheers for JEFF. DAVIS, when the applause shook the building. The Abolitionists then called for three cheers for LINCOLN, which met with a faint response. Four hundred rioters were arrested and sent to Fort Norfolk.

A body of Confederate cavalry had made a raid to Poolville, Maryland, and captured about forty Yankee cavalry. BANK'S expedition passed Hilton Head on the 16th. A despatch from Nashville, of the 16th, says there were no signs of a rebel advance.

The Federal Generals JACKSON and BAYARD, and Colonel DICKENSON, were killed at the battle of Fredericksburg.

The Confederate war steamer Alabama is still operating successfully on the commerce of the United States. A ship has arrived at New York from Port Petrie, brought the crew of the ship Levi Starbuck, which was captured and burned by the Alabama on the 2d of November, when five days out. On the 8th of November the Alabama captured and burned the ship T.B.Watts, of and for Boston, from Calcutta, with a valuable cargo of saltpetre, gunny cloth, &c. The Alabama put into Point Petrie on the 17th, and landed the Captains and crews of these ships. The same afternoon the U.S. steamer San Jacinto arrived outside to wait for the Alabama, but the latter vessel escaped during the night. Capt. SEMMES boasts that he has been within seventy miles of New York.

The *Charleston Mercury*

December 23, 1862

Letter from Richmond
(Correspondence of the *Mercury*)

Richmond, Thursday, December 18
How terrible was that defeat at Fredericksburg which our General modestly heralded as a '! From many points we hear that the enemy loss was from 18,000 to 20,000. Three thou-

sand of his dead he left unburied, after laboring hard all Saturday night and all day Sunday in the sad work of interment and the removal of the wounded. Leesburg has been re-enacted on a grand scale, as we shall learn ere long, although Washington papers of the 16th received this morning, do not admit even a defeat, but declare that General Burnside is satisfied with the result of Saturday fight. "I shouldn't wonder' – as the showman remarked when asked if the Siamese twins were brothers.

I learn, on good authority, that Gen. Lee was so confident that the battle would be renewed on Monday, that he had disposed his forces to meet the shock in a manner that would have horrified those who thought they tested the whole rebel strength on Saturday. A story is floating about to the effect that Jackson, who generally goes to sleep at councils of war, was quite excited on Saturday night, and insisted that the Yankees should be driven into the river forthwith, without waiting for morning. My information is that near 200,000 of the enemy were more or less actively engaged, against only 22,000 on our side – 14,000 of Jackson corps and 8,000 of Longstreet.

All the talk of the town is about the great victory which we achieved almost without knowing it, and I could fill a dozen letters with the accounts, all joyous, of parties who have come down from Fredericksburg. But everybody seems to be at a loss in regard to the next move of the enemy. Reports say he has gone down the left bank of the river, but there is not a point between Fredericksburg and the mouth of the river where he would be likely to fare any better than he has done. He is, to the best of everybody's knowledge and belief, a up man, and we have made a long step towards independence. Government authorities say Burnside will go home, and his army return to Washington. We shall see.

The *Examiner* has some statements about the treatment of the wounded, which conflict with those made in a recent letter of mine; but the mass of evidence shows that there is more system and attention than heretofore.

A singular feature in this war is the youthfulness of many of our distinguished artillery officers. The Pelham, as Gen.

Lee calls him, is an Alabamian about 20 years old; Pegram, of the Purcell Battery, is hardly 21; Latimer, the Captain of the Letcher Artillery, is only 17; and Dearing, of Lathamold battery, is not above 22 or 23.

Clear freezing weather. We will get plenty of ice.

HERMES

The *Charleston Mercury*

December 25, 1862

Interesting Facts in Regard to the Battle of Fredericksburg

The *Richmond Dispatch* presents the following statement off acts in regard to the late battle, which it obtains from sources in every respect trustworthy:

A small proportion of our army only was engaged, not more than 25,000 men at farthest. Burnside rates his own force engaged at 40,000. It was certainly double that figure. Burnside writes that he lost but 5,000 men. General Armistead, of the Confederate service, took the precaution to count the dead bodies left on the field by the Yankees, and they were rather more than 3,500. This was on Tuesday, after the Yankees had employed two whole days in burying. At the lowes tcalculation, then, we must have killed at least 5,000 of their men, and this may be what Burnside means when he says his loss was 5,000. The wounded, after a battle, usually stand to the dead in the proportion of five to one, so that 25,000 of the Yankees must have been wounded, and their whole loss, exclusiveof 1,300 prisoners, must have been 30,000 men. Any person who saw the field of battle and Fredericksburg after the retreat, would readily credit the estimate. At the place where General Cobb was killed, within the enclosure of a stone fence, a regiment of his brigade was posted. It was assaulted by a whole brigade of Irishmen, who behaved with the most determined bravery, and were repeatedly led to the assault. Only four of this regiment – exclusive of General Cobb himself – were killed, and they killed more than five hundred of their enemy, whose bodies were left on the field. In Fredericksburg across one of the streets, the Yankees dug a trench, and left beside it five hundred dead bodies piled up. Our informant had no doubt that they intended to make a breastwork of these bodies, as they had placed them on the edge of the ditch and covered them with dirt, as if they had been logs. All about the streets in every direction, dead bodies of the Yankees were lying in piles of two, three, and as high as a dozen. In the porch of Mayor Slaughterhouse, there were no less than five dead Yankees. The night of the battle, the dry grass in a portion of the field took fire, and many of the Yankee wounded were burned. The explosion of their cartridge boxes, as the fire reached them, and the shrieks of the sufferers were heard all night long by our pickets, who had it not in their power to relieve the sufferers.

That the Yankees were greatly averse to the fight, and that they could be brought to engage in it with great difficulty, is absolutely certain. A section of the 1st Howitzers (Richmond) was placed upon an eminence which commanded a full view of the whole Yankee army. Before the cannonade began, on their part, they were of course all busy in looking at the advancing enemy. They distinctly saw large bodies of men marching behind the advancing columns, with fixed bayonets, evidently forcing them into battle. On more than one occasion they saw the officers fire on their own men, and repeatedly they saw them riding after and endeavoring to bring them up. Little idea had we of the tremendous defeat we had inflicted on the enemy.

The battles of the war have hitherto been fought in the woods. The battle of Fredericksburg, like European battles, was fought in a clear space, which might be taken in at a single glance. It formed the grandest panorama ever witnessed on this Continent. It continued after nightfall, and the long line of fire was visible for miles around. It was one of the most sublime sights it is possible to see.

The *Charleston Mercury*

December 29, 1862

The Slaughter at Fredericksburg

The army correspondent of the *Savannah Republican*, writing after the late battle on the Rappahannock, says:

I went over the ground this morning, and the dead still remaining there, after two-thirds of them had been removed, lay twice as thick as upon any other battlefield I have ever seen. On a piece of ground not exceeding two hundred yards square, it is estimated that the enemy left between thirteen and fourteen hundred dead! Allowing five wounded for every one man killed (the usual proportion), it would be safe to put down their loss in killed and wounded on this bloody square of two hundred yards at 6,500! The blood may still be seen in puddles on the ground, as in a butcher pen, and the way along which their wounded were carried back into the town is still red with blood, notwithstanding the rain this morning.

Just in front of our line is a thin plank fence, behind which the enemy sought shelter as they advanced up the hill. Some of the planks in this fence were literally shot away from the posts to which they were nailed, and one can hardly place his hand upon any part of them without covering a dozen bullet holes. At the foot of the stone wall behind which the Confederates fought, thousands of flattened musket balls may be seen, whilst the hills behind it have been converted into a partial lead mine.

The Sack of Fredericksburg

The same correspondent writes of the appearance of Fredericksburg:

I have often read of the scenes attending the sacking of a city, but was never able to realize the full import of the term until this morning when I rode into Fredericksburg. The number of houses destroyed by fire is not so great as at first reported, but otherwise the ruin is complete. Chimneys were knocked down, roofs torn away, great gaps made in the walls, streets barricaded, furniture hacked to pieces or used for firewood, store houses opened and rifled of their contents, tables were stolen, mattresses taken into the streets and alleys for the vandals to sleep upon, books, paintings and looking-glasses scattered over the ground, provisions consumed, cellars ransacked, and the enclosures around private residences and lots pulled down and used for firewood or to rest upon. There is hardly a structure in the whole city that does not bear some traces of the fearful struggle in the streets and suburbs. The floors of many of the houses into which the wounded were taken are covered with blood, and in some instances the dead still remain in the silent chambers, their eyes fixed in death, yet glaring wildly up at blackened and blood stained walls. A few of the inhabitants concealed themselves in cellars, and now and then they may be seen timidly peeping out from their hiding places, or flitting across the streets like mysterious shadows. The churches and better descriptions of buildings seem to have been the mark of the enemy spite. But nothing escaped their fury, and it will be a long while before the town can recover from the terrible ordeal through which it has passed.

From *The New York Times*

December 15, 1862

Headquarters of the Army of the Potomac
Saturday, Dec. 13, 1862
11 o'clock A.M.
The great battle, so long anticipated between the two contending armies, is now progressing.

The morning opened with a dense fog, which has not entirely disappeared.

Gen. REYNOLDS' Corps, on the left, advanced at an early hour, and at 9:15 A. M., engaged the enemy's infantry. Seven minutes afterward the rebels opened a heavy fire of artillery, which has continued so far without intermission.

Their artillery fire must be at random, as the fog obstructs all view of almost everything.

Our heavy guns are answering them rapidly.

At this writing, no results are known.

ATTACK ON THE REBEL WORKS AT FREDRICKSBURG (WAUD). LIBRARY OF CONGRESS.

Headquarters of the Army of the Potomac
Saturday Dec. 13, 1862
IN THE FIELD – 11 o'clock A.M.
The fog began to disappear early in the forenoon, affording an unobstructed view of our own and the rebel positions.

It being evident that the first ridge of hills, in the rear of the city, on which the enemy had their guns posted behind works, could not be carried except by a charge of infantry, Gen. SUMNER assigned that duty to Gen. FRENCH'S Division, which was supported by Gen. HOWARD'S.

The troops advanced to their work at ten minutes before 12 o'clock at a brisk run, the enemy's guns opening upon them a very rapid fire. When within musket range, at the base of the ridge, our troops were met by a terrible fire from the rebel infantry, who were posted behind a a stone wall and some houses on the right of the line. This checked the advance of our men, and they fell back to a small ravine, but not out of musket range.

At this time another body of troops moved to their assistance in splendid style, notwithstanding large gaps were made in their ranks by the rebel artillery. When our troops arrived at the first line of the rebel defences, they "double quicked," and with "fixed bayonets" endeavored to dislodge the rebels from their hiding places. The concentrated fire of the rebel artillery and infantry, which our men were forced to face, was too much for them, and the centre gave way in disorder, but afterwards they were rallied and brought back.

From that time the fire was spiritedly carried on, and never ceased until after dark.

Gen. FRANKLIN, who commanded the attack on the left, met with better success. He succeeded, after a hard day's fight, in driving the rebels about one mile. At one time the rebels advanced to attack him, but were handsomely repulsed, with terrible slaughter and loss of between four and five hundred prisoners belonging to Gen. A. P. HILL'S command. Gen. FRANKLIN'S movement was directed down the river, and his troops are encamped to-night not far from the Massaponox Creek.

Our troops sleep to-night where they fought today. The dead and wounded are being carried from the field.

The following is a list of officers killed and wounded as far as yet known:

Gen. JACKSON, of the Pennsylvania Reserves, killed.

Gen. BAYARD struck in the thigh by a shell, and afterward died.

Gen. VINTON wounded in the side, but not seriously.

Gen. GIBSON wounded in the hand. Gen. KIMBALL wounded in the thigh.

Gen. CALDWELL wounded in two places, but not seriously.

Col. SINCLAIR, of the Pennsylvania Reserves, wounded seriously.

Capt. HENDERSON, commanding the Ninth New York State Militia, wounded seriously.

The following is the loss of officers in the Fifth New-Hampshire Regiment:

Col. CROSS, wounded in the abdomen. Major STURTEVANT killed. Adjutant DODD killed.

The firing of musketry ceased about 6 o'clock this evening, but the Rebels continued throwing shell into the city until 8 o'clock.

The position of the rebels was as follows:

Gen. LONGSTREET on the left, and holding the main works.

Gen. A. P. HILL and "Stonewall" JACKSON were in front of Gen. FRANKLIN, with JACKSON's right resting on the Rappahannock, and HILL'S forces acting as a reserve.

The troops are in good spirits and not the least disheartened.

OCCUPATION OF FREDERICKSBURG. GENERAL MCDOWELL'S CORPS CROSSING THE RAPPAHANNOCK RIVER ON PONTOON BRIDGE (FORBES). LIBRARY OF CONGRESS.

From Another Correspondent
Headquarters Army of the Potomac
Saturday, Dec. 13 – 10 P. M.

Last night our troops were rapidly pushed across the river, and every preparation made for a battle. Gen. FRANKLIN's Division crossed two miles below the city, while Gen. Sumner's troops occupied a portion of the town. Gen. Franklin's line was moved forward at sunrise, with his right resting on Fredericksburgh, his centre advanced a mile from the river, and his left resting on the river three miles below.

Skirmishing commenced on the left about daylight. Soon after, a rebel battery opened on our lines, and the Ninth New York Militia was ordered to charge, but after a fierce struggle was compelled to retire. The remainder of the Brigade, under Gen. TYLER, then charged the enemy's guns, when the fight became general on the extreme left. Gen. MEADE'S and Gen. GIBBON' S Divisions encountered the right of Gen. A. P. HILL'S command.

The cannonading was terrific, though our troops suffered but little from the enemy's artillery. Gradually the fight extended around to the right.

Gen. HOWE'S division went in, and then Gen. Brook's division. About 10 o'clock A.M. Gen. SUMNER'S troops engaged the enemy back of the city, since which time the battle has raged furiously along the whole line. The enemy, occupying the woods and hills, had a much more advantageous position but were driven back on their right a mile and a half early in the day.

About noon Gen. GIBBON was relieved by Gen. DOUBLEDAY, and Gen. MEAD by Gen. STONEMAN. Afterward Gen. NEWTON'S Division moved round to the support of the left, when the firing ceased in that portion of the field for a short time, and broke out with greater fierceness in the centre, where our troops were exposed to a plunging fire from the enemy's guns and earthworks from the hills.

Along the whole line the battle bas been fierce all day, with great loss to both sides. To-night each army holds its first position, with the exception of a slight advance of our left. Cannonading is still going on, and the musketing breaks out at intervals quite fiercely.

Gens. GIBBONS, VINTON, BAYARD and CAMPBELL are wounded. Gen. BAYARD was struck in the hip by a solid shot, while conversing with Gen. FRANKLIN and his staff, and cannot survive. His right leg has been amputated, but the operation will only serve to prolong his life a short time.

Several hundred prisoners have been taken, who report that Gen. LEE'S entire army is in the immediate vicinity. Gen. HILL'S troupe were withdrawn this morning and started down the river, but afterwards relented. Gen. FRANKLIN is to-night opposed to Stonewell JACKSON.

It is impossible to form an accurate idea of the loss on either side, as the firing is still going on, rendering it extremely difficult to remove the killed and wounded.

The city suffered terribly from the enemy's artillery, and is crowded with our troops, the front extending but a short distance beyond.

The balloon has been up all day. During the morning but little could be seen, owing to the dense fog; but the afternoon was remarkably clear.

This evening the rebels have been shelling Fredericksburgh, endeavoring to drive our troops out of the place, but without success.

The Operations of Sunday

Headquarters Army of Potomac
Dec. 14 – 11:30 A. M.
There is no fog to-day, the sun shining brightly, with a strong breeze. At daylight this morning there was a heavy fire of artillery and infantry in front of the first line of work, where Gens. SUMNER and HOOKER were engaged yesterday. The fire slacked about an hour afterward, and was heard only at intervals until now. The same occurred in front of Gen. FRANKLIN'S Divsion down the river. The object of both parties was evidently to feel the other.

During last night and this forenoon the rebels have considerably extended their work and strengthened their position. Large bodies of troops now to be seen, where but few were to be seen yesterday.

Our dead which were killed yesterday while charging in front of the enemy's works, still remain where they fell. When attempting their removal last night, the rebels would open fire with infantry but the wounded have all been removed from the field, and all the dead obtained are now being buried.

The indications are that no decisive battle will be fought today, unless the rebels should bring on the engagement, which they will not probably do.

Reports by Way of Washington

December 14, 1862

It is thought here that about 40,00O of our troops were engaged in yesterday's battle.

From information received early this morning, preparations were making all night for a conflict today, Gen. BURNSIDE remaining on the field giving orders, looking to the position and condition of his forces.

Additional surgeons, and everything which the necessities of the wounded require, have been dispatched from Washington to the battle-ground.

It is proper to caution the public against hastily crediting the many unsupported rumors concerning yesterday's battle. Some of them here prevalent have no other basis than surmise, and are mere inventions in the absence of facts. Rebel sympathizers are responsible for not a few of these fictions.

Gentlemen in high public positions repeat the assertion, as coming from Gen. Burnside, that *he has men enough, and therefore, desires no further reinforcements.*

Details of Operations to Saturday Morning

Camp Opposite Fredericksburgh
Saturday, Dec. 13, 1862
Affairs are rapidly culminating here, the crisis of battle, the grandest – probably most decisive – of the war, approaches apace.

The nation may well pause and hold its breath in the terrible suspense now impending. The prelude of the conflict has passed. The taking of the town by assault, and after a determined fight with the enemy's sharpshooters and skirmishers, and the crossing of the river by a considerable portion of the Union force, are fast bringing the two great armies face to face. To-day – to-morrow at furthest – must witness events which will long live in history. May we hope that the battle will be as decisive as it now promises to be bloody and terrible.

STUDY OF INFANTRY SOLDIER ON GUARD – WILLIAM J. JACKSON, SERGEANT MAJOR 12TH N.Y. VOLS – SKETCHED AT STONEMAN'S SWITCH NEAR FREDRICKSBURG (FORBES). LIBRARY OF CONGRESS.

The events of yesterday may be briefly summed up as follows:

Gen. SUMNER'S corps, the Right Grand Division, were across and occupied the town; one division took possession the first night, and the remainder of the column passed across the upper bridge in the morning. They filled the whole length of Caroline or Main street to the lines of the railroad, and by degrees extended their front to Commerce street, and the streets running up from the river, until the body of the town was filled up. They remained under cover of the houses, the streets running nearly North and South being parallel to the line of the enemies' batteries behind the town. The completion of a second pontoon bridge during the first night greatly facilitated the passage of the troops. The first artillery thrown across were the Napoleon batteries attached to Gen. SUMNER'S Division.

The enemy's pickets stubbornly occupied the outskirts of the town, and a fusilade between them and our own advance pickets was kept up during the day. The remainder of FRANKLIN'S column crossed their two pontoon bridges during the forenoon, two miles below the centre of the town. Their passage, as well as that of Gen. SUMNER'S Corps, was disputed by occasional but not very persistent firing from the rebel batteries, which are chiefly to the South and rear of the town, so to command the line of the railroad, and also the Bowling Green.

Gen. REYNOLDS' First Corps brought up the rear of FRANKLIN's column, and occupied the broad plateau south of the town, extending for miles down the river

Gen. HOOKER'S Grand Division, which had been on foot since Thursday, when they broke camp, remained with the head of its column pointed toward the upper bridges, but up to 3 o'clock awaited Gen. BURNSIDE'S orders to advance.

Three times during the day the enemy's battery commanding this crossing opened fire upon the troops which came down, their shells exploding with uncomfortable accuracy just at the hither end of the bridge, on the slope of the hill, and even beyond on the level plain by which they approached.

Shortly after 3 P. M. HOOKER'S column began to move down the river, as if with the design of crossing on the bridges below, where FRANKLIN crossed. Up to a late hour, however, they had not gone over. It is believed they passed the river during the night.

This change in the line was no doubt occasioned by the extraordinary activity displayed by the rebel batteries southeast of the town.

At 2½ P. M. the whole semi-circle of batteries in that direction opened fire upon the pontoon bridges, and upon the lower part of the town, where our troops were quartered. Their other batteries, north of the plank-road, and toward Falmouth, simultaneously poured in their contribution upon the upper crossing, and that part of the town lying in front of it.

Five separate batteries below, working ten or twelve guns, and four above, with eight or ten, kept up a fire of shot and shell until near sundown. Many of their shells fell short, but some took effect in the town, and near the river. What damage they did to the troops I could not learn at that late hour.

Several shells burst near the Lacey House, and one close by the north end of the building while I was getting the names of the wounded lying in that place. One man, a few minutes afterward, was brought in with his arm terribly shattered by a piece of shell. A considerable body of cavalry and infantry were partially sheltered behind these buildings, which are of brick. It being used as a hospital, and occupied by the rebels in common with the Union, for wounded soldiers is a guarantee that it will be respected. Its position being only a little to the left of the crossing, and nearly in line of one of the main rebel batteries, probably accounts for these shells bursting so near it.

We must presume that they were accidental shots, as I believe there is no well authenticated instance of their intentionally firing upon a hospital. It is situated only two hundred yards north of Lieut. MILLER'S battery, which is protected by earthworks, and very prominent on the high land below the house. These circumstances render the place unsafe, and it will only be used as a temporary hospital. The wounded will, for the present, be carried to the rear, where tents have been established for their accommodation.

The main body of the rebel army is believed to be in position some five or six, perhaps ten miles west, with a strong rear guard for cooperating with and supporting their batteries.

If estimates which I have heard be correct, we have an aggregate of over sixty thousand men more than the estimated strength of the rebel army. Our artillery figures up over five hundred guns. Considering the difficulties of the situation, the completion of six pontoon bridges and the crossing of such an army in twenty four hours, is worthy of all military achievement. The events of the last two days have increased the enthusiasm of the whole army toward its Commander, and strengthened confidence in the Generals leading the Grand Divisions. With town and river behind, we must fight – there is no backing out.

The Town – Its Condition

Our shot and shell have riddled a great many of the houses in town; and most of the churches, from foundation to steeple, have been accidentally perforated by the storm of missiles which were sent into the town. As the monuments and representatives of a priesthood and people thoroughly baptized in treason, they deserved no exemption from the common doom, but being larger than any other buildings, and very prominently in the range of our fire, they naturally received their full share of the iron storm. The clock in the steeple of the Episcopal church was untouched, and continues to toll off the eventful hours, for the benefit of the Union forces in the town.

In spite of prompt and general efforts to guard the houses from intrusion and pillage, by the establishment of guards, a good many residences have suffered more or less spoliation. Household articles, such as cooking utensils and crockery, pickles, sweetmeats and ditches of bacon, were observed among the troops, as I passed through the different streets. The latter, taken from the meat houses of the first families, no doubt, are generally transfixed on the end of bayonets, and carried in triumph on their shoulders.

There has been, as yet, no general pillaging of the town, and it will not be permitted. The principal stores have each a strong guard to protect the small stock of goods left behind in the flight of their proprietors.

Not over twenty houses, all told, have been burned, and the total damage to the place, by the bombardment and flames, I estimate at not over two hundred thousand dollars.

The few dead who were shot in the streets, have been buried, necessarily in the town, near where they fell. Considering all the terrible circumstances of provocation, the preservation of the town from total destruction, and its wholesale pillage by the army, are in the highest degree creditable to the Union troops, and to their discipline. Enclosed is a list of the killed and wounded as far as ascertained.

In haste to send the mail.

E.S.

What the Historians Say

The first battle at Fredericksburg, known also as Marye's Heights, occurred in Spotsylvania County and Fredericksburg on December 11-15, 1862. It was the only battle in the Fredericksburg Campaign of November and December, 1862.

The principal commanders were Maj. Gen. Ambrose E. Burnside leading 172, 504 Union troops and Gen. Robert E. Lee commanding 72,497 Confederates. Casualties were 13,353 and 4,576 respectively.

On November 14, Burnside, now in command of the Army of the Potomac, sent a corps to occupy the vicinity of Falmouth near Fredericksburg. The rest of the army soon followed. Lee who reacted by entrenching his army on the heights behind the town. On December 11, Union engineers laid five pontoon bridges across the Rappahannock under fire. On the 12th, the Federal army crossed over, and on December 13, Burnside mounted a series of futile frontal assaults on Prospect Hill and Marye's Heights that resulted in staggering casualties. Meade's division, on the Union left flank, briefly penetrated Jackson's line but was driven back by a counterattack. Union generals C. Feger Jackson and George Bayard and Confederate generals Thomas R.R. Cobb and Maxey Gregg were killed. On December 15, Burnside called off the offensive and re-crossed the river, ending the campaign. Burnside initiated a new offensive in January 1863, which quickly bogged down in the winter mud. The abortive "Mud March" and other failures led to Burnside's replacement by Maj. Gen. Joseph Hooker in January, 1863.

10

Gettysburg

The High Water Mark of the Confederacy

Author's Commentary

The fog of war obscured much on the battlefield. Both the coverage of the *Charleston Mercury* and *The New York Times* claimed victory for their respective sides at the great battle in Pennsylvania.

Coverage of the battle at Gettysburg was obviously much easier for *The New York Times* to arrange than for the *Charleston Mercury*. But it still wasn't easy. It was particularly hard for Sam Wilkeson of *The New York Times*. Jeb Stuart's cavalry had ripped out telegraph lines and disrupted the army's rail communications with Washington and Baltimore. Wilkeson, trying to get to the Army out of Washington, along with several other correspondents from other papers, left for Baltimore at eleven in the morning to discover, upon arrival, that the train they were hoping to catch was not available. He returned to Washington and learned the next day that the track had been repaired as far as Frederick, Maryland, so he returned to Baltimore then went on to Frederick reaching it on June 30. He then tried to reach Meade's Army by way of the Western Maryland Railroad to Westminister.

Successfully catching the Westminister train, Sam Wilkeson finally arrived at the battlefront on July 2, the second day of battle. But his difficulty would take a great emotional turn. He was advised upon his arrival that his son, Bayard, a young officer, had been severely wounded, having lost his leg from cannon fire. He learned the next day that his son had died. Wilkeson stayed to write his dispatch, reportedly by his son's grave site.

When the fog of war lifted, and Robert E. Lee's Army of Northern Virginia was forced to retreat southward, *The New York Times* still claimed victory for the Union, but the *Charleson Mercury* never admitted that the Confederate Army lost the great battle in Pennsylvania.

July 7, 1863: From the *Charleston Mercury*

Telegraphic News of the Battle of Gettysburg

Richmond, July 5 – Accounts from the *Baltimore American* of the 2d instant state that at 9 o on the lst, the 11th Corps of the Army of the Potomac entered Gettysburg, the cavalry of the rebels falling back and passing out of the west end of the town. The rebels, under LONGSTREET and HILL, advanced steadily, and, in a few minutes, a heavy fire of artillery and musketry opened along the whole Federal line against the advancing rebels. Several unsuccessful charges were made by the rebels on our lines. At 3 o the enemy massed his entire forces, and endeavored to turn our right wing. A heavy fight ensued, both sides suffering severely. The field between the contending armies was strewn with the dead and wounded. It is said the enemy suffered quite as heavily as we did. The effort to flank our right wing entirely failed. The advantage on the field is said to have remained decidedly with the Northern forces; but officers who arrived last night with prisoners describe the result of the fight as rather unfavorable to our arms. The enemy held the field at the close of the day, our forces having fallen back, after the fall of General REYNOLDS. On Thursday there was heavy skirmishing but no general engagement. The enemy is rapidly concentrating his troops. Yesterday MEADE'S whole army had reached the field. In the battle General WADSWORTH was severely wounded. The Union losses were enormously heavy, especially among field and line officers.

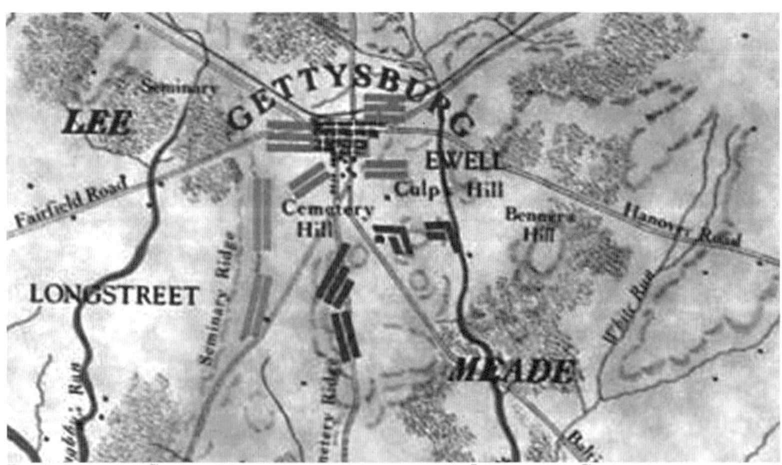

BATTLE MAP OF GETTYSBURG CAMPAIGN ON DAY ONE. LIBRARY OF CONGRESS.

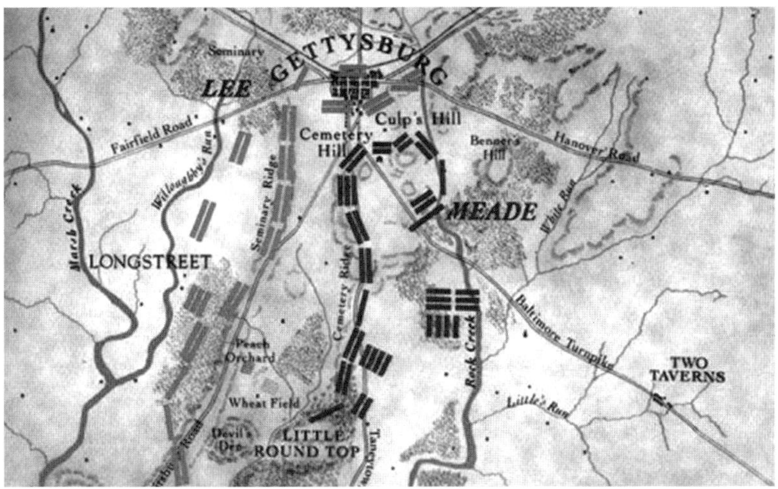

Battle map of Gettsyburg campaign on day two. Library of Congress.

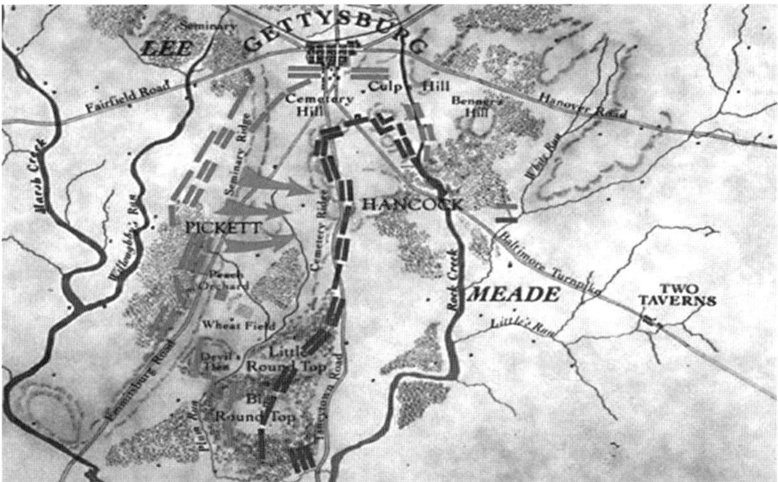

Battle map of Gettysburg campaign on day three. Library of Congress.

The Yankees on the flag of truce boat last night state that General MEADE was severely wounded in the battle of Gettysburg, and that four Federal Generals were killed. They say it was a drawn battle.

The Situation in Pennsylvania

As the crow flies, Gettysburg is about forty miles north from Washington, and about fifty miles from Baltimore, and it is on the direct route to Philadelphia, via York and Columbia, where the road crosses the river. Our advance has been to Columbia; EWELL'S corps was at York; LONGSTREET between York and Gettysburg, some twenty miles apart; and A.P. HILL'S corps has reached Gettysburg. LONGSTREET and HILL, at that place it seems, met and repulsed the enemyattacking columns with slaughter. And EWELL'S advance corps, as a reserve, has returned to reinforce, and we trust complete a victory which Yankee accounts call a battle.

If LEE succeeds in crushing MEADE'S army, Philadelphia will be at his mercy, or he may come down upon Washington in its rear. In either case, something brilliant and effective will have been accomplished, which, if vigorously used, may greatly tend to peace. But nothing except complete victory can make LEE master of the situation. So far the Yankee accounts we publish are very encouraging. Concealment of the extent of their distress, we regard as a matter of course; and, therefore from what they admit, feel confident they are badly hurt.

The *Charleston Mercury*

July 8, 1863

Telegraphic News
Great Battle in Pennsylvania
Our Forces Victorious

RICHMOND, July 7. – The latest despatches received from Martinsburg report that the enemy has been completely routed.

Forty thousand prisoners were taken on Sunday.

I will send fuller despatches this afternoon.

Later

RICHMOND, July 7 – The following telegrams have just been received here:

MARTINSBURG, VA, July 5 – At 5 p.m. on Saturday Gen. LEE had changed his front, occupying the ground from which the enemy had been driven on the 1st and 2d instants. The whole army was in splendid spirits and masters of the situation.

Gens. RHODES and PICKETT were wounded. Col. AVERY, of N. C., was killed, and Cols. BENNETT and PARKE wounded.

MARTINSBURG, July 6, a.m. – A courier just in reports that the enemy was defeated yesterday, and driven three miles.

A vast number of prisoners are reported to have been taken by LEE. The prisoners refused to be paroled, and are now on their way to Richmond.

This has been the bloodiest battle of the war. Our loss was very great. That of the enemy was immense.

JULY 6, p.m. – On Saturday night our centre fell back, drawing on the enemy. By our movement we had gained a good position on the heights. A general fight then ensued, resulting in the rout of the Yankees. LEE (as all accounts agree) captured 40,000 prisoners.

Fighting was going on at Williamsport between IMBODEN'S cavalry and several regiments of infantry, with a division of Yankee cavalry under PLEASANTON.

Another telegram, dated Martinsburg, June 6, says:
The latest accounts which seem to be trustworthy, state that the fight of Sunday was the bloodiest of the war. A. P. HILL fell back in the centre, causing the enemy to believe that he was retreating. The enemy thereupon advanced, when EWELL and LONGSTREET, with the right and left wings, closed in upon him, surrounding him completely.

We took the heights for which we had been contending, and captured 40,000 prisoners. They refused to be paroled. PICKETT'S division is guarding the prisoners on their way to Martinsburg.

From the West – Reported Fall of Vicksburg

BOLTON STATION, MISS., July 5 – Yesterday, about 12 o, the Yankee cavalry crossed the Big Black at Budsong Ferry. They advanced into the interior, but were promptly met by WHITFIELD'S Brigade and driven back across the river.

A courier, just in from EdwardDepot, says that AUSTERHAUS'whole command crossed near that place last night. If so, we will have warm work today.

GRANT is evidently very uneasy in regard to events transpiring in his rear. There was but little firing at Vicksburg yesterday.

Later
JACKSON, MISS., July 6. – The mail carrier has just arrived, and states positively that Vicksburg has fallen.

The *Charleston Mercury*
July 8, 1863

This same news has been received this morning from different sources, but not by any one here officially.

The War in North Carolina

WILMINGTON, July 6 – The damage to the Wilmington and Weldon Railroad during the recent Yankee raid was but trifling, and will be repaired tonight. Through trains will be run tomorrow. FOSTER is retreating to Newbern.

JULY 7 – A letter from a reliable source, dated Kinston, last night says: 'A courier just arrived reports that an engagement is now progressing between the retreating enemy and our forces near Freebridge. The enemy is supposed to be cut off.'

The *Charleston Mercury*
July 13, 1863

From General Lee's Army
A wounded officer of WRIGHT'S brigade, who arrived in Richmond on Thursday gives highly interesting particulars of the battles of Gettysburg. He left Gettysburg at 11 o on Saturday morning. From his statement we gather the following particulars:

In the fights of Wednesday and Thursday we whipped the enemy badly. On Friday the fight again commenced, being chiefly done by our centre, which was composed of Longstreet corps and two divisions of General A. P. Hillcorps. Neither the right nor left wing was seriously engaged. We drove the enemy back five miles to the heights, which he had fortified. In driving them this five miles we broke through two of their lines of battle formed to receive the onset of our troops, and finally charged them to the heights. Here our men were ordered to charge the heights, and the order being executed, resulted in our repulse.

VIEW FROM THE SUMMIT OF LITTLE ROUND TOP. THE ADVANCE OF GENERAL LONGSTREET'S CORPS ON THE UNION POSITION (5TH CORPS) THURSDAY EVENING AND FRIDAY AFTERNOON (FORBES). LIBRARY OF CONGRESS.

On Friday night our wagon trains were ordered to fall back, and commenced going to the rear. It is supposed that our army fell back from want of provisions. There was no scarcity of ammunition, for there were many trains of ordnance out of which not a single cartridge or shell had been taken. Some of them were attacked by the enemy, but Imobodencavalry successfully drove them off. Those of our men who were slightly wounded and could walk were sent off Saturday about noon. Those who were severely wounded were left in hospitals near the battle field.

In the fights of Wednesday, Thursday, and Friday, General Lee took about 10,000 prisoners, who were promptly sent to the rear, and who, our informant thinks, will reach Virginia safely. During the same time we lost about 4,000 prisoners and about 11,000 killed and wounded – making our loss 15,000 in all. The battle was the most furious that has taken place in this country, and the losses of the enemy in killed and wounded must exceed ours. In the charge upon them which drove them five miles, their loss, while flying before our troops, was enormous. Wrightbrigade suffered severely. One of the regiments which went into action with a Colonel, Lieutenant Colonel, and five or six Captains, came out in charge of a Second Lieutenant, the ranking officers having been either killed or wounded.

Our informant says that our army fell back with the greatest deliberation and order, to use his expression, there was no demoralization. None of the officers have any idea that Gen. Lee intends to recross the Potomac, nor has that intention been even hinted at by the officers commanding corps. It was generally and distinctly understood that the falling back was caused by the difficulty in obtaining provisions through so long a line of communication as that from Gettysburg to Williamsport, and no one in the army believed that it was intended to evacuate Maryland. The men were in good spirits, and ready for another fight with the enemy.

The Potomac, when our informant crossed, was very high. It is proper to state that the officer from whom the above information was obtained was a very intelligent, cool and deliberate person, and one not likely to exaggerate any fact which he might have learned.

From *The New York Times*

Saturday, July 4, 1863

Special Dispatches to *The New York Times*
Battle-Field Near Gettysburgh
Thursday 4:30 P. M. Via Baltimore, Friday A. M.
The day has been quiet up to the present moment. The enemy are now massing a heavy force on our left, and have just began the attack with artillery. The probability is that a severe battle will be fought before dark.

The rebel sharpshooters have been annoying our batteries and men all day from the steeples of the churches in Gettysburgh.

We hold the Emmetsburgh and Baltimore roads. L. L. CROUNSE.

Friday morning July 3,- three A.M. Via Baltimore, one P.M.
At the close of my last dispatch at 4½ P.. yesterday, the enemy had just opened a heavy attack by artillery on our left and centre. The tactics of the enemy were soon apparent – a massing of their main strength on our left Bank, which covered the Frederick road, with the determination to crush it. So intent were the enemy on this purpose, that every other part of the lines was left alone.

THE PURSUIT OF GENERAL LEE'S REBEL ARMY. THE HEAVY GUNS – 30 POUNDERS – GOING TO THE FRONT DURING A RAIN STORM (FORBES). LIBRARY OF CONGRESS.

Battle Field Near Gettysburgh

The fighting was of the most desperate description on both sides. Our gallant men fought as they never fought before. We had against this great onslaught of the enemy three corps – the Second, Third and Fifth. The Third and Fifth joined hands, and fought heroically. The Second ably supported them, and at the same time held its own position. One division of the First was also engaged.

The fighting was so furious that neither party took many prisoners. We captured about 600 in one or two charges.

The losses, considering the duration of the conflict, are more than usually heavy on both sides. Many of our most gallant officers have fallen. Gen. SICKLES' right leg was shot off below the knee. Amputation has been performed, and he is doing well.

Late in the evening, Gen. MEADE called a council of his corps commanders, and it was resolved to continue the fight so long as there was any one left to fight.

L. L. CROUNSE.

Baltimore, Friday, July 3. Via Washington. Friday, July 3

Our correspondent has just arrived from the battle-field at Gettysburgh, having left there at 3 o'clock this morning. The reports of the occurences in that vicinity, as thus far rendered in the Philadelphia and Baltimore papers, are almost totally incorrect. A brief and candid statement of the situation up to this morning is this:

In Wednesday's fight we were repulsed, simply because we were overpowered and outflanked. We fell back to the rear of Gettysburgh, and held that position. The action was not general, and was not intended to be by Gen. MEADE. It was brought on by Gen. REYNOLDS, under the impression that his force exceeded that of the enemy.

There was no fighting yesterday until 4½ o'clock, P. M. A bloody engagement was then fought, lasting until dark, *resulting in a substantial success to our forces, the enemy being repulsed with great loss.* The particulars I have already sent you by a special courier.

Neither Gens.WADSWORTH, VAN STEINWEHR nor DOUBLEDAY are wounded.

The total number of prisoners taken up to this morning was about fifteen hundred – eight hundred and fifty on Wednesday and six hundred on Thursday. This is reliable.

The enemy made the attack yesterday. *It was terrific, and they threw their whole force into it, but they were finally repulsed with great slaughter.*

At daylight this morning the battle was renewed, the cannonading being rapid and heavy. It was the determination of our Generals to fight to the bitter end.

L. L. CROUNSE.

PRISONERS BELONGING TO GENERAL LONGSTREET'S CORPS, CAPTURED BY UNION TROOPS, MARCHING TO THE REAR UNDER GUARD (FORBES). LIBRARY OF CONGRESS.

Official Dispatches from Gen. Meade

WASHINGTON, Friday, July 3
An official dispatch was received this afternoon from Maj.-Gen. MEADE, dated Headquarters Army of the Potomac, July 2, 11 o'clock P.M., which says:

"The enemy attacked me about 4 P. M. this day, and, after one of the severest contests of the war, was repulsed at all points. We have suffered considerably in killed and wounded. Among the former are Brig.-Gens. PAUL and ZOOK, and among the wounded Gens. SLOCUM BARLOW, GRAHAM and WARREN, slightly. We have taken a large number of prisoners."

Second Dispatch

WASHINGTON, Friday, July 3
A later dispatch has been received from Maj.-Gen.MEADE, dated 8 o'clock this morning, which says:

" The action commenced again at early daylight upon various parts of the line. The enemy thus far have made no impression upon my position. All accounts agree in placing their whole army here. Prisoners report that LONGSTREET'S and A. P. HILL'S forces were much injured yesterday, and had many general officers killed. Gen. BARKSDALE. of Mississippi is dead. His body is within our lines. We have thus far about 1,600 prisoners, and a small number yet to be started."

The Battle of Wednesday

Special Dispatch to *The New-York Times.*
Battle-Field near Gettysburgh
Thursday, 12( ) M... July 2, via Frederick, July 3
The engagement yesterday was quite severe, though confined to our advance, the First and Eleventh corps; the action being mainly fought by the First corps, under Gen. Reynolds, who was killed by a sharpshooter early in the fight. We first attacked the enemy's advance just beyond Gettysburgh, and repulsed it. when the whole corps became engaged, and subsequently the Eleventh corps, which came up to support by the Emmetsburgh road. The opposing forces were the rebel corps of HILL and EWELL. Our men gallantly sustained the fight, holding their own until 4 o'clock, when they retired to a strong position just to the eastward and southward of Gettysburgh.

This was maintained until the arrival of reinforcements at night, and our lines are now well formed.

No general engagement has yet taken place, but the probability is that a great battle will be fought this afternoon or to-morrow. The enemy is in great force. Our troops are now all up and well in hand.

The battle yesterday was sanguinary in the extreme. WADSWORTH'S division sustained the early portion of it with great valor, charging the enemy and taking a whole regiment of prisoners with Brig.- Gen. ARCHER. We have taken fully one thousand prisoners and lost many, most of them being wounded and in Gettysburgh, the greater portion of which the enemy now hold.

The rebels occupy Pennsylvania College as an hospital. ROBINSON'S division and one brigade of DOUBLEDAY'S supported WADSWORTH with great gallantry. The Eleventh corps, most of it fought well, and redeemed the disgrace of Chancellorsvllle. Among the general officers we lose beside Maj.-Gen. REYNOLDS. Gen. PAUL killed, and Gen. BARLOW wounded. Gen. SCHIMMELFENNIG is a prisoner. An estimate of yesterday's casualties cannot now be made.

Gettysburgh was injured by shells to a considerable extent. Most of the inhabitants remain in the burgh; many got away yesterday. It is a beautiful place, surrounded by a beautiful open and rolling country.

There has been more or less skirmishing all the morning, but no engagement of dimensions. Both parties are preparing for the great contest before them. Our troops are in splendid condition and fight like veterans.

Reports from Philadelphia

Philadelphia, Friday, July 3

The *Evening Bulletin* learns from parties who have arrived in this city the following particulars:

The fight opened at Gettysburgh on Wednesday, when our forces were about half a mile beyond the town.

But one brigade of the corps of Major-Gen. REYNOLDS was in position to do service at the opening of the struggle.

Gen. REYNOLDS gallantly pushed that brigade to a commanding position on Seminary Hill, and endeavored to hold it until the rest of the corps could come up.

Reinforcements were, however, delayed, and our forces subsequently fell back of the locality called Seminary Hill.

About 10,000 of our men in this fight were engaged with 30,000 of the enemy.

The last position taken by the Union forces was held up to the latest dates.

Gen. REYNOLDS was killed very early in the action, while placing the brigade in position.

During Wednesday night, about seventy-five thousand of Gen. MEADE'S troops came up and took favorable positions for reopening the battle on Thursday morning, while at that period some twenty-five thousand other Union troops belonging to the Army of the Potomac were so near at hand as to be immediately available for the conflict.

The rebels had mainly concentrated their forces near Gettysburgh on Wednesday night and there was but little doubt that the great battle of yesterday would involve every available man of both armies.

The Battle of Thursday

Special Dispatch to *The New York Times*
Battle-Field near Gettysburgh, Penn., Via Baltimore
Friday, July 3

My brief dispatches regarding the desperate engagement of yesterday have hardly conveyed a true idea of its magnitude and character. We have now had two days' fighting. Nearly the whole of Wednesday was thus employed by the First and Eleventh Corps, with varying success, they finally being obliged to fall back before greatly superior numbers.

This morning there were strong premonitions of an early engagement with the enemy in force, but as the day wore away no positive exhibition was made by the enemy. We began to think that perhaps there would be no immediate battle after all. We were hardly in a condition to give battle, as all our dispositions had not been made, Gen. MEADE not having arrived on the ground until 2 o'clock in the morning. The position of our forces after the fight of Wednesday was to the eastward and southward of Gettysburgh, covering the Baltimore Pike, the Taneytown and Emmttsburgh roads and still being nearly parallel with the latter. The formation of the ground on the right and centre was excellent for defensive purposes. On our extreme left the ground sloped off until the position was no higher than the enemy. The ground in front of our line was a level, open country, interposed here and there with an orchard or a very small tract of timber, generally oak, with the underbrush cut away. During the day, a portion of the troops threw up temporary breastworks as an abbattis. Gen. MEADE'S headquarters were at an old house on the Taneytown road, immediately in rear of the centre.

Our line was not regular in shape. Indeed the centre protruded out toward the enemy so as to form almost the two sides of a triangle. Before sundown Gen. MEADE'S headquarters proved to be the hottest place on the battle-held, so far as careless shelling was concerned.

Gen. HOWARD occupied, with his corps, a beautiful cemetery on a hill to the south of Gettysburgh. Cannons thundered, horses pranced, and men carelessly trampled over the remains of the dead. From this hill a beautiful view could be obtained of the valley, and also of a goodly portion of the enemy's line of battle.

Our forces had all been concentrated on Tuesday night, save the Fifth and Sixth corps. The former arrived during the morning, and the latter soon after noon. They were all massed immediately behind our centre. Whether or not it was Gen. MEADE'S intention to attack, I cannot say, but he was hardly ready before the afternoon of yesterday. The day had become almost dull. Skirmishing was now and then brisk, and the sharpshooters in the steeples and belfries of the churches persistently blazed away at officers and artillery horses. It was by sharpshooter in a barn just opposite WADSWORTH'S Division, yesterday, that Capt. STEVENS, of the Fifth corps was killed.

***The New York Times*, Saturday, July 4, 1863**

Gen. REYNOLDS was killed very early in the action, while placing the brigade in position. During Wednesday night, about seventy-five thousand of Gen. MEADE'S troops came up and took favorable positions for reopening the battle on Thursday morning, while at that period some twenty-five thousand other Union troops belonging to the Army of the Potomac were so near at hand as to be immediately available for the conflict.

The rebels had mainly concentrated their forces near Gettysburgh on Wednesday night, and there was but little doubt that the great battle of yesterday would involve every available man of both armies.

APPEARANCE OF CEMETARY HILL JUST PRIOR TO PICKET'S CHARGE (WAUD). LIBRARY OF CONGRESS.

The New York Times

July 6, 1863

The Great Battle of Friday
Our Special Telegrams from the Battle-Field
Near Gettysburgh, Saturday, July 4

Another great battle was fought yesterday afternoon, resulting in a magnificent success to the National arms.

At 2 o'clock P. M., LONGSTREET'S whole corps advanced from the rebel centre against our centre. The enemy's forces were hurled upon our position by columns in mass, and also in lines of battle. Our centre was held by Gen. HANCOCK, with the reliable old Second army corps, aided by Gen. Doubleday's division of the First corps.

The rebels first opened a terrific artillery bombardment to demoralize our men, and then moved their forces with great impetuosity upon our position. Hancock received the attack with great firmness, and after a furious battle lasting until (?) o o'clock, the enemy were driven from the field, Longstreet's corps being almost annihilated.

The battle was a most magnificent spectacle. It was fought on an open plain, just south of Gettysburgh, with not a tree to interrupt the view. The courage of our men was perfectly sublime. At 6 P. M. what was left of the enemy *retreated in utter confusion,* leaving dozens of flags, and Gen. HANCOCK estimated at least *five thousand killed and wounded on the field.*

The battle was fought by Gen. HANCOCK with splendid valor. He won imperishable honor, and Gen. MEADE thanked him in the name of the army and the country. He was wounded in the thigh, but remained on the field.

The number of prisoners taken is estimated at 3,000, including at least two Brigadier-Generals OLMSTEAD, of Georgia, and another—both wounded.

The conduct of our veterans was perfectly magnificent. More than twenty battle flags were taken by our troops. Nearly every regiment has one. The Nineteenth Massachusetts captured four. The repulse was so disastrous to the enemy that LONGSTREET'S corps is perfectly used up. Gen GIBBON was wounded in the shoulder. Gen. Watts was wounded and remained on the field. Col. HAMMELL, of the Sixty-sixth NewYork, was wounded in the arm.

At 7 o'clock last evening, Gen MEADE ordered the Third corps, supported by the Sixth, to attack the enemy's right, which was done, and the battle lasted until dark, when a good deal of ground had been gained.

During the day EWELL'S corps kept up a desultory attack upon SLOCUM on the right, but was repulsed.

Our cavalry is to-day playing savagely upon the enemy's flank and rear.

L. L. CROUNSE

From Another Correspondent

Gettysburgh, Friday, July 3

The experience of all the tried and veteran officers of the Army of the Potomac tells of such desperate conflict as has been in progress during this day. The cannonading of Chancellorsville, Malvern and Manassas were pastimes compared with this. At the headquarters, where I write, sixteen of the horses of Gen. MEADE'S staff officers were killed by shell. The house was completely riddled. The Chief of Staff, Gen, BUTTERFIELD, was knocked down by a fragment of case-shot. Col. DICKINSON, Assistant Adjutant-General, had the bone of his wrist pierced through by a piece of shell. Lieut. OLIVER, of Gen. BUTTERFIELD'S Staff, was struck in the head, and Capt. CARPENTER, of Gen. MEADE'S escort was wounded in the eye. While I write, the ground about me is covered thick with rebel dead, mingled with our own. Thousands of prisoners have been sent to the rear, and yet the conflict still continues.

The losses on both sides are heavy. Among our wounded officers are HANCOCK, GIBBON and a great many others whose names I feel restrained from publishing without being assured that they are positively in the list of casualties.

It is near sunset. Our troops hold the field, with many rebel prisoners in their hands. The enemy has been magnificently repulsed for three days – repulsed on all sides – most magnificently to-day. Every effort made by him since Wednesday morning to penetrate MEADE'S lines has been foiled. The final results of the action I hope to be able to give you at a later hour this evening.

S. Wilkeson

What the Historians Say

The battle at Gettysburg occurred on July 1-3, 1863 in Adams County, Pennsylvania. It was the pivotal battle in General Robert E. Lee's Gettysburg Campaign, which lasted through June, July and August The principal commanders were Maj. Gen. George G. Meade commanding the United States forces consisting of 83,289 troops and Gen. Robert E. Lee with his Army of the Confederacy consisting of 75,054 men. The casualties were enormous on both sides, the Confederacy suffering 28,000 and the Union 23,000.

Gen. Robert E. Lee concentrated his full strength against Maj. Gen. George G. Meade's Army of the Potomac at the crossroads county seat of Gettysburg. On July 1, Confederate forces converged on the town from west and north, driving Union defenders back through the streets to Cemetery Hill. During the night, reinforcements arrived for both sides. On July 2, Lee attempted to envelop the Federals, first striking the Union left flank at the Peach Orchard, Wheatfield, Devil's Den, and the Round Tops with Longstreet's and Hill's divisions, and then attacking the Union right at Culp's and East Cemetery Hills with Ewell's divisions. By evening, the Federals retained Little Round Top and had repulsed most of Ewell's men. During the morning of July 3, the Confederate infantry were driven from their last toe-hold on Culp's Hill. In the afternoon, after a preliminary artillery bombardment, Lee attacked the Union center on Cemetery Ridge. The Pickett-Pettigrew assault (more popularly, Pickett's Charge) momentarily pierced the Union line but was driven back with severe casualties. Stuart's cavalry attempted to gain the Union rear but was repulsed. On July 4, Lee began withdrawing his army toward Williamsport on the Potomac River. His train of wounded stretched more than fourteen miles.

The Union victory was of major significance in reversing the forward movement of Lee's invasion of the North.

ENTRANCE TO GETTYSBURG–SHARPSHOOTING FROM THE HOUSES (WAUD). LIBRARY OF CONGRESS.

11

Vicksburg

The Mississippi River Falls Under Federal Control

Author's Commentary

The New York Times was well represented on the battlefield. Its reporters were usually in the thick of it when the cannons roared, but it was not so on that day in July when Vicksburg fell to General U.S. Grant and the besieging United States Army and Navy. The defeat *The New York Times* felt that day could only be surpassed by the surrendering Confederates.

The *Times* war correspondent, Franc Bangs Wilkie, known for his integrity and reliability, had charge of the reportage of all the military operations in the Western Theater. He chose to be away from the army for a few days at a time when Grant's ongoing siege had been under way for more than forty days. He left his two aides to cover events per his intructions if, indeed, Vicksburg ever fell. When Vicksburg did fall during Wilkie's absence, the assistant assigned to carrry the dispatches and reportage to the newspaper, while enroute, was forced to switch trains at Indianapolis. As he waited at a hotel for his connecting train, he encountered two newspaper competitors and bragged openly that he could drink them both under the table. The challenge was accepted, the drinking bout began, and so did the legerdemain of the two competitors, who apparently were less concerned about drinking than about beating the competition to press.

Wilkie's assistant awoke the next day in the care of the chambermaid. *The New York Times*, instead of having a first-hand report of the surrender at Vicksburg, was forced to run stories of the celebrations in such cities as Philadelphia, Boston, and Syracuse, New York.

July 4, 1863 – From the *Charleston Mercury*

The Administration on Johnston

The *Richmond Sentinel*, the organ of the Administration, says:

From Vicksburg the news is calculated to increase our solicitude. Grant has not retired as we had hoped he would; nor has General Johnston struck his blow yet. We cannot for a moment think of Vicksburg falling without an effort on the part of Johnston to relieve it. The enemy say he has less than twenty thousand men – for with that force he would strike. We are sure he has many more than twenty thousand men, and we believe he will strike. Doubtless he is surrounded with many disadvantages. But this has been the fate of all our Generals in every great battle of the war. If we had declined battle whenever the odds were against us, we would never have fought a battle. Johnston must at least try and show that the fault wasnot his—that victory was not in reach of an effort. If Vicksburg falls without a blow from him, his reputation, were it ten times what it is, would not survive it. It would be impossible to imagine Jackson, were he alive, sitting by inactive while his gallant brethren were being assailed by night and by day, and starved into capitulation; and Jacksonexample and his great success have taught our people to attach great value to daring and activity, and to place large calculation on such qualities. On the other hand, the sleeping fox catches no poultry. Let Johnston bestir himself.

The *Charleston Mercury*

July 9, 1863

Telegraphic News—Surrender of Vicksburg

RICHMOND, July 8 – The following despatch was received at the War office today.

JACKSON, July 7. – To Hon. J. A. Seddon, Secretary of War: Vicksburg capitulated on the 4th inst. The garrison was paroled and are to be returned to our lines, the officers retaining their side arms and personal baggage. This intelligence was brought by officers who left on Sunday, the 5th.

(Signed) J. E. JOHNSTON, General.

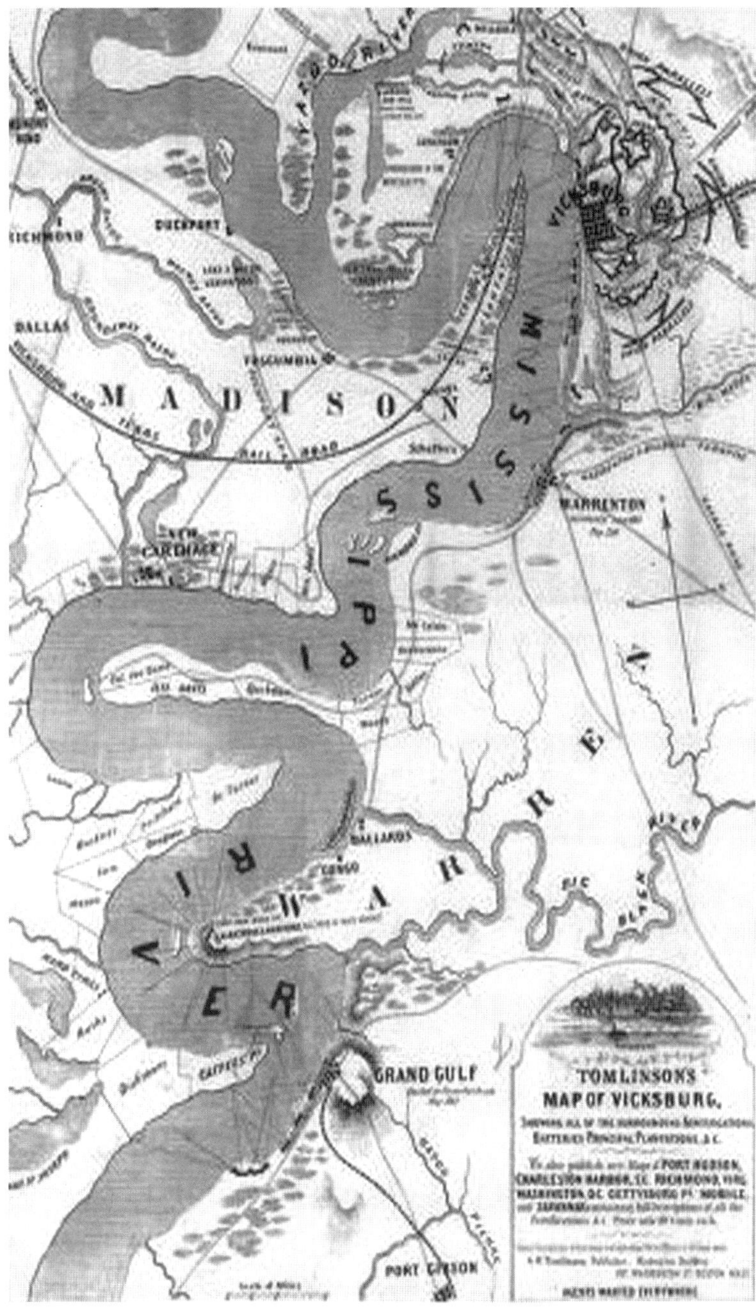

Map of Vicksburg showing the surrounding fortifications, batteries, and principal plantation (Tomlinson). Library of Congress.

JACKSON, MISS., July 7—General LORING attacked AUSTERHAUS yesterday near Edward Depot, and, after threehours hard fighting, drove him across the river. Our loss is reported to have been heavy. The enemyloss is not known.

An officer from the vicinity of Port Hudson says that General DICK TAYLOR crossed under cover of our guns at that point last Saturday. He joined his forces with GARDNER and attacked BANKS, routing him with heavy loss. GARDNER and TAYLOR are now moving to reinforce JOHNSTON.

We have nothing further in regard to the fall of Vicksburg.

JACKSON, July 7. – Vicksburg has fallen. It was surrendered on the morning of the 4th, the men being in a starving condition, and completely worn out with excessive fatigue. The terms of capitulation are that officers be allowed their side arms, horses and all private property—they and the men to be paroled immediately, and allowed to march out with all their colors flying. Immediately after the surrender GRANT sent a boat load of supplies to the famished garrison. Some of the officers have arrived here.

Later

But little more is known of the fall of Vicksburg. Officers who have come out say that had Gen. JOHNSTON reached there twelve days sooner, he could not have relieved the garrison, as they could not muster over 7,000 men for duty.

Many citizens are leaving here with their families, negros and stock. The Mississippian newspaper is packing up to leave.

JACKSON, July 8. – Everything here is in the wildest state of excitement. The citizens are flying in every direction, and the streets are filled with stock, negros, families, oxcarts and every species of conveyance. There was a terrible storm last night, with very heavy rain.

The citizens from beyond Clinton report that the enemy is burning every dwelling he passes. A fight here is looked for hourly.

NATCHEZ, July 6 – A transport, towing two barges loaded with coal, passed down this morning; also one last night. An officer on General SMITH'S staff reports that

PRICE was ordered on Sunday, June 28th, to take Helena, Ark. He moved immediately.

An extra of the *Natchez Courier* says: 'A letter has been-received from a member of CONNOR'S Battery, dated last week, near Lake Providence, Louisiana, reporting a battle to have just occurred, in which the enemy was severely punished, with a loss of 1,500 prisoners. CONNOR'S Battery was in the fight, and met with no loss.'

A gentleman from the vicinity of Port Hudson reports that the movements there indicate that BANKS is about to raise the siege. All flats and skiffs were burned at Natchez, by order of Colonel SMITH. The river is rising. We have plenty of rainhere. The crops and weather are fine. Thermometer 91 degrees.

Latest from the Border

WINCHESTER, VA., July 7. – There has been four days' fighting in Pennsylvania, beginning on the 1st and lasting till the 4th instant. Our men carried the immense fortifications of the enemy by assault. Our loss is estimated at 10,000. Between 3,000 and 4,000 of our wounded arrived here tonight. Generals SCALES and PENDER were among our wounded, and are here. The hills around Gettysburg are covered with the killed and wounded of the Yankee army.

The *Charleston Mercury*

July 14, 1863

Local Intelligence from the West
Movements of Grant and Johnston

JACKSON, July 11. – Another day has passed without any engagement. In the morning the enemy threw a force over our right, threatening to flank FEATHERSTONE, but BUFORD having been sent to reinforce him, drove the enemy back after a half hour of hard fighting. BUFORD lost sixty men, chiefly from the 7th and 8th Kentucky regiments. The enemy withdrew from our right, but in the afternoon made a demonstration upon our left and centre. DAN ADAM'S brigade repulsed them after a hard fight. Our loss today was about 200. The enemy is still fortifying.

JACKSON, July 11 – 11, p.m. – The enemy is still concentrating on our right to reach a supply of water at Pearl River. Our forces are driving them back in the centre. We have burned the houses occupied by their sharpshooters.

JACKSON, July 12. – The enemy opened fire on six batteries upon our left at 8, a.m., and rained shells upon the city. The enemy finally made a charge, but the Washington Artillery and COBB'S Battery repulsed him with heavy loss. Three hundred prisoners and three stands of colors were taken by our troops. ADAMS' and STOVALL'S brigades acted most gallantly. The enemy is moving around our right. Our scouts report that BURNSIDE, with two divisions, is crossing at Birdsong Ferry. Colonel WITHERS, an old citizen of Jackson, was killed in the trenches by a shell. General JOHNSTON, on the 10th instant, issued to the troops the following battle order, which was read along the line amid deafening shouts from the soldiers:

Headquarters on the Field
July 9, 1863
'Fellow Soldiers! An insolent foe, flushed with hope by his recent success at Vicksburg, confronts you, threatening the people, whose homes and liberty you are here to protect, with plunder and conquest. Their guns may even now be heard at intervals, as they advance.

'This enemy it is at once the mission and the duty of youbrave men to chastise and expel from the soil of Mississippi.The Commanding General confidently relies on you to sustain hispledge, which he makes in advance, and he will be with you inthe good work, even unto the end.

'The vice of 'he begs you to shun, and to frown on. If needs be, it will be checked by even the most summary remedies.

'The telegraph has already announced a glorious victory over the foe, won by your noble comrades of the Virginia army on Federal soil; may he not, with redoubled hope, count on you, while defending your own firesides and household goods, to emulate the proud example of your brothers in the east?

'The country expects, in this, the great crisis of its destiny, that every man will do his duty.'

Latest News from General Lee's Army

HAGERSTOWN, July 11 – To the *Savannah Republican.* There was considerable skirmishing yesterday. The enemy are reported as advancing by the Boonsboro and Sharpsburg Pikes. Brigadier General Paul J. SEMMES died of his wounds at Martinsburg yesterday.

MARTINSBURG, July 12 – The telegraph wires were cut near this place yesterday. Constant skirmishing is going on between LEE'S and HOOKER'S armies. The enemy occupies the line of the Antietam River. General LEE is near Hagerstown. Our army has been in line of battle since Friday evening. A fight is expected every day. The Potomac is falling at Williamsport.

The *Charleston Mercury*

July 15, 1863

Telegraphic News

Sufferings of the Vicksburg Garrison

JACKSON, July 8 – A number of the Vicksburg heros arrived here to-day. I have conversed with a number of them, privates as well as officers. The privates praise General PEMBERTON in the highest terms. They say they went into Vicksburg prejudiced against him, but no man could have done more than he did. One man shed tears when he told me of what they had suffered, with no relief, and then for Vicksburg to fall. The Yankees were led to believe that if they took Vicksburg the war was ended, and they could all go home, and they would remark to our troops, 'boys, we can all go home now.' An officer who arrived from Vicksburg says that the garrison had been living on pea bread and mule meat for two weeks. He says that if it had been known that relief was coming, it would have held out longer. It is stated that all the officers of PEMBERTON urged him to surrender.

THE SIEGE OF VICKSBURG. APPROACH OF MCPHEARSON'S SAPPERS TO THE REBEL EARTH WORKS (DAVIS). LIBRARY OF CONGRESS.

The *Charleston Mercury*
July 13, 1863

From General Johnston's Army

The *Jackson Mississippian* of July 7th says:

We are profoundly pained to learn, as we do on good authority, that the noble garrison at Vicksburg capitulated last Saturday morning, the 4th instant. There was no assault from the enemy, but some of his mines were sprung, which rendered further resistance useless. The terms of the capitulation are that the garrison, 17,500 in number, are to be moved out to some acceptable point on the Big Black to wait exchange. The officers were allowed to retain their side arms. We had up to this mournful event an excess of 30,000 prison ers,and an exchange will soon be effected.

The Yankees sent word to all the planters on theMississippi River above Vicksburg, whose negros they have taken, to send or come after their negro women and children, stating that they cannot afford to feed them any longer. The negro men they retain, to be slaughtered in battle! The women and children must starve, or be thrown upon the mercy of their owners!

THE FEDERAL RAM, QUEEN OF THE WEST, ATTACKING THE REBEL GUNBOAT VICKSBURG OFF VICKBURG (HARPER'S WEEKLY) U.S. NAVAL HISTORICAL CENTER.

The Jackson correspondent of the *Mobile Register*, writing on the same date, says:

Our troops and stock are suffering greatly for the want of water. There is little or none between here and the Big Black, and unless Johnston can obtain sufficient advantages over the enemy to enable him to hold that river, or a portion of it, he will be compelled to fall back to Pearl River, where he can obtain it. The railroad bridge over Pearl River will be completed this week, and the cars once more running into the city of Jackson.

For the last few hours the wagon trains of Johnston have been filing through the city to Pearl River. His army is reported to be falling back, and his rear skirmishing with the enemy. What an hour will bring forth I am unable to conjecture. Johnston is expected here, and is said to be here. A want of water forces this movement, and while it compels Johnston to fall back, it is equally as great an impediment to the advance of Grant.

I hope that Gardner will be warned in time to get away from Port Hudson. If true that he has whipped Banks off, he will be enabled to do so; if not, then look out, for the fall of Vicksburg leaves idle a large portion of Grant forces, whose mission is to open the Mississippi River to the Gulf. As I have before stated, when the enemy shall have these places, and the open navigation of the Mississippi River, he will have found his prize valueless for the want of Southern trade, and when the West finds out that the sword will not bring back the trade of the South, then you will hear a cry raised for peace in the West more potent and powerful than heretofore.

From *The New York Times*

The New York Times July 8, 1863
WASHINGTON, Tuesday, July 7, 1-P.M.
The following dispatch has just been received
U. S. MISSISSIPPI SQUADRON,
FLAGSHIP Black Hawk July 4, 1863
Hon. Gideon Welles, Secretary of the Navy
SIR : I HAVE THE HONOR TO INFORM YOU THAT VICKSBURG SURRENDERED TO THE UNITED STATES FORCES ON THE 4TH OF JULY.
Very respectfully,
Your obedient servant,
D. D. PORTER,
Acting Rear Admiral.

Unofficial Reports from Cairo

Cairo, Ill., Tuesday, July 7.
The dispatch boat has just arrived here from Vicksburg. She left at 10 o'clock on Sunday morning. The passengers announce that Gen. PEMBERTON sent a flag of truce on the morning of the 4th of July, and offered to surrender if his men were allowed to march out.

Gen. GRANT is reported to have replied that no men should leave, except as prisoners of war. Gen. PEMBERTON then, after consultation with his commanders, unconditionally surrendered.

This news is perfectly reliable.

THE RAMS SWITZERLAND AND LANCASTER RUNNING THE BLOCKADE AT VICKSBURG, MARCH 25, 1863 (HARPER'S WEEKLY). U.S. NAVAL HISTORICAL CENTER.

Special Dispatch to *The New York Times*

Washington, Tuesday, July 7

The Cabinet was in regular session to-day. Admiral PORTER'S Vicksburgh dispatch was received by Secretary WELLES, and read to the President. The news immediately spread throughout the city, creating intense and joyous excitement. Flags were displayed from all the Departments and crowds assembled with cheers. Secretary STANTON issued an order for a salute of one hundred guns.

The fall of Vicksburgh, conjoinly with the Gettysburg successes, is regarded as the turning point in the war. The President and high officials express a determination that the campaign shall not slacken off in consequence, but be carried on with renewed vigor. This sentiment is urged upon them by MESSRS. HAMLIN, WILSON, CHANDLER, WASHBURNE and other prominent loyalists now in town.

The President congratulates himself on his inflexible resistance to the efforts once made to induce him to remove Gen. GRANT. He always believed in GRANT'S genius and energy, and is now rewarded for his decision in his favor. HON. ELIHU WASHBURNE, GRANT'S nearest personal friend, who defended him last Winter in the House, is overjoyed at the result of the siege.

Rejoicing in New York

Albany, Tuesday, July 7
By order of the Adjutant-General, two salutes of thirty-four guns each were fired to-day—one in honor of our victorv in Pennsylvania, and the other for the fall of Vicksburgh. To-night there is an impromptu demonstration by the citizens. Guns are exploding, bells ringing. and with music and fireworks. The demonstration will be kept up until a late hour by an immense gathering of both sexes.

Syracuse, Tuesday, July 7
A grand impromptu celebration is taking place here, to-night, in honor of our victories. There is a mass-meeting in Hanover square. A salute of 100 guns is thundering. All the bells of the city are ringing. There is a parade by the Davis Guards, and fireworks, bonfires, and illuminations flame in all the principal streets. Such a scene of enthusiasm and rejoicing was never known.

Utica, Tuesday, July 7
The fall of Vicksburgh has been celebrated here by the ringing of bells, firing of cannon, and every display of popular joy.

Rejoicing in New Jersey

Burlington, N. J., Tuesday, July 7
The glorious news of the surrender of Vicksburgh was received here amid the ringing of the church bells and a salute of one hundred guns. The most intense enthusiasm prevails. The Union League rooms and several private residences are are iluminated.

Rejoicing in Massachusetts

Boston, Tuesday, July 7
The news of the surrender of Vicksburgh appeared to cause more joyous excitement in Boston than any previous event of the war. Bells were ringing, cheers and congratulations exchanged generally. At Newburyport the bells were rung, and a salute of one hundred guns fired. Dispatches from many quarters describe similar demonstrations of joy and gratitude for the glorious result.

HEADQUARTERS OF THE UNION ARMY, COMMANDED BY GENERAL GRANT, ON THE BANKS OF THE MISSISSIPPI RIVER NEAR VICKSBURG. STEAMBOATS IN THE BACKGROUNAD (LOVIE). LIBRARY OF CONGRESS.

Rejoicing in Philadelphia

Philadelphia, Tuesday, July 7 – 2 P. M.
The State House bell is ringing a joyful peal over the capture of Vicksburgh. All the fire-bells in the city are also now ringing, by direction of the Mayor, sent through the police telegraph.

Philadelphia, Tuesday, July 7
The newspaper offices are illuminated this evening. The *Ledger* building has stars placed along the entire front. The *North American* has the word "Victory." The *Bulletin* and other offices are tastefully decorated in honor of the victory. Numerous private dwellings and other edifices are illuminated.

Rejoicing in New Haven

New Haven, Conn., Tuesday, July 7
There is great rejoicing in this city over the news of the capture of Vicksburg. A National salute is now being fired upon the Public Square by direction of the Mayor.

What the Historians Say

The siege of Vicksburg occurred during May 18–July 4, 1863, in Warren County, Mississippi. It was the campaign objective of Grant's 1863 Operations against Vicksburg.

The principal commanders were Maj. Gen. Ulysses S. Grant leading his Army of the Tennessee against Lt. Gen. John C. Pemberton commanding the Confederate garrison. The estimated casualties were 4,550 and 31,275 respectively.

In May and June of 1863, Maj. Gen. Ulysses S. Grant's armies converged on Vicksburg, entrapping a Confederate army under Lt. Gen. John Pemberton. On July 4, Vicksburg surrendered after prolonged siege operations. This was the culmination of one of the most brilliant military campaigns of the war. With the loss of Pemberton's army and this vital stronghold on the Mississippi, the Confederacy was effectively split in half. Grant's successes in the West boosted his reputation, leading ultimately to his appointment as General-in-Chief of the Union armies.

The Union victory effectively split the Confederacy in two and gave control of the Mississippi to the Union Army and Navy.

12

The Wilderness

Grant Comes to the Eastern Theatre

Author's Commentary

The Wilderness was a frightening place. Because of the tangled mass of underbrush, neither army had a clear perspective on where the enemy was in strength. It was virtually impossible to maneuver large forces. It tested the nerves of the men in the field and certainly the officers who were trying desperately to adjust to the difficult situation.

General Grant, who was in his first major encounter with General Lee on the Overland Campaign, had an additional concern added to his list–one which demonstrated a tolerance for the press not shared by most general officers in either the Union or Confederate armies.

One night during the battle, General Grant, General Meade, and some staff officers were seated around a campfire discussing tactical procedures for the following day. One of the officers spied a shadowy figure hiding behind a nearby tree stump and quickly approached him. It was William Swinton of *The New York Times* who was scribbling the overheard plans as discussed by Grant, Meade, and their officers. Hauled before the officers, Swinton, who surely would have been shot if it were Sherman or Halleck he spied upon, was let off with a reprimand by Grant.

Swinton was not unknown to Grant. He had previously misrepresented himself to Grant, through an intermediary, to be not a correspondent of the press but rather a literary gentleman who wished to write a history of the war when it was over. Grant discovered Swinton's true identity when a Richmond newspaper, which Grant read with regularity, contained a verbatim report of instructions he had given a subordinate officer while crossing the Rapidan River.

May 9, 1864 – From the *Charleston Mercury*

Latest from the Seat of War
The Battles on the Rapidann
Continued Success of Our Arms
Official Despatches from Gen. Lee
General Jenkins Killed, and Generals Longstreet and Pegram Severely Wounded
Fighting Continued All Day Friday and Saturday
Movements on James River

ORANGE C.H., May 6 – We have the following additional particulars of the fighting on Thursday:

HETH'S and WILCOX'S divisions were engaged. They checked and drove back three corps and two divisions of the enemy.

LANE'S North Carolina brigade last night surprised and captured three hundred prisoners.

From 3 p.m. until nightfall there was very heavy musketry fighting. But little artillery was engaged.

COOK'S brigade fought well and suffered a heavy loss.

THOMAS' and McGOWAN'S brigades (the latter consisting entirely of South Carolina troops) also suffered considerably. ROSSER, with his single brigade, fought WILCOX'S whole division of Yankee cavalry, driving them back at all points.

The fighting has been resumed this (Friday) morning. It is reported and believed that we are driving them. About 300 more prisoners have been received here, and more are on the way.

Gen. BENNING was slightly wounded this morning, in the arm, and Gen. PEGRAM in the knee.

The battle field is about twenty-five miles below here.

The Richmond ambulance committee have arrived here. The Press correspondent left for the battle field this morning.

Later – The Battle on Friday

ORANGE C.H., May 6 – 9 p.m. – The attack of the enemy this morning was very violent, but it was repulsed in every instance. A strong effort was made to turn our right. We drove them on our left; but their line resisted stubbornly on the right. LONGSTREET, however, finally forced them to give way.

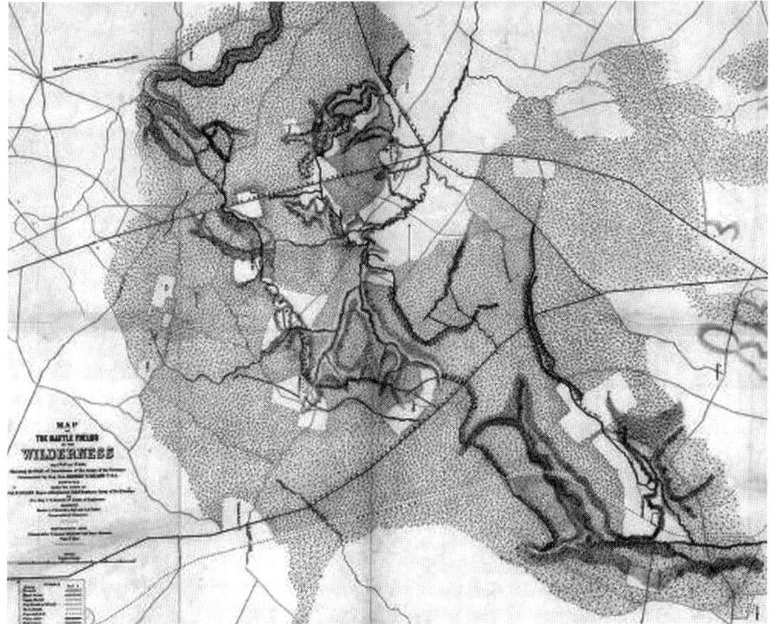

Map of the battle fields of The Wilderness, May 5, 6, and 7, 1864. Shows field of operations of the Army of the Potomac commanded by major General George B. Meade. Library of Congress.

General LONGSTREET received a severe wound in the shoulder, and General JENKINS, of South Carolina, was mortally wounded. Col. BROWN, of Georgia, of the Virginia Artillery, was killed.

Amongst the other casualties reported are the following:

Colonel JAMES D. NANCE, South Carolina regiment, killed; Colonel MILLER, 12th South Carolina regiment, killed; Lieutenant Colonel BOOKTER, 12th South Carolina regiment, mortally wounded; Lieutenant Colonel FRANKLIN GAILLARD, 2nd South Carolina regiment (and formerly editor of the Columbia Carolinian) killed.

The fighting was principally with musketry, the ground being unsuitable for the use of artillery. The battle was fought near the 'Wilderness,' and the enemy has been pushed back nearly to Chancellorsville. Everything looks well. The Yankee General WADSWORTH, who was the Abolition candidate for Governor, against SEYMOUR, in the last New York election, was killed. Up to this time seventeen hundred prisoners have been received here.

General Lee's Official Despatch

Richmond, May 6 – The following has just been received at the War Office:

Headquarters
Army Northern Virginia, May 6
To the Secretary of War

Early this morning, as the divisions of General HILL, engaged yesterday, were being relieved, the enemy advanced, creating some confusion; but the ground lost was recovered as soon as our fresh troops got into position, and the enemy was driven back to the original line. Afterwards, we turned the left of his fresh line and drove it from the field, leaving a large number of dead and wounded in our hands – amongst them General WADSWORTH.

A subsequent attack forced the enemy into his entrenched lines on the Brook Road, extending from the Wilderness Tavern, on the right, to Trigg Mill. Every advance on his part, thanks to a merciful God, has been repulsed.

Our loss in killed is not large; but we have many wounded – most of them slightly, the artillery having been little used on either side. I grieve to announce that Lieutenant General LONGSTREET was severely wounded, and General JENKINS killed.

General PEGRAM was badly wounded yesterday. General STAFFORD, it is hoped, will recover.

(Signed)
R.E. LEE

Saturday's Despatches

RICHMOND May 7 – The chief Monitor of the enemy fleet in James River is the Onandaga, which has just been finished in New York. The Yankee gunboat destroyed by one of our torpedoes yesterday was blown into fragments. The official despatch says that hardly a piece as big as a rowboat was left. After the explosion, the rest of the fleet was stopped.

Nothing has been heard of the situation of affairs on the Rappahannock this morning. GRANT'S plan was to turn our right and get between LEE and Richmond. LONGSTREET turned the enemy left and was pushing him back steadily when he received his severe wound. He was shot, owing to a mistake, by some of our own men, of MAHONE'S brigade, and Gen. JENKINS was killed by the same brigade. Gen. KERSHAW commanded McLAWS' division with distinguished honor. BATTLE'S Alabama and GORDON'S Georgia brigade suffered severely.

Saturday's Fighting

An interruption of telegraphic communication with Richmond on Saturday afternoon, which was not restored until a late hour Sunday night has prevented the receipt of the expected press despatches in regard to the operations of Saturday. Private telegrams, however, received on Saturday, before the interruption took place, render it certain that the conflict still continued on that day, with encouraging results.

Ed. *Mercury*

Latest Official Despatch from General Lee

RICHMOND, SUNDAY, May 8 – The following was received at the War Office this morning:

Headquarters
Army Northern Virginia
May 8, 1864
To the Secretary of War

Gen. GORDON turned the enemy extreme right yesterday evening, and drove him from his rifle pits.

Amongst the prisoners captured are TRUMAN, SEYMOUR and SHALLOE. A number of arms were also taken.

The enemy has abandoned the Germania Ford Road, and removed his pontoon bridge towards the ElyFord Road.

There has been no attack to-day; only slight skirmishing along our line.

(Signed)
R.E. LEE.

A despatch from ChaffinBluff says that one of the enemy gunboats had been attacked and disabled, and afterwards boarded and burned on the 7th instant. Two iron clads bore down on our forces, but subsequently withdrew. We have no further particulars.

THE 6TH CORPS – BATTLE OF THE WILDERNESS – FIGHTING IN THE WOODS (FORBES). LIBRARY OF CONGRESS.

(Note – In order that our readers may comprehend the state of affairs, we will explain the position of the roads and fords alluded to in General LEE'S despatch. Germania and Ely Crossings, on the Rapid Ann, are on the roads leading from Culpeper to Fredericksburg. Germania is the crossing for the plank road, and Ely, which is lower down the river, for the old wagon road. These are the roads formerly used by the country people in passing from Culpeper to Fredericksburg. When the enemy crossed, he occupied both roads and both fords. But it seems that, on Saturday evening, our forces turned the right of his line, which was drawn up along the plank road, and at right angles to the course of the river. Being thus cut off from the south bank of the river at Germania Ford, the enemy appears to have withdrawn his line of battle to the old wagon road, lower down, at the same time removing his pontoons from Germania to ElyFord.)

Ed. *Mercury*

The *Charleston Mercury*
May 9, 1864

GENERAL JENKINS – Among the heavy casualties which our country will be called to mourn when the sad list of those killed on the field of battle shall have appeared, South Carolina will weep the extinction of no more distinguished name than that of the lamented Gen. M. JENKINS, who fell mortally wounded on the 6th, whilst leading his victorious troops against the enemy near The Wilderness. We fear, too, that he fell by the hands of our own men, another victim of the carelessness which deprived us on the same ground, and by the same misfortune, of the illustrious Stonewall JACKSON.

In a few days we shall attempt to give a sketch of the life and services of the General, whose loss our whole State will deeply deplore. She has given few names to the history of this awful contest, of more unsullied or enduring luster, and none more generally respected and beloved, than his which has been forever stricken from the roll of living men.

The *Charleston Mercury*
May 10, 1864

The Defeat of GrantArmy

In the devout language of the Commander-in-Chief of the Army of Northern Virginia, which he has so often led to victory, Thanks to the Giver of all Victories, that wise General and that invincible host have again triumphed, and once more the hirelings of the North, baffled and demoralized, are in full retreat along the historic banks of the Rappahannock.

Cheered by glad tidings from every quarter of our extended frontier, nerved to the highest pitch of resolute courage and endeavor by the consciousness that our all was at stake, and supported by an unwavering confidence in the discipline, spirit and intelligence of our troops, the whole country has awaited, with undisturbed confidence, the issue of this last, long threatened and tremendous assault upon the Capital. Though the details that have thus far reached us are meagre, and though the conflict may yet be prolonged for days, we know enough to be certain that the new 'On to Richmond,' like those which preceded it, has met with signal and humiliating disaster.

A brief review of the operations which led to this splendid triumph of our arms will enable our readers, with the aid of their maps, to form a tolerably correct idea of the campaign. The Yankee forces at Culpepper Court House, it appears, moved by the old Plank Road and crossed the Rapidan at Germania Ford. Those at Brandy Station, Catlett, Warrenton and Manassas, on the Orange and Alexandria Railroad, moved by the old Turnpike and crossed the Rappahannock at

ElyFord, four miles below the junction of the Rapidan and Rappahannock Rivers, and eight miles, in an air line, from Germania Ford.

Germania Ford is about twelve miles and ElyFord about four miles from Chancellorsville. Orange Court House is about twenty-seven miles and Wilderness Tavern about twenty-two miles from Chancellorsville. From points between Chancellorsville and Wilderness Tavern, roads lead to Gordonsville, Louisa Court House and FrederickHall, on the Virginia Central Railroad, at distances varying from twenty and thirty miles. From these places there are good roads leading direct to Richmond, which is distant between forty-two and fifty-four miles; and also good roads to Hanover Junction.

The enemy having clearly developed the direction of his advance, our forces, marching parallel with the courses of the river, rapidly moved to meet him, LONGSTREET'S corps starting from Gordonsville, HILL taking the Plank Road, and EWELL the Old Turnpike, which joins the Plank Road a few miles above Chancellorsville. The conflict opened at noon on Thursday, May 5th, in a considerable engagement between EWELL'S Corps and the Fifth Corps of Yankee infantry, including SYXE'S Regulars.

General Wadsworth's division in action in The Wilderness near where the General was killed (Waud). Library of Congress.

The collision took place near PACKER'S store, where the Germania Ford road debouches into the old turnpike. This point is in Spottsylvania county, about eight miles above Chancellorsville and twenty miles below Orange C.H. The whole face of the country in that neighborhood is thickly covered with an undergrowth of field pines, cedars and scrub oaks, and therefore utterly unfit for the use of cavalry or artillery.

The night of the 5th instant closed with the complete repulse of the enemy on all sides, and the capture of seventeen hundred Yankee prisoners, and four pieces of artillery. The fighting was resumed on the next morning (Friday), 6th inst.

The battlefield was about five miles lower down, at the Wilderness, or, as Gen. LEE states in his despatch to the War Department, near Wilderness Tavern. The enemy were soon driven back on Chancellorsville, so that the principal fighting must have taken place at or near the old Chancellorsville battle ground. The attack of the enemy was desperate and violent, but was repulsed in every instance. GRANT'S plan, it seems, was to turn our right and get between LEE and Richmond. This maneuvre was frustrated by LONGSTREET, who had turned the enemy left and was pressing him back steadily when he received the severe wound in the shoulder by a shot from MAHONE'S Brigade through mistake. With this mishap, the fighting of Friday seems to have substantially ceased. On Saturday, however, the battle was renewed, and while the enemy's whole line was steadily held in check. GORDON'S Brigade, by a brilliant charge, turned his right, cutting him off from Germania Ford and necessitating a hasty withdrawal of his force towards Ely. Our accounts of the subsequent operations are scanty; but a severe cavalry engagement having occurred on Sunday, in which the enemy was with great slaughter, GRANT, at last accounts, had abandoned the position to which he had been driven, and in which his right rested upon ElyFord, and was marching off down the river, in the direction of Fredericksburg. So ends the advance of the great column, which was to crush LEE and deliver Richmond to the mercies of BUTLER, the jackal of Yankee conquerors. We trust, however, that the chapter of GRANT'S reverses is not yet closed, and that his victor has yet to strike the closing blow of the campaign.

WOUNDED ESCAPING FROM THE BURNING WOODS OF THE WILDERNESS (WAUD). LIBRARY OF CONGRESS.

But, if our people be wise, they will indulge in no exaggerated fancies as to the probable consequence of our victory. Let them be satisfied that the latest and most formidable aggressive movement of the public enemy has been completely baffled. A force, much superior to ours in numbers and equipment, bearing upon its banners the last hope of the infatuated Northern rabble, and led by their idol of the hour, 'Man on Horseback,' has been hurled back, shattered and demoralized, by our gray clad veterans. The lying presses of the North may palliate the disaster, but the world will not fail to recognize the glory and the importance of our triumph. Taken in connection with our late brilliant successes everywhere, by sea and land, West as well as East, the defeat of GRANT must still further relax the energies and sap the strength of our already tottering opponent.

For us, meantime, there is but one course – to press on our victorious standards everywhere, sparing no effort, abating no hope, but yielding to no false confidence until the goal of an acknowledged Independence be fairly won, trusting the issue to Him, who has so marvelously befriended us in our dread struggle against the unholy aggressions of a powerful and malignant foe.

THE WILDERNESS, ON THE BROCK ROAD, 2ND CORPS, MAY 11, 1864 (FORBES). LIBRARY OF CONGRESS.

From *The New York Times*

Special Dispatches to *The New York Times*
First Dispatch
Washington, Sunday, May 8, 1864
The latest news from the army received here is up to seven o'clock yesterday evening, at which time GRANT fully maintained his position. The fighting on Thursday and Friday was very severe, with skirmishing only on Saturday. LEE'S first onset was made upon our left, but failing, he then fell upon our centre and finally upon our right, where the hardest contest took place. Here the rebels charged upon our lines twice. but were repulsed each time with severe loss. HANCOCK'S corps charged back twice, and at one time entered that portion of the enemy's entrenchments commanded by A. P. HILL but were at length compelled to fall back. SEYMOUR'S division of HANCOCK'S corps was badly cut. Gens. WADSWORTH and BARTLETT were badly wounded, the former having been knocked off his horse by a spent minié ball. The rebels were reported retreating yesterday morning. The number of wounded is reported at about ten thousand; the killed at two thousand. The loss of the enemy exceeds this. He left his dead and disabled on the field, in our hands. The

Ambulance Corps, with its admirable organization, is working up to its full capacity, carrying the wounded to Rappahannock Station. Sixteen trains of cars, dispatched from Alexandria to-day, will receive them. It is expected that they will return, with their bruised and mangled freight, about daylight. Several car-loads of ice were also sent down for the comfort of the wounded. The Sanitary and Christian Commissions are on the field, with a full force of assistants, and with plentiful supplies of everything necessary for the wounded. The Government has hospital accommodations here for thirty thousand, which will probably meet all demands.

Second Dispatch
Washington, Sunday, May 8 – Midnight
Your special correspondent, writing from headquarters at Wilderness Tavern, Friday evening, May 6, gives the following intelligence of the great battle on Friday:

The day has closed upon a terribly hard-fought field, and the Army of the Potomac has added another to its list of murderous conflicts. LEE'S tactics, so energetically employed at Chancellorsville and Gettysburgh, of throwing his whole army first upon one wing and then upon another, have again been brought to bear, but I rejoice to say that the army of the Potomac has repulsed the tremendous onslaught of the enemy and stands to-night solidly in the position it assumed this morning. The first attempt was made upon HANCOCK, upon the right, somewhat weakened in numbers by the battle of yesterday, but the iron old Second Corps nobly stood its ground. Then the enemy hurled his battalions upon SEDGWICK, and once or twice gained a temporary advantage; but our veterans were nobly rallied, and the rebels repulsed with awful slaughter. About half past four P.M., LEE made a feint attack upon the whole line, and then suddenly fell, with his whole force, upon SEDGWICK, driving him back temporarily; but the advantage was soon regained, and the rebels hurled back with great loss. Night had now come on, and it is believed at headquarters, at this hour, that LEE has withdrawn from our front. Although the nature of the ground has been of a terrible character, most of it being so thickly wooded as to render movement all but impossible, and to conceal entirely the operations of the enemy, yet he has been signally repulsed in all his attacks, and nothing but the nature of the battle-field has been preventing it from being a crushing defeat. The loss on both sides has been very heavy, but at this hour of hasty writing, I cannot even give an estimate.

What the Historians Say

The battle in The Wilderness, known also as Combats at Parkers Store, Craig's Meeting House, Todd's Tavern, Brock Road and the Furnaces, occurred in Spotsylvania County, Virginia, May 5-7, 1864. It was the first of the eleven major battles in Ulysses Grant's Overland Campaign, which occurred during May and June, 1864. The principal commanders were Lt. Gen. Ulysses S. Grant and Maj. Gen. George G. Meade of the Union Army and Gen. Robert E. Lee of the Confederate. The forces engaged were 101,895 Federal troops and 61,025 Confederate. The estimated casualties were 18,400 and 11,400 respectively.

The opening battle of Grant's sustained offensive against the Confederate Army of Northern Virginia, known as the Overland Campaign, was fought at The Wilderness, May 5-7. On the morning of May 5, 1864, the Union V Corps attacked Ewell's Corps on the Orange Turnpike, while A.P Hill's corps during the afternoon encountered Getty's Division (VI Corps) and Hancock's II Corps on the Plank Road. Fighting was fierce but inconclusive as both sides attempted to maneuver in the dense woods.

Wounded soldiers crossing the Rappahannock River at Fredricksburg on a flat-boat. After the battle of The Wilderness (Forbes). Library of Congress.

General U.S. Grant at The Wilderness, May 7, 1864 (Forbes). Library of Congress.

Darkness halted the fighting, and both sides rushed forward reinforcements. At dawn on May 6, Hancock attacked along the Plank Road, driving Hill's Corps back in confusion. Longstreet's Corps arrived in time to prevent the collapse of the Confederate right flank. At noon, a devastating Confederate flank attack in Hamilton's Thicket sputtered out when Lt. Gen. James Longstreet was wounded by his own men. The IX Corps (Burnside) moved against the Confederate center, but was repulsed. Union generals James S. Wadsworth and Alexander Hays were killed. Confederate generals John M. Jones, Micah Jenkins, and Leroy A. Stafford were killed. The battle was a tactical draw. Grant, however, did not retreat as had the other Union generals before him. On May 7, the Federals advanced by the left flank toward the crossroads of Spotsylvania Courthouse.

It was a major battle but with significant but inconclusive results. Grant was not deterred from proceeding on the offensive.

13

Cold Harbor

The Ninth Major Battle in Grant's Overland Campaign

Author's Commentary

William Swinton, *The New York Times* correspondent, who was pulled from the shadows as he was eavesdropping on Generals Grant and Meade during the battle of The Wilderness, was a writer of recognized literary skill. *The Army and Navy Journal* hailed him as such. Like most, if not all, correspondents during the Civil War, his facts sometimes conflicted with reality. At Cold Harbor, General Ambrose Burnside, normally a taciturn individual, confronted Swinton and laid out Swinton's short-comings in this regard. Burnside arrested Swinton with the intention of rendering a swift judgment, for Swinton had the temerity to misrepresent the conduct of his Ninth Corps in actions at the Battle of Bethesda Church on May 31, 1864.

Swinton had reported that Burnside's Ninth Corps had participated in artillery only and did not engage in any close encounter action. The official report stated otherwise. The Ninth Corps had actually suffered over twelve hundred casualties. Burnside was livid. According to Grant, in his memoir, Burnside had given the order for Swinton to be shot that afternoon. But Grant intervened through General Meade and ordered Swinton to be expelled from the Army.

Following Swinton's expulsion, *Times* editor Henry J. Raymond, on July 14th, editorialized:

"Judging from Gen. Meade's previous action in similar cases, and from the general temper he exhibits toward the press, Mr. Swinton is quite as likely to have been excluded for being too accurate as for any other offence."

Ironically, Raymond's facts, too, conflicted with reality. General Meade, who also had a reputation as an antagonist of the press, was being taken to task for General Grant's action.

June 9, 1864 – From the *Charleston Mercury*

Telegraphic

The Campaign Against Richmond

BATTLEFIELD, NEAR GAINES' MILL, June 7 – 5 p.m. – The press telegram sent last evening should have read 'EARLY followed the enemy two miles,' and not 'After pursuing two miles, and finding the enemy entrenched on Tolpotomy Creek, with a swamp in their front, EARLY went no further.'

The condition of affairs on our left is unchanged today. The enemy is still in front of HILL'S and ANDERSON'S corps, but is reported moving to the right.

Last evening GRANT sent another flag of truce asking permission to bury the dead. This was granted, and three hours (from 7 until 10 p.m.) fixed as the time. But it seems GRANT did not get General LEE'S answer in time; and the dead are still unburied. Another flag of truce has come in this morning.

Some artillery and picket firing is going on today.

Second Despatch

RICHMOND, June 8. - GRANT sent Gen. LEE the flag of truce yesterday for the purpose of returning a detail of ours, improperly captured, while burying the dead last night, and apologized for taking them.

Nothing of interest has transpired today.

The Latest from the United States

RICHMOND, June 7 – The *Washington Chronicle* of the 2d instant says that GRANT'S communications with the White House are complete. A railroad will be put into operation between West Point and the White House.

Brownsville, Texas, at last accounts, was threatened by 2,000 rebels.

Gold in New York 89 1/2.

We have European dates to May 20. Parliament had reassembled. PALMERSTON'S health was restored. There are alarming accounts of the health of the Pope. Some credit was attached, on the London Stock Exchange, to the report of GRANT'S victories over LEE. The Confederate loan declined 3 per cent, and the news caused unsettled feeling in commercial circles.

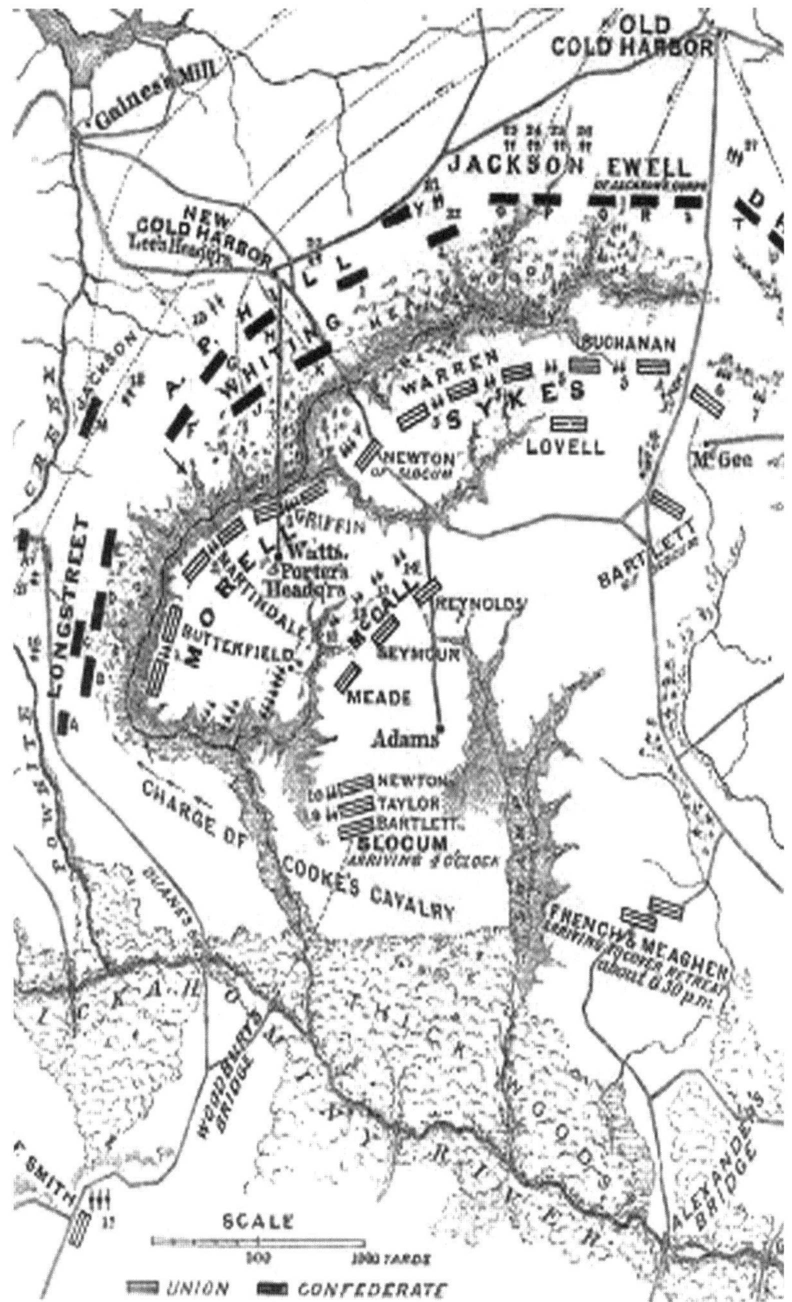

Union and Confederate battle lines at Cold Harbor. Library of Congress.

Later
RICHMOND, June 8 – United States papers of the 4th instant have been received. They quote gold at 192.

GRANT, in his despatches of May 2d, claims that the rebel works at Cold Harbor were carried on the afternoon previous. The rebels' repeated assaults, he says, were repulsed with loss in every instance. Several hundred prisoners, he adds, were taken.

Other despatches, equally false, from BUTLER and other sources, are published, probably with a view of influencing the action of the Republican Convention, which met in Baltimore yesterday.

The *Charleston Mercury*

June 14, 1864

Letter from Richmond
Correspondence of the *Mercury*
Richmond, Friday, June 10
While his gabions are being prepared, GRANT amuses himself by sending out raiding parties. That sent to Petersburg yesterday succeeded about as well as SHERIDAN did when he got inside the outer line of works around Richmond. A engineer from Petersburg declared that the enemy got as far as Main street, but were mown down there by cannon which the plucky Petersburgers keep planted in all their streets.

Can Grant reduce Turkey Ridge by regular approaches? I put this question to a military man a week ago; he said it could not be done, and explained why it could not – because the sappers could be flanked and enfiladed. To prevent this, Grant gets up his gabions, etc., and yet this is a long-taw siege with a vengeance. Turkey Ridge is ten or twelve miles from here. There is a ruse somewhere.

The proposition to pay the President $50,000—he does not prefer to exercise his legal right to demand his present salary of $25,000 in constitutional money, or gold—excites a good deal of ridicule and serious irony on the part of the independent newspapers of this city. It is a monstrous proposition. Twenty-five thousand dollars in gold, at present rates, viz: for 1, would make the President's salary $350,000 in Confederate money.

Sheridancavalry, 6,000 strong, is moving up the country, either to cut off Breckenridges' trains, or to join Hunter and

Crook in the Valley. Should the three unite, the joint force would be about 18,000. This would give us trouble. Hampton is close up to Sheridan. Our loss in the fight near Staunton, in which General W. E. Jones fell, was 1,300 killed, wounded and missing.

The Yankee practice of shooting at our wounded was carried to a villainous extent during the late battle at Cold Harbor. I hear of an artillery officer who was shot seven times after he had fallen. On the field in front of Kershaw, where the blue coats lay so thick, the Yankee sharpshooters killed many of their own wounded, and left the rest to die at leisure.

The Bureau of Conscription has decided that after the 15th of July, all the able bodied men employed by the Express Company shall be put en permanence into the army.

The engorgement of the City Postoffice has abated in a measure, yet we get few Southern papers, except such as are sent from the Express office in this city.

HERMES

The *Charleston Mercury*

June 16, 1864

Telegraphic

From Gen. Lee's Lines

Headquarter's Army Northern VA, June 14, 9 p.m.

The force of the enemy mentioned in my last despatch as being on the Long Bridge Road disappeared during the night. It was probably advanced to cover the movement of the main body of his forces, most of which as far as I can learn, have crossed the Chickahominy at Long Bridge and below, and have reached the James River at Westover and Wilcoxlandings. A portion of Grantarmy, upon leaving our front at Cold Harbor, are reported to have proceded to the White House, and embarked at that place. Everything is said to have been removed. The depot at White House was broken up. The cars, engines, railroad iron and bridge timber brought to that point were also all removed.

RICHMOND, June 14 – Our cavalry yesterday evening gave back some two miles above RIDDLE'S shop, towards Richmond, until strengthened by WILCOX and part of MAHONE'S infantry, when the enemyforce, consisting of two divisions of infantry, artillery and cavalry, were encountered and driven back some three or four miles below RIDDLE'S shop, towards the Long Bridge, thus recovering the road to Malvern Hill, which the enemy at one time held. This movement of the enemy was a mere feint. Last night they again withdrew from our front, and are reported today to be moving towards James River, at Shirley, on both sides of the Chickahominy. Some seventy more prisoners have been brought in. GRANT'S exact whereabouts or intentions have not been ascertained.

The *Charleston Mercury*

June 16, 1864

Letter from Richmand
(Correspondence of the *Mercury*)
Richmond, Wednesday, June 8
Believed that Master GRANT has come back to his work, after trying in vain to fool LEE into the opinion that he was off on another file left movement. But you can hear anything you want from the army. For example, it was currently reported yesterday that the heaviest battle of the war was raging below Cold Harbor.

RICKETT'S DIVISION, 6TH CORPS, ATTACKING AT COLD HARBOR (FORBES). LIBRARY OF CONGRESS.

Prisoners taken on Monday say Grant is receiving large numbers of horses; so we may expect another great raid, perhaps on the north side of the city, around Leeleft, to the canal, and perhaps over the river to the Danville road.

Preparations have been made for Grantreception on the Southside. Beauregard is watchful as a lynx, and if Ulysses is not careful, he will find a lion in his path the moment he sets foot on shore at City Point.

The vulnerable points on the Danville Road are not numerous. Raiding parties will have to venture very far from their base in order to do much damage; nearer at hand, they will be apt to catch a Tartar. The Danville Road is well supplied with rolling stock and doing good work, but I was surprised to hear this morning that only two locomotives were in use on the Greensboro connection. I doubt whether the authorities are aware of this fact.

I have wondered that none of my letters have appeared in late numbers of the *Mercury*. A visit to the Postoffice yesterday explained matters. One hundred thousand letters for the South were lying on the floors, window sills, etc., and have been there for nearly a week. Let every heart, from the James to the Rio Grande, break with anxiety. What matters it to the impractical Washington hacks in power in this city, so six clerks are added to the army?

Hunter will not be able to spend an undisturbed summer in Staunton. Fact is, he will be annoyed to death in less than a week from this time. You take the hint. Weather strangely cool and cloudy.

HERMES

The *Charleston Mercury*

June 17, 1864

Grant Moving Towards James River
(From the *Richmond Dispatch*, June 14)
At an early hour Monday morning the reports of cannon in the direction of BottomBridge gave warning that active hostilities had been resumed, though to what extent was not known until a later hour of the day. A rumor was soon in circulation that GRANT was moving his whole army towards the James, and abandoning his position near COLD HARBOR, which he had taken so much pains to fortify and render impregnable.

This report was afterwards fully confirmed.

It appears that a force of the enemy, during the night of Sunday, crossed the Chickahominy at Long Bridge, eight miles below BottomBridge, and drove in our cavalry pickets.

Report says that they also crossed at Forge Bridge and Turner Ford, still lower down the river. Our pickets fell back to RiddleShop, a point thirteen miles below Richmond, at the intersection of the Charles City and Long Bridge roads, where a brisk skirmish took place between a detachment of Gen. W.H.F. Leecavalry, under Col. Gary, and the enemy.

This fight was progressing at two o p.m., though with what result we are not informed. A report was in circulation that the enemy had gained possession of Malvern Hill, but this lacks confirmation.

Later advices state that our men, owing to the difference in numbers, were compelled to fall back.

Army Northern Virginia

June 13th, 5 p.m.

Grant, after digging six heavy lines of entrenchments on his old front, near Gaines' Mill, suddenly abandoned them last night, moving again on our right. This morning about day he suddenly appeared at the Long Bridge on the Chickahominy, about eighteen miles below Richmond. Here his forces found a small picket of ours, which was readily driven in, and the enemy proceeded to cross. Our cavalry fell back to RiddleShop, and the enemy pushing us there was a considerable fight until our men were forced to give back before the enemycombined force of infantry, artillery and cavalry.

The enemy are also reported moving on the river road, as well as the Charles City road. Our scouts also say that Grant is landing troops and supplies from his gunboats near Malvern Hill, and it is supposed that he is in possession of those heights. This accords with the information previously received, and now confirmed, that the enemy have been tearing up and destroying the York River Railroad.

Up to this hour there has been no collision of the two armies, but it is not improbable that one will occur late this evening or early in the morning. Our troops are marching rapidly to thwart and check the enemy.

Grant may intend to go to the southside, but it is more likely that he will make another effort this side of the James and the Chickahominy.

Our men captured a few prisoners this morning. They were principally from the 9th and 18th corps.

Grant is not so near Richmond as when he was south of the Chickahominy, but he has certainly now made across that river.

The enemy, when they abandoned their breastworks this morning, left them guarded by a line of skirmishers, some one hundred and fifty of whom fell into our hands, among them a mail carrier attached to the 6th corps.

Sunday Evening
June 12, 1864

On the left of our lines nothing at this time is occurring of either an exciting or important character. Scouts today were down the Chickahominy River Road, below HaweShop. The only Yankees seen were pickets on the Topotomy River, two miles below HaweShop. I have learned from parties who have just returned from the vicinity of the White House that the enemy are destroying the York River Railroad, and moving towards James River, carrying the railroad iron with them.

Cold Harbor Tavern (Forbes). Library of Congress.

The section the enemy passed through has been ditched and fortified extensively. When ever they halted an hour they entrenched themselves. Feathers, broken jars, corks, bottles, ETC., trailed their tracks, telling the depredations they committed and showing their thievish and brutal propensities.

Yesterday several squadrons of their cavalry thought they would test the strength of our pickets some miles out from the Meadow Bridge. They trotted up and were fired upon by our pickets, we killing three, capturing two, and, it is thought, wounding five times that number. Their horses are unusually poor.

J.S.H.

From *The New York Times*

June 7, 1864

Headquarters, Army of the Potomac,
Cold Harbor, Near the Chickahominy
Friday, June 3–10 P.M.
General View of the Battle
Judged by the severity of the encounter and the heavy losses we have experienced, the engagement which opened at gray dawn this morning and spent its fury in little over an hour, should take its place among the *battles* of the war; but viewed in its relations to the whole campaign, it is, perhaps, hardly more than a grand reconnoissance – a reconnoissance, however, which has cost us not less than *five or six thousand* killed and wounded.

The object of the action was to force the passage of the Chickahominy, on the north side of which, and covering the roads to Richmond, the rebels had planted themselves in a fortified line. What we have done is to feel this line by a vigorous attack, in which, though gaining some temporary successes, and at one or two points actually carrying the enemy's works, we have, on the whole, reached the conclusion that any victory that could here be won must cost too much in its purchase. I do not say this as speaking with any authority, but only as recording the general conviction of the army. Such conviction, however, when the common judgment of such men as have to-day led their lines against the enemy, is apt to be of itself authority, and hence I think I may safely predict that there will be *no renewal of the assault on the lines of the Chickahominy*; that we must look to the resources of strategy to plant this army in a position where, being at less of a disadvantage, its valor will have a better promise of adequate reward.

It is in this view that the action of to-day assumes to me the aspect of a great reconnoissance. but it might easily have been more. Were prudence not as much a characteristic of Lieut. Gen. Grant's mind as pluck, did he not know as well how and when to cry a halt as to order an advance, he might have pushed the action from a reconnoissance to a bloody battle; but to me it is clear we should have had only another Fredricksburgh and its useless slaughter. Gen. Grant is not so poor in resource that he need do this; and I think already his eyes are turned away from the Chickahominy to lines and combinations more bold than any yet essayed.

Ten Minutes of History

The metaphysicians say that time is naught, is but a category of thought; and I think it must be so, for into ten mortal minutes this morning was crowded an age of action. Ten minutes of the figment men call time, and yet that scant space decided a battle. There are a thousand details, ten thousand episodes, but the essential matter is this: that first rush of advance carried our whole front butt up against a line of works, which we were unable to break through, or, breaking through, were unable to hold. Conceive of this in the large, the fierce onslaught amid deafening volleys of musketry and the thunder of artillery, and the wild, mad yell of battle, and see the ranks mown down, and the lines break here and there, and the sullen, obstinate retreat, every inch contested, and we shall then be able to *descend* to some of the points of action as they individualize themselves along the line.

The Left
Hancock's Corps

Hancock held the left of the whole line of battle; and of his three divisions, that of BARLOW held the extreme left of the army, that of Gibbon was drawn on the right of Barlow, while Birney's division was held in reserve. Of the four brigades of Barlow's division, Brooks had the left and Miles the right, each brigade in double line of battle. SMITH, commanding the Irish Brigade, was placed in support. The left was protected by refusing it – the Third Brigade being disposed so as to cover that flank

The formation of Gibbon's division on the right of Barlow was similar: Tyler's brigade (heavy artillery) holding the right, Smith's the centre and Owen's the left – McKean in rear of Tyler's centre, in two lines. On Hancock's line there were but a few places where artillery could be used with effect.

Barlow had directed that his attacking brigades should, previously to the assault, be moved out, and formed just in rear of the picket line. From this point they advanced for half a mile through woods and over open intervals, under a severe fire, square up to the enemy's works. That portion of his front where the right of Mile's brigade joined with the left of Brooks' – the same brigades that so brilliantly carried the famous salient in the lines of Spotsylvania – succeeded in a similar splendid coup here; they got over and into the enemy's parapet, capturing his guns (four light 13-pounder), his colors and five or six hundred prisoners, about 300 of whom were secured by promptly passing them to the rear. The storming column, in fact, were just turning the enemy's guns on the retreating rebels, when powerful reinforcements from the second rebel line appeared advancing. The first rebel fire was held by Breckenridge's troops and was carried, but Lee is too good a General to leave a point so important thus weakly defended. Breckenridge's men were placed in the fore-front to receive the baptism of fire, but behind these lay the veterans of Hill's corps, and it is these we now see dashing forward to retrieve the honors we had snatched. Barlow's brigades – stout hearts not used to pale before the greatest odds – could have held their own under conditions the least short of desperation, but the situation in which they now found themselves overleaped its limits: It was not merely the overwhelming front that came pressing down upon them, of that they had no fear, but the position they had gained placed them in advance of the whole line of battle, and gave the rebel artillery the opportunity for a deadly enfilading fire. Beside this, they had lost the directing - heads of two of the chief commanders. Brooks and Burns "souls of courage all compact," fell mortally wounded, and all the organizations had suffered fearfully from an unparalleled lose of officers. In this state of facts they fell back, bringing with them the prisoners they had taken and a captured color, but not the guns. They fell back, but not to their original position – to a position far in advance of that they had held, and at different points not more than fifty yards from the enemy. Here they intrenched, and here I leave them to pass on to Gibbons' division of the same corps on the right, and which was engaged at the same time.

Gibbons' advance was simultaneous with Barlow's, but in moving forward, he came upon one of the swamps of the Chickahominy, which had to be turned or overpassed, in the process of which it became very difficult to establish the connection between different parts of his line. This overcome, however, his troops pressed forward with the same vigor that marked the conduct of their companion division on the left. Parts of the brigades of Tyler and Owen gained the rebel works, but for reasons identical with those that forced back Barlow's troops, they also were compelled to give up what they had won. Gibbons' division, too, lost very heavily. Gen. Tyler, of the Eighth New York Heavy Artillery, was killed; immediately after, the Lieutenant-Colonel (Bates) fell dead. Another of his regimental commanders, Col. McMahon of the One Hundred and Sixty-Fourth New York, was struck while planting his color on the rebel works and was left a prisoner in the enemy's hands – his troops not supporting him after he was wounded. Owen's brigade lost two entire companies taken prisoners inside of the enemy's intrenchments. In giving way, Gibbons' division also was far from losing all the ground it had gained. It took up an advanced position, close to the enemy, and just over the crest, the rearward slope of which was held by the rebels. This position it has retained during the day, and McKean's brigade has held all day a position within *fifteen yards* of the enemy's works.

The Key Point of the Battle and How It Was Lost

Not until the splendid attack of Hancock's Corps had been made, not till after its blood-bought victory had been wrested from our hands, was he or any man in this army aware of the supreme importance of the position this morning carried and lost. The key-point in the battle of Gaines' Mills, two years ago, it is strange and mortifying that no one should have appreciated its value. This position is a bald hill, named

Watts Hill, dominating the whole battleground and covering the angle of the Dispatch road. Along this ridge the rebel works formed a salient, and in front of it was a sunken road. Of this road Hancock got possession, and the brigades of Miles and Brooks actually struck and carried the work directly on the salient! Had we held this point, we would have had a position whence the entire rebel line might have been enfiladed; and I think it is not too much to say that the day would have been ours, and Lee pushed across the Chickahominy. Had we even known in advance its commanding importance, very different dispositions for attack would have been made: we would have massed on the left, and made the victory a certainty. These considerations certainly inspire bitter regrets; but who does not know that it is on precisely such contingencies that the fate of battles often hangs?

The Left Centre and Centre – Wright and Smith
Simultaneously with the attack of the Second Corps, the Sixth, under Wright, connecting on the left with Hancock, made a general advance at a quarter before five o'clock – each division assaulting on the entire line. Of this corps, the Second Division, (McNeill) held the right, the Third Division, (Ricketts) the centre, and the First Division (Russell) the left. Five batteries, under charge of the Chief of Artillery of the Second Corps, Col. Tompkins – namely: Adams' First Rhode Island Battery, Cowan's First New York (Independent), Hahn's Third New York (Independent), McCurtin's First Massachusetts, and Rhode's First Rhode Island, were planted in good positions and did effective service in covering the advance. The assault of the Sixth Corps was made with the utmost vigor, and succeeded in carrying the first line of rebel rifle-pits along its entire front, and got up within two hundred and fifty yards of the main works. Smith's Corps, connecting on the right with the Sixth, had advanced in conjunction with it; but the left division, that of Martindale, who led the attack in heavy, deep columns, got disarranged, and was repulsed. Gen. Smith made three different attacks to relieve Martindale, but his last supports did not get up in time to allow him to hold on. The effect of this repulse on the left of Smith had a disastrous effect on the position of Wright. It uncovered the right flank of the Sixth and exposed Ricketts' Division, which was stoutly holding the advanced position, to a savage fire on the prolongation of its line. In this state of

facts, to retain possession of a position somewhat in advance of his point of starting, was the utmost Gen. Wright could possibly do.

Operations on the Right and Right-Centre
Warren and Burnside
Operations along the fronts of Warren and Burnside were of an importance quite subordinate to that of operations on the left. No results were achieved except the carrying of the line rifle-pits occupied by the rebel skirmishers. The Fifth and Ninth Corps nowhere struck the enemy's main work. Burnside kept up a furious cannonade for some hours; but it was nothing – *vox et preterea nihil.* From the tenor of one of Burnside's morning dispatches, it was at one time hoped that he would be able to turn the enemy's left; but this hope also was doomed to disappointment

Chickahominy in History

Notwithstanding that the position of our own line would localize the action of to-day as the battle of Cold Harbor, I have called it the battle of the Chickahominy, for the double reason that this name marks the formation of the rebel line which we assailed; and further, because the supreme object of to-day's action was to force the passage of that stream. In view of the failure to make good this purpose, the thought of the army and of the country will naturally be directed to the future moves on the great chess board. It is a fact of which you may or may not have thought, that Lieut. Gen. GRANT, in his advances on Richmond, has crossed every line of operations that has ever been planned with Richmond as the objective. He has adopt not; he has bisected all. He is at present on the line of McClellan's peninsular campaign; but will he remain on it? May he not swing across that too? It would certainly be in the line of his mode of action to do so. But such considerations belong to an order of speculation in which extreme delicacy is an obligation of duty imposed upon every writer here. Accordingly, let the section of to-day pass into history to hold such relation with the whole campaign as the future.

William Swinton

The New York Times
Wednesday, June 8, 1864
Battle of Sunday
Special Dispatch to *The New York Times*
Near Cold Harbor, Sunday Evening, June 5

The enemy appear to be exceedingly anxious to break up our lines, particularly on the left, so as to cut off all communication with White House Landing. During the last three days they have made several assaults, but in each instance were repulsed with fearful loss. The last attempt of this kind was made just after dark this evening in front of Smyth's brigade, late Carroll's, of Gibbons' Division, Second Army Corps. The weather was peculiarly favorable for the movement, as the rain of last night was succeeded by a hot murky day, and, in consequence, the whole lower strata of atmosphere was a dense mist. Under cover of this impenetrable fog the enemy advanced a strong line of battle, and succeeded in rescuing a point within pistol range of our works before discovered by the advanced pickets. No sooner did the outpost give the alarm than one sheet of fire belched forth from our ranks in front and on both flanks of the enemy. In about half an hour he fell back, leaving the ground covered with his dead and wounded.

A little later moment there was apparently a similar demonstration about to be made in front of Russell's Division of the Sixth Corps, but that was speedily checked.

These night attacks have got to be so frequent that they cease to create an alarm, for the whole army is always on duty, ready at any moment to meet any emergency. Gens. Grant and Meade are constantly on the alert so that a surprise is practically an impossibility.

But while these attacks at night create no alarm, there is something romantically interesting about them. It is a pyrotechnic display of gigantic proportion. The continued explosions of thousands of rockets would be no comparison.

The loss on our side in this last assault was small owing to the fact that the men were behind earthworks.

Lieut. McCone, Fifth Excelsior, of Gen. Hancock's Staff, had his leg shot off while standing near Gen. Hancock's headquarters.

The Second Cavalry Division, Gen. Gregg, gained an important position to-day on the left.

THE BATTLE OF COLD HARBOR. THROWING UP BREASTWORKS (FORBES). LIBRARY OF CONGRESS.

From Our Special Correspondent
Near Cold Harbor
Friday, June 3 – 3 o'clock P. M.

Since my dispatch of 9 o'clock A. M., I have gathered some additional particulars of the contest this morning. Compelled to leave the field to get off that dispatch at the early hour I did, and not foreseeing that our troops might be compelled to give up a portion of the works they had won against such odds, makes my first account under present circumstances rather exaggerated; that is, the object of the movement on the left was not fully accomplished. True, the cavalry on the left of our line rests upon the Chickahominy, and this morning all felt confident that the left of the infantry line would certainly hold that position, by doing which the enemy, taken in flank, would have had their whole line on this side of the Chickahominy rolled up like a piece of parchment, and the entire demoralization of the enemy must have been the result. As it was, the success was only partial. Our extreme left (Barlow's division of the Second Corps) advanced to within three-quarters of a mile of the river – an advance of nearly one mile. Of this gallant movement I wish to speak more in detail. Gen. Barlow's division occupied the extreme left of the line of the army, in fact; Gen. Gibbon's next, while

Gen. Birney's division was held in reserve. The movement was inaugurated by the advance of one-half of the first-named division. Gen. Miles' brigade, composed of the Fifth New-Hampshire, Sixty-first New-York, Eighty-first Pennsylvania, One Hundred and Fortieth Pennsylvania, One Hundred and Eighty-third Pennsylvania, Twenty-sixth Michigan and Second New-York Heavy Artillery, of Barlow's division, occupied the extreme left; while Brooks', brigade, of the same division, composed of the Fifty-third, One Hundred and Forty-fifth, One Hundred and Forty-eighth Pennsylvania, Sixty-sixth and Sixty-fourth New-York, Second Delaware and Seventh New-York Artillery, moved up on the right. The movement was commenced at precisely 4 ½ o'clock A. M. The One Hundred and Forty-eighth Pennsylvania, Col. Beaver, deployed as skirmishers. At first the ground over which the command moved was covered with trees and an undergrowth of bushes passing through which the command emerged into an open space in full view of the enemy. At this moment a terrific fire was opened upon the devoted patriots, but they quailed not. Continuing to advance, one-half the command charged upon and obtained possession of the enemy's works. A battery of six guns was in our hands, and just as Col. Morrris, of the Second New York Artillery, was in the act of turning the guns upon the foe, they advanced in overwhelming numbers, and the braves of the Union were compelled to fall back. The enemy did not then and has not since been able to use these guns. Our men (One Hundred and Forty-eighth Pennsylvania, Col. Beaver) hold a position within thirty-five yards, and every man is shot who attempts to approach the guns. The enemy, composed of HILL's and Breckenridge's troops, are behind a line of earthworks on the crest of a roll of land, while our boys hold a similar position in a depression of the land, having thereby a little advantage as to position, as the reader will readily perceive, for to aim at our men, a rebel must raise his head so far above the earthworks as to look down a hill, while ours look up at an angle of perhaps thirty degrees. The enemy's flag floats defiantly over the parapet, and has been frequently shot away; when this is done the boys banter the enemy to raise their "rag" again. Not a head or the least portion of a man's person can be exposed but what a dozen guns are instantly fired by our men; and various are the expedients resorted to induce some of the enemy to make a show of hands; some of these which have been successfully used a number of times, are to give the word of command as though our men were to advance, about to be relieved, or reinforced; being within a few paces, the enemy hearing every word distinctly, in large numbers peer over their works to take advantage of the supposed order. Scores of them to-day have forfeited their lives by serving a bad cause with such alacrity. In the charge upon the works, Corp. Terrance Bigler, Company D, Seventh New-York Heavy Artillery, snatched the State flag of the Twenty-sixth Virginia Infantry from the hands of the bearer within the enemy's works, and carried it off triumphantly to the rear. The different temperament of men under the excitement of battle is strongly illustrated by the following incident: The Colonel of the Twenty-sixth Virginia was bayoneted on the spot by one of our men, while a Captain at his side was taken prisoner by another – all the work of a moment. Fifteen commissioned officers and 215 non-commissioned officers and privates were captured by this division.

Gibbon 's division, as I have before said, was at the right of Gen, Barlow. His command also had a desperate conflict, assaulting the enemy's works several times, and gaining some ground and capturing about 150 prisoners. McKean's, Owen's, Smith's and Tyler's brigades were all in the fight. A portion of one brigade got so far within the enemy's works that it could not go either way, and there it remains at this moment. The men will be got-out tonight.

What the Historians Say

The battle at Cold Harbor, also known as Second Cold Harbor, took place in Hanover County, Virginia, on May 31–June 12, 1864.

It was the ninth major battle in Grant's Overland Campaign that took place during May and June 1864.

The principal commanders were Lt. Gen. Ulysses S. Grant and Maj. Gen. George G. Meade leading the Union forces of 108,000 men and Gen. Robert E. Lee, the Confederate force of 62,000

The estimated casualties were 13,000 and 2,500 respectively.

THE ARMY OF THE POTOMAC CROSSING THE PAMUNKEY RIVER ON THE MARCH TO COLD HARBOR (FORBES). LIBRARY OF CONGRESS.

On May 31, Sheridan's cavalry seized the vital crossroads of Old Cold Harbor. Early on June 1, relying heavily on their new repeating carbines and shallow entrenchments, Sheridan's troopers threw back an attack by Confederate infantry. Confederate reinforcements arrived from Richmond and from the Totopotomoy Creek lines.

Late on June 1, the Union VI and XVIII Corps reached Cold Harbor and assaulted the Confederate works with some success. By June 2, both armies were on the field, forming on a seven-mile front that extended from Bethesda Church to the Chickahominy River. At dawn on June 3, the II and XVIII Corps, followed later by the IX Corps, assaulted along the Bethesda Church-Cold Harbor line and were slaughtered at all points. Grant commented in his memoirs that this was the only attack he wished he had never ordered.

The armies confronted each other on these lines until the night of June 12, when Grant again advanced by his left flank, marching to James River. On June 14, the II Corps was ferried across the river at Wilcox's Landing by transports. On June 15, the rest of the army began crossing on a 2,200-foot long pontoon bridge at Weyanoke. Abandoning the well-defended approaches to Richmond, Grant sought to shift his army quickly south of the river to threaten Petersburg.

It was a major Confederate victory.

14

Petersburg

The Second Major Battle of the Richmond–Petersburg Campaign

Author's Commentary

They were opposites in many ways. The *Charleston Mercury*, no supporter of Confederate President Jefferson Davis, took every opportunity to criticize the President. As the second Union assault of Petersburg was under way, so too was a proposition in Richmond to increase Jefferson Davis' salary. On June 14th, the *Mercury's* correspondent penned his thoughts regarding Davis' preference for payment in gold, stating that it was the cause of much ridicule in the independent newspapers. "It is a monstrous proposition," it railed, "twenty-five thousand dollars in gold, at present rates. . . would make the President's salary $350,000 in Confederate money."

To the North, on the following day, June 15th, as General Butler's XVIII Corps and General Kautz's cavalry crossed a 2,200-foot pontoon bridge at Appomattox River at Windmill Point and attacked Petersburg, Henry J. Raymond, editor of *The New York Times*, was standing before an overflowing crowd at the Cooper Institute in New York City. He was endorsing, for President and Vice-President, Abraham Lincoln and Andrew Johnson as the nominees of the Republican Party. Raymond, in addition to being the founder and editor of *The New York Times*, was also a founder of the Republican Party and Chairman of the Republican National Committee.

June 17, 1864: From the *Charleston Mercury*

Telegraph from General Lee's Lines
Richmond, VA, June 15

GRANT'S exact whereabouts and intentions are still undetermined. A body of his cavalry attacked GARRY'S cavalry, of our army, this morning, near Malvern Hill, and were driven back. MCINTOSH'S brigade of Yankee cavalry has also been skirmishing with a part of HETH'S division on Charles City road, about two miles below RIDDLE'S shop today. A few prisoners were captured, who say it is the advance of GRANT'S army, which is not, however, believed to be more than a mere reconnoitering party. GRANT is either going to the Southside or is broken down, and has gone below to reorganize and recruit.

Headquarters
Army Northern Virginia
June 15, 6 p.m.
To the Hon. Secretary of War
Sir:
After the withdrawal of our cavalry yesterday evening from the front of the enemy works at Harrison Landing, his cavalry again advanced on Salem Church Road, and he is this morning reported in some force on that road, and at Malvern Hill. Gen. W.F. LEE easily drove back the force at the latter point, which retreated down the river road beyond Carter Mill. A brigade of infantry was sent to support our cavalry on the road to Smith Store, drove the enemy to that point without difficulty. Nothing else of importance occurred today.

(Signed)
R.E. LEE.

The Attack on Petersburg

Richmond, June 16
The *Petersburg Express* of this morning gives a full account of another demonstration against that city, yesterday. The enemy advanced in force by the City Point Road, early in the

morning, and were held in check until sunset, when a furious assault was made upon our outer works, defended by two regiments of WISE'S brigade and STURDEVANT'S battery. Three furious assaults were repulsed, but the fourth was made by such overwhelming numbers, our men were compelled to fall back, and the enemy occupied the works, and captured three guns of STURDEVANT'S battery. The force of the enemy is rumored to be ten or twelve thousand.

The Attack on Petersburg

Ever since GRANT'S move down the Chickahominy to the James River, the public of the Confederate States has looked to the railroad communication with Richmond on the South side as the object of that strategy. The people have been busy with enquiries as to the routes and relative distances to be traveled by the two armies to their new battle ground between the Petersburg Railroad and the James River.

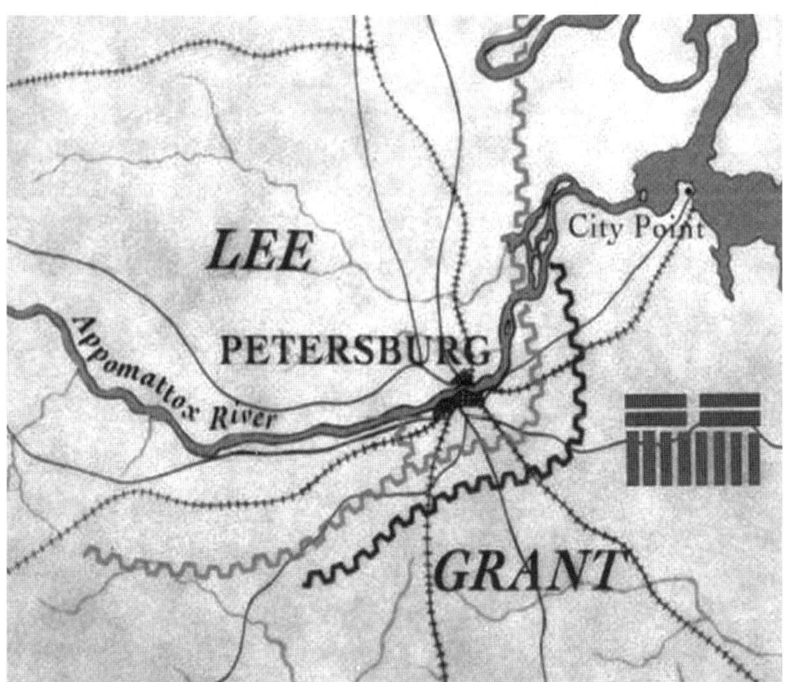

BATTLE MAP OF PETERSBURG. LIBRARY OF CONGRESS.

The existence and location of pontoon bridges, for the passenger of General LEE'S army have been discussed, in full confidence that our Government was on the qui vive to meet the promptest and most energetic attack of GRANT in the expected quarter. This attempt to cut our communications, and hold some portion of this road, is evidently the last effort of the foiled invader. Slow siege and gradual starvation are to be tried for reducing Richmond, rather than the open field and grand assault of the army on the planet. The possession of Petersburg first, followed by a successful attack on the Danville road, would obviously place the Confederate capital in an awkward state of beleaguerment.

When, in the face of these patent facts of some days standing, we learn by telegraph that the outer defences of Petersburg have been attacked by a Yankee column of some twelve thousand men, and unsuccessfully defended by but two regiments of Confederate infantry and one light battery, we are at a loss to account for what appears either a singular dullness inperceiving GRANT'S object, or a strange sluggishness in transferring the army from the north to the southside defence. Appearances, however, are not reliable, and we await the denoument, trusting that time will be allowed to send the required reinforcements – that Petersburg and the railroad communication will be saved, and that GRANT will here meet this final and crushing defeat of all his plans of taking Richmond.

The *Charleston Mercury*

June 18, 1864

Telegraph from Richmond, June 16 – p.m.

There is nothing authentic from Petersburg today. The Yankees have advanced their lines in Chesterfield. Some fighting took place near Chester today. By last advices SHERIDAN was moving through Spottsylvania and was reported crossing the Rapidan.

General LEE has been placed in command of all forces in Virginia and North Carolina.

A regiment of the 18th Corps carrying a portion of Beauregard's line in front of Petersburg (Mullen). Library of Congress.

Latest from Petersburg, June 17

The assault on Battery 16 last evening was handsomely repulsed by BUSHROD JOHNSON'S division. About 450 prisoners were captured, belonging to HANCOCK'S corps. They report General BARTON mortally wounded. Our forces met with a slight reverse at the same point this morning. An assault at the same place this afternoon was repulsed.

It is believed the enemy forces are heavily massed in front of Petersburg. Colonel PAGE, of WISE'S brigade, was killed this morning. Captain FRED CARTER, of the Richmond Blues, who was wounded Wednesday night, died today. Colonel RANDOLPH THOMSON, severely wounded in the same fight, is doing well. Lieutenant Colonel Wise, seriously wounded, is improving.

The *Charleston Mercury*

June 21, 1864

From the Virginia Front

From the *Richmond Dispatch* of the 17th, we get the following additional items:

On Thursday morning the enemy appeared in force near the Richmond and Petersburg Railroad, and drove in our skirmishers, who fell back to the right of the road. About the same hour a division, while marching by the turnpike towards Petersburg, was attacked by the enemy about a mile and a half from Chester. The General commanding the division at once drew up his troops in line of battle, charged, and drove the Yankees back three miles towards the Appomattox River. At last accounts our forces held the fortifications at Chester. A train which arrived from that point about eight o last night brought news that the fight had been renewed, and was in progress when the cars left for Richmond.

Meantime the enemy succeeded in getting possession of the railroad between Port Walthall Junction and Swift Creek, cut the telegraph wires, and, it is presumed, indulged in their favorite amusement of tearing up the track. Of this, however, we have no definite account, as no train has passed over the entire length of the road since early yesterday morning.

A business despatch, dated Petersburg, 1:45 p.m., received yesterday, makes no mention of any fighting there. It proves, however, that the city was safe at that hour.

In connection with the fight on Wednesday, there are painful rumors relative to the casualties of the Richmond Light Infantry Blues, 46th Virginia Regiment, Wise Brigade. It is reported that they suffered heavily, and that their gallant commander, Captain Fred Carter, received a mortal wound.

Army Correspondence of the *Savannah Republican*

Army of Northern Virginia
Cold Harbor
June 11, 1864
There has been no change in the position of the two armies since the date of my last letter. Grant has availed himself of the protection afforded by an almost impassable swamp, and to this he has added very strong entrenchments. His conduct since the sanguinary battle of the 3d points to a defensive policy, at least until he can reorganize and recruit his beaten army. Meanwhile, he hopes to be able to accomplish by raids what he has failed to do by open battle. Mixed columns of

cavalry, light artillery and infantry will be, and have already been, sent out to operate upon our communications and cut off our supplies. Of this character was the late demonstration against Petersburg, where, as you have been informed, the enemy was signally repulsed by the militia and such regular forces as could be brought up in time.

You have heard also of the expedition of Sheridan, who ha moved with a mixed force of ten or twelve thousand men in the direction of Gordonsville. It may be that he will seek to unite with Hunter, now at Staunton, or to sweep around and destroy the bridges on the Danvile Railway. The two expeditions set out about the same time – a coincidence which gives some color to the suspicion that the design of both of them is to interrupt our communication. The party that marched against Petersburg has already been defeated and driven off, and we are hourly expecting information that Hampton, who was sent towards Gordonsville, has done the same thing with Sheridan. At last accounts Hampton was between Gordonsville and the enemy, in a position to guard the railway lines that intersect at that place, to join our forces operating in the Valley, or strike Sheridan, as may seem best.

The advance of Hunter up the Valley of the Shenandoah and his occupation of Staunton were designed to create a diversion in favor of Grant. The latter hopes, by threatening Richmond in that quarter, to compel General Lee to detach a considerable force from his main army, and so weaken himself as to be no longer capable of coping with his adversary in the field When he shall have done this, the Federal commander will either make another desperate effort to bear down all opposition and reach the capital, or to gain the banks of James River, and finally the south bank of the Appomattox. He might now retire across the Pamunkey, take water at West Point, and move around by Fortress Monroe to City Point; but Lee would have sufficient notice of such a movement to put his own army in a position to checkmate it, and that is just what Grant desires to prevent.

SHARPSHOOTERS FROM THE 18TH CORPS (WAUD). LIBRARY OF CONGRESS.

Breckinridge was sent back to the Valley some days ago. What with the forces he took with him, the cavalry already there under Imboden and others, and the column now moving thither under Hampton, it is hoped we shall be able to make the country too hot for the Federals. It must not be disguised, however, that the latter are concentrating at Staunton also, and perhaps in larger numbers than the Confederates. The latest official information from Breckinridge was dated yesterday, at which time the enemy was aware of his presence, and was making suitable dispositions to receive him. Morgan, unfortunately, seems not to be yet cured of his love of raids; in other words, he has gone into Kentucky, where he can do no good but much harm, instead of remaining in Virginia, where every stroke of his sabre would be a stroke to some purpose. It is well enough to capture enemy trains and destroy his communications, but mere raids, such as that of Morgan into Ohio and this one into Kentucky, answer no valuable purpose, but rather invite, and to some extent justify, those retaliatory measures by the enemy from which our noncombatant population has suffered so much.

The troops are now receiving full rations of salt meat and bread, coffee and sugar, and pretty fair supply of West Indian onions and greens. The vegetables are very acceptable, and will check, it is hoped, the manifest tendency to scurvy and disorders of the bowels. The men are also well clothed and shod, and the morale of the army is excellent. The condition of the animals of the army is improving rapidly, in spite of Gen. Grant and his bridge burning raiders. Indeed, the Quartermaster General, the Commissary General, the Chief of Railway Transportation and the railroad authorities, deserve much credit for the skill and energy with which they have discharged their several duties under very embarrassing circumstances.

P. W. A.

Telegraphic from Virginia

Richmond, June 20

Unofficial information from Lynchburg states that the Yankees were overtaken in their retreat at Liberty, and a large number of them captured.

SHERIDAN is reported in Hanover today, moving towards the James River with the remnant of his command. The capture of the entire party is confidently anticipated.

Petersburg, June 20

Since yesterday nothing of interest has transpired. Today there has been some cannonading and slight skirmishing.

Yesterday General MEADE sent a flag of truce to General BEAUREGARD requesting permission to bury the dead, which was not granted.

The City Council held a meeting today, and sent a committee to General Beauregard to ask advice in regard to the removal of noncombatants. General BEAUREGARD replied that no notice had been given by the enemy of a purpose to shell the city, but it would be prudent for those who could leave the lower part of the city to do so, and for women and children to remain in the cellars. Very few shells have been thrown into the city today.

GRANT'S lines reach from James River, across the Appomattox, to within two miles of the Weldon Railroad.

Advices from Liberty, received this morning, say that HUNTER had been pursued through that place, and that he was retreating towards Buford Gap in considerable confusion. Some prisoners had been taken, and more, doubtless, would be captured.

The enemy, at this writing, seem to be moving towards the Weldon Railroad. Our Generals will, doubtless, be prepared for them.

From *The New York Times*

Important: Petersburg Captured

The Fortifications Stormed by General Smith.BOTH LINES CARRIED.Four Hundred Prisoners and Sixteen Guns Taken Distinguished Gallantry of the Black Legion.Gen. Smith Tenders His Thanks to Them.PETERSBURG UNDER OUR GUNS.The Rebels on the West Side of the Appomattox.The Army All Across the James.HANCOCK IN JUNCTION WITH SMITH.GRANT WELL AHEAD OF LEE.SECRETARY STANTON TO GENERAL DIX
[OFFICIAL.]

Washington, Sunday, June 17, 1864
To Major Gen. Dix:
The following dispatches have been received by this Department:

CITY POINT, June 15, VIA JAMESTOWN ISLAND, 5:30 A.M., 1864.

SMITH, with 15,000 men, attacked Pittsburgh this morning.

Gen. BUTLER reports, from his observatory near Bermuda Hundred, that there had been sharp fighting and that the troops and trains of the enemy were, as he writes, moving from the City across the Appomattox as if retreating.

HANCOCK is not near enough to render Gen. SMITH any aid.

The Richmond papers have nothing to indicate a suspicion of our crossing the James River. They expect to be attacked from the direction of Malvern Hill.

CITY POINT, Va., 5:30 P.M., June 15, 1864.

Our latest report from SMITH was at four P.M. He had carried a line of entrenchments at Beatty's House, the colored troops assaulting and carrying the rifle-pits with great gallantry, but he had not yet carried the main line. He describes the rebel artillery as very heavy.

He expected to assault this line just before dark. HANCOCK is within three miles of SMITH.

City Point, VA, 7 a.m., June 16, via Jamestown Island, 11:45 A.M.

At 7:20 P.M. yesterday, SMITH assaulted and carried the principal line of the enemy before Petersburgh, taking thirteen cannon, several stands of colors, and between three and four hundred prisoners. This line is two miles from Petersburgh. HANCOCK got up and took position on SMITH'S left at 3 A.M. to-day. There was heavy firing in that direction from 5 to 6 o'clock. No report has been received yet.

Don't Hard Landing, VA

June 16 – 1 P.M.

After sending my dispatch of this morning from the heights southeast of Petersburgh, I went over the conquered lines with Gen. GRANT and the engineer officers. The works are of the very strongest kind, more difficult to take than was Missionary Ridge, at Chattanooga. The hardest fighting was done by the black troops. The forts they stormed were the worst of all. After the affair was over, Gen. Smith went to thank them, and tell them he was proud of their courage and dash. He says they cannot be exceeded as soldiers, and that hereafter he will send them in a difficult place as readily as the best white troops.

They captured six out of the sixteen cannons which he took.

The prisoners he took were from BEAUREGARD'S command. Some of them said they had just crossed the James above Drewry's Bluff.

I do not think any of LEE'S army had reached Petersburgh when SMITH stormed. They seem to be there this morning, however, and to be making arrangements to hold the west side of the Appomattox.

The town they cannot think of holding, for it lies directly under our guns. The weather continued splendid.

THE BATTLE OF DARBY TOWN ROAD (WAUD). LIBRARY OF CONGRESS.

City Point, VA

June 16, 1864 – 4:15 P

Gen. Butler reports from Bermuda Hundred that the enemy have abandoned the works in front of that place. His troops are now engaged in tearing up the railroad between Petersburgh and Richmond.

Grant's Last Movement

Its Military Aspects and Objects
Its Probable Effect upon the Campaign
From Our Special Correspondent

WASHINGTON, THURSDAY, JUNE 16, 1864. The clear and succinct dispatches of the Secretary of War have made the country acquainted with the outline facts of the last great move of Gen. GRANT – the transfer of the Army of the Potomac from the Chickahominy to the James River. I can add no details of fact to the official statement, having been absent from the army since the battle of Chickahominy on the 3d inst. There are, however, some suggestions of moment that may not be out of place.

Your readers will recollect that in my letter on the battle of the Chickahominy, in which I endeavored to recognize the true military character and bearings of that battle, I put on record the opinion that Gen. GRANT would make no further effort to pass the Chickahominy, and hinted that his eyes were even then "turned away to lines and combinations more bold than any yet essayed." Well, what could then only be thus obscurely foreshadowed, is to-day a realized fact. Indeed, I may now go further, and state that from the very start, the transfer of the army to the south side of Richmond has formed an integral part of Gen. Grant's plan of campaign; and while the battle of Chickahominy was still in progress, the whole question of the pontooning of the James River was elaborately discussed. And now recognizing the relations which that section holds to the general plan of operations – noting that it now stands defined as the pivotal point of the whole campaign – would it be too much for me to ask those presses that abused me for having so recognized it a fortnight ago, to take back their abuse?

The battle of the Chickahominy was an experiment made for a specific purpose – to test the feasibility of an assault on Richmond from the northern side. It was an experiment perfectly proper to be made; and it was satisfactory. It convinced every reflecting mind that nothing was to be gained in that direction. This was obvious to every one; and every one waited to see what card GRANT would play next. But it was only those who knew something of the boldness of his military conception, that could have ventured to anticipate a repetition of the Vicksburgh strategy—the same strategy, the same audacity, only on a far grander scale!

This splendid stroke, comparable only to MOREAU'S passage of the Rhine and flank march on Ulm, stands to-day an accomplished fact; the Army of the Potomac, taken up, as in the arms of a giant, is transported from the Chickahominy and planted south of the James River and south of Richmond. Now begins a new act in the grand war drama. We shall operate on new and unattempted lines, looking to new and hitherto unattainable results. I think there are a few military men who do not now feel that *the present position of the Army of the Potomac gives us reason to indulge in brighter hopes of ultimate success than has been possible any time since the war began.*

The south side is the true line of operation against Richmond looking to great ulterior results. Of the three cardinal maxims of strategy, the most important of all prescribes "to operate on the enemy's communications without endangering your own." Now, the operations of the Virginia campaign have been conducted under circumstances that made it impossible to apply this principle. Gen. GRANT has aimed assiduously to bring on a great decisive field fight with the hope of crushing the rebel army. But from the nature of the country, its prodigious facilities for defence, and the kill of the opposing General, this has been impossible. We gained victories, steadily pushed the enemy back, and in an unparalleled campaign of twenty-nine days, forced LEE from the Rapidan to the front of Richmond. But no decisive results were accomplished. LEE'S army is an army of veterans; it is an instrument sharpen to a perfect edge. You turn its flanks; well, its flanks are made to be turned; that effects little or nothing. All that we can reckon as gained, therefore, is the loss of life inflicted on the enemy, and of having reached a point thus near the objective; but brilliant military results. In loss of life we were undoubtedly suffering more severe than the rebels; I think we may fairly say in the proportion of five to their three. Now it is obvious that we could not have long stood thus. Whatever preponderance of numbers we might have would soon disappear – would soon become an equality, and presently an inferiority. The rebel army might have been wore away by attrition; but we should ourselves have been exhausted in the process. The hammer would have been broken on the anvil.

By the present move a new order of operation begins. We not only threaten the communications of the enemy, we plant ourselves across his communications. The communications of the rebel army are the great lines of railroad by Petersburgh and Danville and their connections.

Richmond, as a city, Richmond, as a military center, is strictly dependent on these lines for its supplies. Cut it off from these and you have a tourniquet around its throat. It may have a month's supplies, or three months', or six months'; but these exhausted, and it must succumb. If LEE allows himself to be shut up within Richmond, therefore, the problem reduces itself to a repetition of Vicksburgh over again. Will he do so? That is a question.

But this is the pitiless alternative to which LEE is now reduced: to stay in Richmond and suffer the fatal lines of circumvallation to be drawn around him, or to come out of his works and give battle. Now a fair field-fight is precisely what the Army of the Potomac invites and welcomes; it will gladly give the rebel man for man, and engage to defeat them withal. If LEE is unwilling to run this risk, he retires within the defences of Richmond, and we then hold precisely the relations held by the Allies to Napoleon defending Paris in 1814. It was in vain then that the consummate master put forth a generalship that recalled the splendors of the first great Italian campaign; in vain he threw his masses on different points of the investing line. If LEE is not a better General than NAPOLEON, he can hardly hope for a much better fate.

With the army of the Potomac planted at the north of Petersburgh, we there tap the great railroad line connecting Richmond with the Atlantic seaboard and Gulf States. When there, Grant may be able to throw his left across the Danville Road, and in this case Richmond is isolated. If his plan does not contemplate so great a development of front, he will at least provide for the effectual destruction of the latter road; and this, as well as the destruction of the Western (Lynchburgh) Road and the James River Canal, will be an easy prey to our cavalry, which, under the hands of SHERIDAN, has almost put the rebel cavalry out of existence. The reduction of Fort Darling is an incidental piece of work, which will be gladly contended for by some of the able engineering heads of the Army of the Potomac. In the meantime, we have a perfectly secure and convenient base – the James River – to which all the transportation lately at White House has been forwarded.

There is another aspect of the move to the south side of the James, which from the point of view of its relation to the whole theatre of war, is not less important than its bearing on the problem immediately before us. It is a division of the two great rebel armies, and gives us an interior position relative to the army of Lee in Virginia, and the army of Johnston in Georgia. It has been reported that large detachments of JOHNSTON'S army are already en route to reinforce LEE, and, if not actually under way, we may depend upon it that the able military heads that rule the war councils at Richmond, thoroughly imbued with the conception of concentration, and willing to risk everything to save Richmond, would willingly have sacrificed Southwestern territory to secure the great point in Virginia. But how does it stand now? JOHNSTON coming to reinforce LEE would find his progress to Richmond barred by the same opponent who stopped his junction with Pemberton in Vicksburgh! We secure this, therefore: that the enemy shall receive no addition to his strength, while our position effects a concentration of both the forces of BUTLER and HUNTER with the main operating force.

While, however, we have reason to look forward to great and important results as coming from the new position of the army, I am very far from looking on our success as a foregone conclusion. We have opposed to us an enemy of the highest skill, handling an army of sufficient strength still to attempt great things, and animated by a spirit of desperation. I fully expect some bold, audacious initiative on the part of LEE, and the greater the straits in which he finds himself, the more energetically he will attempt to retrieve himself, and the fortunes of the Confederacy bound up with him.

WILLIAM SWINTON

What the Historians Say

The battle at Petersburg, known also as the Assault on Petersburg, took place in the city of Petersburg, Virginia, on June 15-18, 1864. It was the second major battle in the Richmond-Petersburg Campaign of June 1864-March 1865.

The principal commanders were Lt. Gen. Ulysses S. Grant and Maj. Gen. George G. Meade leading 62,000 Union forces and Gen. Robert E. Lee and Gen. P.G.T. Beauregard commanding 42,000 Confederates. The estimated casualties were 8,150 and 3,236 respectively.

Marching from Cold Harbor, Meade's Army crossed the James River on transports and a 2,200-foot long pontoon bridge at Windmill Point. Butler's leading elements (XVIII Corps and August Kautz's cavalry) crossed the Appomattox River at Windmill Point and attacked the Petersburg defenses on June 15. The 5,400 defenders of Petersburg, under command of Gen. PG.T Beauregard, were driven from their first line of entrenchments back to Harrison Creek. After dark, the XVIII Corps was relieved by the II Corps. On June 16, the II Corps captured another section of the Confederate line; on the 17th, the IX Corps gained more ground. Beauregard stripped the Howlett Line (Bermuda Hundred) to defend the city, and Lee rushed reinforcements to Petersburg from the Army of Northern Virginia. The II, XI, and V Corps from right to left attacked on June 18 but were repulsed with heavy casualties. By now the Confederate works were heavily manned and the greatest opportunity to capture Petersburg without a siege was lost. Now the siege of Petersburg began. Union Gen. James St. Clair Morton, chief engineer of the IX Corps, was killed on June 17.

It was an important Confederate victory that allowed Lee to reinforce the railroad center that supplied Richmond.

15

Atlanta

The Union Victory That Saved Lincoln's Presidency

Author's Commentary

For a variety of reasons, many general officers disliked the press, but none more so than General William T. Sherman. An antagonist to those who sent dispatches to their newspapers revealing Union troop movements, Sherman held them in contempt. Many newspapers reacted by questioning his state of mind. Franc Wilkie of *The New York Times* wrote that Sherman demonstrated his "madness" for selecting landing sites at Chickasaw Bluffs in December 1862 that resulted in a Union defeat. The *Times*' editorial referred to the approach as "the insane attack." And the *Times* was not alone in that sentiment. Other newspaper editors were equally hostile to Sherman. Thomas Knox of the *New York Herald* admonished the General, ". . . you are regarded as the enemy of our set, and we must in self-defense write you down."

It was disconcerting then when Sherman's troops took Atlanta and the Union press started writing his praises. In a letter to his brother, John, on August 12th, he penned, "I was hoping to remain unpopular, but I see even the newspapers begin to point out the good points in my character. This is the certain presage of a downfall."

July 22, 1864: From the *Charleston Mercury*

Telegraphic

Important from Atlanta – Heavy Skirmishing along the Lines

Atlanta, July 20 – General REYNOLDS' brigade attacked the enemyline of skirmishers last evening at Peach Tree Creek, and took possession of their breastworks. He then charged their reserve picket support by VILWORTH'S corps and captured one hundred and fifty prisoners. The Eighty-fifth Regiment of Illinois Volunteers lost in killed and wounded alone, one hundred, while the loss in the Fifth Ohio was severe.

ATLANTA, July 20. The enemy made a strong demonstration yesterday and this morning on our right, near Decatur.

Gen. HOOD attacked their right at 4 o this afternoon, at Peach Tree Creek, near the Chattahoochee. In a few minutes the enemy were driven into their works. The colors of the 33d New Jersey and about 300 prisoners were captured from HOOKER'S corps. Our loss not heavy, mostly slightly wounded. Brig. Gen. CLEMANT H. STEVENS, of South Carolina, was wounded, it is feared, mortally. Maj. PRESTON, formerly of Gen. JOHNSTON'S staff, was killed.

There was some skirmishing on our right, where the enemy attacked our entrenchments, but were repulsed with heavy loss. Our cavalry, under Gen. WHEELER, followed up the retreating Yankees, driving them with repeated charges towards Decatur.

Yesterday evening REYNOLDS' North Carolina and Virginia Brigade, which had already crossed Peach Tree Creek, drove them back, taking two stand of colors and 130 prisoners. Our troops are in fine spirits.

The *Charleston Mercury*

July 25, 1864

IMPORTANT FROM GEORGIA – SHERMAN'S RAIDERS AT WORK ON THE RAILROADS – While the main armies of SHERMAN and HOOD are confronting each other around Atlanta, the Yankee raiding parties are very active in their depredations upon the railroads. The *Augusta Constitutionalist* of Saturday, in noticing the raid on the Georgia Road, says:

By passengers that arrived on the train this morning we learn that the Federals captured two trains, yesterday morning, at Conyers. One of the engineers escaped, and procuring a mule, made his way towards Covington. When he arrived there he saw a force of the enemy approaching the place, and continued on down to Rutledge. All the stock of the company, we learn, was moved from Rutledge to Union Point last night. Rumor also says the enemy have burned Yellow River and Alcova Bridges, and the depot at Covington. We give place to these reports in order to satisfy the anxiety of our people for intelligence of operations from Atlanta and vicinity, not that we give them full credit, but in order that they may not be deceived and unnecessarily excited by wild and unfounded rumors.

Atlanta Campaign: Army operations showing battles of Peach Tree Creek, Atlanta, and Ezra Church (Western and Atlantic Railroad Company). Library of Congress.

The same paper, in its issue of Sunday, tells us that a despatch from General Hood states that the Yankee raiding force now making havoc along the Georgia Railroad numbers three brigades of cavalry. A Confederate cavalry force had left Atlanta in pursuit. Ample preparations have been made to give the raiders a warm reception in case they progress much farther in this direction. A gentleman who came from Athens yesterday evening states that the enemy had not been seen this side of Alcova bridge. The rumor that the Yankees were in force at High Shoals nine miles from Athens, on Friday, needs confirmation.

The Columbus Ga. *Sun Extra*, of Thursday, says, that the citizens of that place were all agog and under arms to repel a raid expected from the direction of the Montgomery and West Point Railroad. The negro men had all been ordered to work on the fortifications. The *Sun* gives the following account of the doings of the raiders:

From the best information that our reporter could obtain, who returned last evening from the front, the raiders most thoroughly did their work of destruction of the superstructure of the Montgomery and West Point Railroad, from a point near Chehaw to another some two or three miles east of Opelika, and also of one and a half miles of the Columbus branch road. The stringers and ties were piled first, the iron rails on top, fire applied underneath, and as the rails became sufficiently heated other means were applied to aid in distorting them. The number of miles of road thus destroyed is probably between thirty and thirty-five. The raiders destroyed no private property, so far as now known, and committed no robberies excepting, perhaps, those of live stock and provisions. They destroyed Government property wherever found. They said that they came solely for the purposes of damaging the road and destroying Government property. They also said that they came with the expectation of being captured. This accounts for their having destroyed so much within the short space of two days. The raiders left the railroad Tuesday evening, and the last news from there is that they had passed through Lafayette, Chambers county,

Alabama, that night. It is reported that Col. Lary, with a detachment of General Clanton's Alabama brigade, was in pursuit of them; and also that a detachment of General **[????]** brigade, from West Point, is trying to intercept the raiders.

The *Charleston Mercury*
July 27, 1864

Telegraphic
The Latest News from Atlanta
ATLANTA, July 25 – The enemy made an attempt last night to break our lines, but were repulsed by CHEATHAM, after a conflict of one hour duration. During the day quiet prevailed around the city, the only demonstration being occasional picket firing. On Monday the Yankees opened with shell again upon the city, shelling for an hour with some vigor. No notice of their intention to shell the city was given, to enable the women and children to be removed to a place of safety. The result of the enemy's barbarous conduct was the murder of a few noncombatants. Most of the shells were thrown from a 20 pounder Parrot gun on the line of the Western and Atlantic Railroad, with an occasional missile from another gun east of the city. The gallant operations of Wednesday and Friday seem to have impressed the Yankees with a wholesome desire to strengthen their flanks, which they are now doing. Their display of rockets and signals this evening is brilliant. The following address to the troops was read this morning:

In the Field, July 25
Soldiers! Experience has proved to you that safety in time of battle consists in getting into close quarters with the enemy. Guns and colors are the only unerring indications of victory. The valor of troops is easily estimated, too, by the number of those secured. If your enemy be allowed to continue the operations of flanking you out of position, your case is in peril. Your recent brilliant success proves the ability to

prevent it. You have but to will, and God will grant us the victory your commander and country confidently expect.

(Signed)

J. B. HOOD, General

The *Charleston Mercury*

July 29, 1864

THE SITUATION OF AFFAIRS AROUND ATLANTA – WHAT THE GEORGIA PAPERS SAY

We gather some interesting paragraphs from our latest Georgia exchanges in regard to the situation of affairs along the front:

The Late Fight – Hardee's Dash

The general impression is that our entire loss in the recent battles will not amount to more than five thousand. The loss of the enemy in killed and wounded has also been overrated, as they fought for the most part behind entrenchments. Our army is unbroken in strength and spirit, and ready to move forward whenever their gallant chief shall give the word. Our wounded are well cared for, and bear their misfortunes like heroes. Seldom is a complaint heard in the hospitals.

The movement of Hardee against the enemy left wing was one of the most dashing of the war, and a complete surprise. His men dashed upon the enemy as a storm from the clouds, and so panic stricken were the vandals that the first line threw down their arms and ran towards our lines, shouting at the top of their voices: 'Donshoot, we surrender!' The prisoners sent to the rear, Hardee attacked the second line and carried it, but with considerable loss to his corps. He held their works for more than a day, no serious effort being made to molest him, and then moved to a more fruitful portion of the field.

The Enemy Suffering for Food

A gentleman from Atlanta says he was informed by a good many of our soldiers, and the testimony was so concurrent that he could not doubt it, that the Yankee prisoners reported themselves in a famishing condition. They stated that had received no rations for three days. They also reported that no trains had come down for four or five days. As these prisoners were captured on the extreme left of Shermanline, it may well be that their case was exceptional, and as to the arrival of railroad trains to Sherman, they may well have been entirely ignorant of what was taking place across the river.

The Last Repulse of the Yankees

On Sunday night the enemy made a heavy demonstration on our centre, with the apparent object of forcing our lines, and to gain a certain advantage of position which would make their operations much more effective. They were repulsed by Gen. Cheathamcorps. The enemy suffered disastrously during the hour that they fought against the impenetrable lines held by that veteran General and his invincible soldiers. After discovering the futility of their operations, Sherman resumed his former position and strengthened his works, especially the wings. We presume he will patiently try the effect of parallels and siege approaches – those offensive operations that have been so eminently characteristic – a peculiarity of his plans and very successful hitherto. But we suspect that he will be foiled completely and his strategy overwhelmed by the rapid movements of an active rival whose enterprise is not inferior to his own.

The Bombardment of Atlanta

A great many houses in Atlanta have been pierced by Yankee shells. A dozen shells have struck Wesley Chapel and the Parsonage. Two batteries have the range of the Car Shed and the Wesley Chapel, and they peg away night and day, making line shots in the direction of the State R. R. bridge. The women and children fly to the cellars, and the men walk about watching where the shells strike. The Atlanta Relief Committee are busy distributing rations to destitute women and children.

The Georgia Militia Moving to the Front

Sixteen hundred of the Georgia militia started from Macon for Atlanta Tuesday. The Telegraph says they made a fine appearance as they marched through the streets, were in the very best spirits and appeared ready to meet the enemy in defence of their homes. The material of this brigade is as good as that of any in the South, and we are certain they will do honor to the State when brought into action. The Telegraph also states that a similar number will go down to Atlanta each day during the week from this place. There is now a large force of militia at Macon, which, when sent to the front, will prove a valuable accession to our gallant army.

Miscellaneous

His Excellency Gov. Joseph E. Brown, Gens. Joseph E. Johnston, B. Bragg, Anderson of Tennessee, Wayne and Hindman, were all in Macon on Sunday.

Reinforcements from Gen. S. D. Lee have arrived, and a large number of troops from the same direction are on their way.

SHERMAN'S CAMPAIGN—PROVOST MARSHAL'S OFFICE, ATLANTA—CITIZENS GETTING PASSES TO GO NORTH, IN CONSEQUENCE OF GENERAL SHERMAN'S ORDER FOR THE DEPARTURE OF ALL CITIZENS (FRANK LESLIE). LIBRARY OF CONGRESS.

The army is in fine spirits, eager for a fight, and confident of success; and while they deplore the removal of General Johnston, have implicit confidence in Gen. Hood and a fixed determination to stand by him and never allow Atlanta to fall into the hands of the Yankees.

The *Charleston Mercury*

August 2, 1864

The news of the defeat and capture of the most famous of all the Yankee raiders comes in like a welcome gleam of sunshine upon what was fast growing to be a very dark picture. It need not be disguised that the aspect of affairs in Georgia, viewed in the list of the rumors and advices that had reached us up to yesterday afternoon, was far from cheering. Vague reports of another battle in front of Atlanta had indeed gone abroad; but we listened in vain to hear, through the smoke of the conflict, those shouts of triumph we had expected from the veterans of HOOD. Meanwhile, SHERMAN, with his multiplied bands of mounted vagabonds, was traversing the fairest regions of Georgia, working his will with her magnificant railroads and, seemingly unresisted, brginging fire and sword to the very gates of her capital.

But the scene has changed. The Army of Tennessee, after inflicting another terrible chastisement upon the foe, still stands, like a wall of fire, around Atlanta; and SHERMAN, baffled and disappointed, is as far as ever from the mastery of the city. The Grand Raid, too, has come to grief. Its main force, doubtless already broken down with fatigue, has been swept like chaff before our pursuing squadrons; its chief aims have all been defeated; and its bold and skilful leader, with many of his officers and men, are captives in our hands.

The contradictory despatches leave us in doubt as to whom we have to thank for this gallant and timely achievement. But of the achievement itself, there is, happily, no doubt whatever. No matter whose the arm that dealt it, truly it was a right lusty blow, and struck at the happy moment.

The *Charleston Mercury*

August 2, 1864

The Great Georgia Raid

The *Savannah Republican* of yesterday gives the following review of the recent operations of the Yankee raiders in the region east of Macon:

On Thursday the telegraph reported a party of raiders at Clinton, in Jones county. At eleven o Friday night this party made its appearance suddenly at Gordon, on the Central Railroad, twenty miles this side of Macon, and the point of junction with the Milledgeville and Eatonton Road. There was no force to meet them, and the raiders proceeded to destroy everything that fire could burn. The railroad depot, Wayside Home, and passenger shed were all consumed, with the houses immediately in their neighborhood. The greatest loss, however, was in rolling stock. Thirteen locomotives and twenty passenger cars, belonging to the State Road, were destroyed, together with a train belonging to the Central Road, known as the train. The track was torn up in every direction, both on the Central and on the Milledgeville Road.

The day following, about 10 a.m., the raiders reached the Central Railroad bridge over the Oconee river, about thirty miles this side of Gordon, and this was also destroyed without, so far as we can learn, any effort to save it. A guard from Savannah had been posted there for several days, up to Friday morning, when, on information from the military authorities in that quarter that the raiders had retired toward Atlanta, they were, unfortunately, withdrawn, leaving that important work wholly without protection. This mischief accomplished, the raiders are said to have struck off in a northerly direction.

From the best information we can obtain, the raiders numbered only two or three hundred, and any sort of organization might have worried them out of the country, and saved us from harm. It does not appear that we had out even scouts to watch and report their movements, or that our planters in the most populous section of the State took any steps to meet them. The whole thing is strange, indeed, and anything but creditable to our State.

In addition to the foregoing, despatches have been received here, in military circles, stating that a large body of Yankee cavalry, to the number of about 4,000, made their appearance at Griffin on Friday. No particulars are given.

These parties are said to be off-shoots from a main body, under Stoneman, numbering 8,000 men, with 16 or 18 pieces of artillery. When last seen they were in the vicinity of Covington, on the Georgia Railroad, when Stoneman sent out his raiders in various directions, with instructions for all to meet at Macon, where they would be joined by Rosseau, with 3,000 more, and after the Union march on Andersonville. Such is the report, and military circles receive it with some degree of faith.

Details of the Damage on the Central Railroad

A despatch dated Gordon, July 31, from Mr. BRENNER, of the Telegraph Company, to President CUYLER, of the Georgia Central Railroad, says:

From 152 mile post to 153, three pieces of the track have been burnt, about the length of three cars in all, in two places across stock gaps. From 154 mile post to No. 15, the track is all right. At No. 15 the side track is partially burnt. From No. 15 to 157 mile post all right. Between 157 and 158 mile post two tressels have been slightly damaged and five uprights burnt, which will cover all the damage. All the track to No. 16 is perfect. The side track at No. 16 partially burnt. From No. 16 to the gates at Gordon, all is right.

All the cars at Gordon except those containing families were burnt; also the warehouse and some small houses near by. The passenger shed is not burnt. The engines were all burnt, but not much damaged. The sideling is mostly injured at Gordon; only about fifty yards of the main track is burnt. All the information we learn at this point is that the force at the stations above number 260, and that they left No. 15 for Milledgeville at 4 o p.m. yesterday.

There was fighting near Macon yesterday; report says we repulsed them. Walnut Creek Bridge (near Macon) is damaged.

I will give you the condition of the rest of the road as I pass over tomorrow. Hope to have the lines working through then.

The *Charleston Mercury*

August 3, 1864

Telegraphic
Official Accounts from Petersburg and Georgia
The Latest Accounts from Georgia

ATLANTA, **August 2**
All is quiet along the lines this morning. The enemy shelled the city for a half hour last evening.

The army is much elated at the defeat of the raiders in their rear. The enemy is still massing his forces on our left.

MACON, **August 2**
Atlanta trains arrive and depart regularly, in schedule time.

Yesterday affairs wore their usual aspect at Atlanta. There was some picket firing and shelling yesterday afternoon, which did no damage. The Yankees have apparently abandoned their advance across the Georgia Railroad, and are massing on their centre and right, endeavoring to work their way down between the city and the river.

The raiders who cut the Macon and Western Railroad were driven towards Newnan by JACKSON'S division of cavalry. Their advance reached Newnan just after the arrival of the train carrying RODDY'S command to Atlanta. He immediately attacked them in front, and the pursuing forces of JACKSON having come up, the Yankees broke and fled, leaving about 500 prisoners, 700 horses, and all their artillery (three pieces) in our hands. The rest sought to escape across the Chattahoochee. It was supposed that more would be taken.

The three pieces of artillery captured from STONEMAN have been brought here. It is also reported that we also captured 600 horses and 800 mules from STONEMAN'S force.

The State militia forces are pouring in, and are being rapidly sent forward to Atlanta.

The *Charleston Mercury*

August 6, 1864

Our Position at Atlanta

Every day delay, in which our enemies at Atlanta are kept at bay, it appears to us, is favorable to the Confederate cause. They draw their supplies for subsistence from an immense distance through an exhausted country, at a period of the year when the rivers in their possession are obstructed in their navigation, by the fall of waters; we, on the contrary, with our railroads repaired, are in the midst of our resources to support our army. The disasters of their late raid, to isolate Atlanta from these resources, will, in all probability, prevent the repetition of such an expedition; whilst it has stimulated the population of Georgia, under the patriotic call of GOV. BROWN, to hasten to the defence of their homes and their native State. We take it to be a matter of course, that our troops will be reinforced, not only by the militia of Georgia, but by Confederate troops, if not from the army of Virginia, from the army under General PRICE, or KIRBY SMITH, or by FORREST, or by MORGAN. It appears to us to be quite impossible that, with such large resources for reinforcing the army at Atlanta, disencumbered from any immediate pressure of our foes, the army at Atlanta will not be reinforced. Independent of the interests of the Confederacy, the promotion of General HOOD to the command of that army, we have not doubted, would secure to it the necessary reinforcements. Since he took the command of it three conflicts have taken place, in two of which he attacked the enemy behind their entrenchments. In both, the wonted valor of our troops hase been displayed.

They carried two lines of entrenchments, but failed to carry the third; and our troops returned to the positions they occupied before the conflicts took place. We cannot doubt that, in these engagements, our losses were heavy. Indeed, we would suppose, from the fact that our enemies fought behind entrenchments, which were stormed by us, that our losses, in killed and wounded, must have been heavier than those of our enemies. These battles, however, teach us an important lesson. They show that, with the number of troops we have at Atlanta, we cannot assume aggressive war with any hope of driving our enemies before us. A defensive warfare is our policy, until reinforcements shall arrive, which shall put us on something like a numerical equality with our foes. General JOHNSTON being removed from the command, because he would not assume aggressive war, we suppose General HOOD was obliged, in some way, to try it. He has tried it; and the result plainly proves, that if he persists, in it, without reinforcements, he will be carrying out the policy of GRANT, without the safety of GRANT, who had a living reservoir of blood, to supply his losses. The policy of every General with inferior numbers, is to fight only when he can fight at advantage. He cannot afford to lose man for man. He must injure his enemy more than his enemy injures him, or he will be ruined. Time, if he can obtain it, is his great ally; which, whilst his enemy is at bay, brings to him reinforcements and strength. And whilst reinforcements, we cannot doubt, will soon gather in front against our foes, may we not also hope that LEE or FORREST will burst upon their rear; and our whole force gathering together its united power, will roll up the Yankee army like a rotten scrowl.

The *Charleston Mercury*

August 9, 1864

Atlanta and its Environs

The *Macon Confederate* has a long article on this subject, from which we derive the following interesting facts:

There are four railroads terminating in Atlanta – the Georgia Railroad, the Western and Atlantic, the Macon and Western, and the Atlantic and West Point. The first of these, the Georgia, was completed in 1828, and then terminated at Whitehall, a small country tavern near the centre of Fulton County. Commencing at Augusta, it ran in a northwesterly direction to that point. Then the Macon and Western was constructed from Macon to the same point, and soon after the village of Whitehall was named Atlanta. The West Point Road was the next constructed, running to the Chattahoochee River over the western boundary of the State. The Western and Atlantic, running northwest to Chattanooga, followed.

Atlanta soon became a city, with factories, shops, merchants, mechanics, traders, speculators, and whatever pertained to a first class commercial emporium.

The Chattahoochee River rises in the Black Mountains, a spur of the Blue Ridge, in Habersham county, and not far from the headwaters of the Savannah. It runs west one hundred and fifty miles, and empties into the Apalachicola and the Gulf of Mexico.

Seven miles north of Atlanta is the Chattahoochee Bridge, where the Western and Atlantic Railroad crosses the river. This bridge, destroyed by the Confederates, has been rebuilt by the Yankees. A few hundred yards above this bridge Peach Tree Creek comes into the Chattahoochee from the east. A little creek, called Nance, runs into the Peach Tree just above the mouth of the latter. Farther up the Chattahoochee, sixteen miles northeast of Atlanta, is Roswell, the present base of the left wing of Shermanarmy. Stone Mountain is an isolated peak, several hundred feet high, sixteen miles from Atlanta. Decatur is a depot on the Georgia Railroad, four miles from Atlanta. Stone Mountain is the only elevation of any importance anywhere about Atlanta.

It is 138 miles from Atlanta to Chattanooga; 171 to Augusta; 84 to West Point; 168 to Montgomery; 110 to Macon. East Point is six miles west on the West Point Road. The Macon and Western and the Atlanta Roads form a junction at East Point. At one place Peach Tree Creek runs within five miles of the city. The enemy, at last accounts, were all along this petty stream.

The surface of the country in Fulton county is generally flat, with here and there small ridges.

The *Charleston Mercury*

August 16, 1864

Telegraphic
Latest from Atlanta

ATLANTA, August 14
The enemy opened fire upon the city with six batteries at 8 o last night, their batteries being stationed on the Marietta street, Peach Tree and Williams' Mill Roads, and in front of the Medical College Rolling Mills. The fire was very heavy, and continued until 4, a. m. About midnight a shell entered the frame storehouse of BIGGERS & CO., on Marietta street, between Peach Tree and Church streets, setting fire to some loose cotton. The flames spread rapidly, and the building was soon enveloped. The alarm was given, and Engine No. 3 responded promptly.

The enemy immediately concentrated their fire on that point, yet the firemen nobly held their ground despite the rain of shells. They succeeded in saving the building and the large warehouse of KYLE & CO. Some few other buildings were consumed. Not a citizen was injured. The women and children sought safety in the bomb proofs.

But little shelling has taken place along the line today. No movement of the enemy is reported.

ATLANTA, August 15
At a late hour yesterday evening the enemy drove in our pickets on the centre, and, after a sharp skirmish, were repulsed. There was desultory firing along the line throughout the night and today, but few shells have been thrown into the city.

A body of the enemycavalry dashed into Decatur this evening, moving in the direction of CobbMills. A small force of infantry is reported to be posted in Decatur. Their actions indicate another movement on our right. Lively skirmishing was going on along our centre.

Everything looks brighter and more hopeful than at any time since the siege began.

The *Charleston Mercury*

August 16, 1864

Operations in Sherman's Rear

It is stated that WHEELER has destroyed the bridges across the Etowah and Oostanaula Rivers, and burnt the track the whole way from Marietta. A large amount of stores are said to have fallen into his hands at Resaca, which was destroyed after our cavalry had appropriated all that was needful to them. At last accounts, the report says General WHEELER was rapidly marching in the direction of Dalton, where an immense amount of stores, both subsistence and ordnance, has been congregating for some time.

From the *Macon Confederate* of Friday we learn that General WHEELER massed his cavalry corps near Covington, on the Augusta Railroad, and on Monday morning the grand cavalcade of gay cavaliers started for adventure and SHERMAN'S rear. It was rumored in town yesterday that he had captured Marietta and burned the Federal stores there, and had taken an immense number of prisoners. Be it as it may, it is certain that the long expected effort to cut SHERMAN'S communication is now about to be realized. The Federal cavalry have nearly all recently been destroyed, and Gen WHEELER is now out just at the right time.

We are assured by gentlemen direct from headquarters that there is not the slightest intention entertained there of a retrograde move or the evacuation of Atlanta. On the other hand, it is expected that SHERMAN will be forced to retreat.

General sherman's Campaign. Burning the railroad bridge at Resaca (Davis). Liabrary of Congress.

The *Charleston Mercury*
August 16, 1864

The Approaching Battle

The movements of the enemy in front of Atlanta indicate that a final and decisive engagement for the possession of that city will shortly take place. The heavy columns of troops being massed on our left will soon compel us either to attack or to evacuate Atlanta, and neither prudence nor policy could impel General Hood to yield the city without a desperate struggle. Under such circumstances we should feel no surprise if at any hour our army assumed the aggressive and the struggle – fraught with the destinies of Georgia, and filled with the greatest importance to the Confederacy – should commence for the possession of a city whose importance to us cannot be overestimated. That General Hood will fight, we have the strongest assurances in the dogged resolution with which he has held the enemy in check for the past three weeks, and in a series of partial engagements, repulsed every effort of the enemy to force us out of Atlanta, either by direct assault or by the more prudent method of flanking.

These partial engagements have been but the prelude to a bloody carnival which must soon be held in the vicinity of Atlanta. Perceiving that his attack on portions of our lines have all proven unsuccessful, and that the raids which he inaugurated have met a similar fate to those of his colleagues in Virginia, Sherman appears to have changed his tactics, and by persistently massing his forces on our left, invites the attack which necessity must soon compel us to make. There is no doubt that in so doing he has acted with considerable prudence and materially decreases the danger of his position.

By forcing us to assume the offensive, with an army inferior to his in numbers, he will have gained a decided advantage. His columns are steadily pushed forward in the direction of East Point, and, unless we force them back, the possession of the railroads leading to Macon and West Point will fall into his hands, and necessitate the abandonment of Atlanta for the preservation of our army. This must be prevented at every hazard; and we are certain that the effort will be made. Still the question arises whether the strength of our army will warrant an attack on the enemy, entrenched as he will be in powerful works and possessing a vast superiority in numbers.

The hour is fast approaching when a bloody and desperate battle will be fought. In fact it cannot be delayed many days. The odds are against us, so far as numbers are concerned, but we must trust to the tried valor of our men to make up all deficiencies. In the meantime, it is the duty of every man who is absent with or without leave that he shall promptly rejoin his command and help to swell our ranks. The very crisis in the fate of Georgia and of the South is at hand; and this is the time for every man to perform the obligation he owes his country. Furloughs can temporarily be laid aside, and a patriotic promptness in reporting to their respective commands, be substituted by our soldiers. We are aware that the pleasures of home and the society of relatives and friends possess great allurement, and are fascinating to the veteran, but he must be willing to forego the happiness of being with his loved ones for a while.

Duty must be obeyed and when victory is achieved and the enemy is sent howling back to the Tennessee, they can repose on the laurels won by their patriotism and heroism.

The battle will be fought in a few days and every additional man will add a tower of strength to the army. We trust for the sake of the cause in which you are engaged that no man will so far ignore the claims of his country by absenting himself from the battlefield at the present time, when his presence and that of thousands who are absent, might turn the scale of battle and wrest victory from the banners of our enemy. Sherman is now playing his last card. If we can beat him back the result will be undoubted. Beaten once more he will be compelled to seek safety in flight, and the lowering clouds which now threaten to overwhelm us in disaster will be dispelled by the bright sunshine of a glorious triumph.

The *Charleston Mercury*

August 19, 1864

Telegraphic
Important from Atlanta
Wheeler in the Enemy's Rear

Atlanta, August 18

Heavy skirmishing began at midnight on our left and centre and continued until 2 a.m., without any result. At daybreak this morning the artillery of STEWART'S corps opened on the enemy, whose batteries replied feebly. The firing on our side was very heavy, and produced consternation amongst the enemy forces.

Prisoners report that our cavalry captured a large number of beeves at Kingston a few days since. Numerous reports are in circulation regarding the operations of WHEELER'S cavalry; but, beyond the fact that they have cut the road at Ackworth, and were destroying the track between the Etowah Oostanoula Rivers, and, thus far, had been entirely successful, nothing official has been received.

The enemy seems ignorant of the magnitude of WHEELER'S operations. They were preparing another raiding expedition, under KILPATRICK, which had rendezvoused at Sweet Water, preparatory to starting, which has been recalled, and is now going in pursuit of our cavalry.

From *The New York Times*

July 25, 1864

Special Dispatch to *The New York Times*

Washington, Sunday, July 24 – 10 P. M.
Official dispatches of another battle before Atlanta, fought on Friday, were received by the authorities last night. At the time of sending the dispatch the contest was still going on, but the results, so far as developed, were favorable. A position had been gained from which SHERMAN was able to bring his siege guns to bear on the city. Extensive fires were raging within its limits as though the rebels were burning stores. &c.

During this engagement Gen. MCPHERSON was killed. This sad report it was at first hoped might prove unfounded, but it has been fully confirmed. In this brilliant young officer the country loses one of its ablest Generals. Gen. Granti has always placed the very highest estimate on his talent, and after the Vicksburgh campaign addressed him a letter, in which he stated that after SHERMAN, no man in his army had rendered him such service, and done so much for the success of the campaign as he.

Gen. McPherson's Death
A Battle on Friday
Fighting Still Going On

Louisville, Sunday, July 23
Major NORCROSS, local Paymaster at Chattanooga, telegraphs Major ALLEN, Chief Paymaster here, that Major Gen. MCPHERSON was killed yesterday before Atlanta. Another correspondent says he was shot fatally through the lungs.

Baltimore, Sunday, July 23
A PRIVATE DISPATCH RECEIVED BY A RELATIVE OF GEN. MCPHERSON in this city last night, dated near Atlanta, July

23, announces that that gallant officer was killed in battle the day previous, and that his remains would be sent home in charge of members of his staff,

Washington, Sunday, July 24

The latest official dispatches from Gen. Sherman represent repeated fighting and give the circumstances attending the death of Gen. McPherson, who fell in battle in the severe contest of Friday.

Gen. Hooker's Corps
Movements of the Army up to July 18
Kenesaw Mountain
Marietta
Chattahoochee River

CHATTAHOOCHEE RIVER. Ga., Monday. July 18, 1864 – The first act of the grand drama which Sherman has been performing this Summer has been played. The Chattahoochee has been reached by the Army of the West. The curtain rests upon the stage, while the actors pause to take breath and arrange their costumes for the inauguration of Act II – the struggle for Atlanta – which the distant booming of cannon announces is about to begin. That it will be prolific of battle scenes and bloody encounters none can doubt who reflect upon the importance of the position to be wrested from the foe.

Thus far Gen. Sherman's campaign has been mainly marked by irregular conflicts, prolonged skirmishing, by arduous marches, flanking operations, and the advance and attack of certain corps to conceal and protect the movements of others. Although the army has frequently been in line of battle and sometimes engaged for a week at a time in heavy skirmishing, if we except 'Resaca' of the 14th and 15th of June, no general engagement has been fought between the opposing armies. But our columns have arrived at last at the river behind which the enemy has all along boasted that his main defence would be made. We are now so close to the city of Atlanta that the decisive conflict cannot be delayed much longer. If the army moves at all beyond the river, the north bank of which is now its line, it will be a movement characterized by very heavy fighting.

In a previous letter the prediction was ventured that the most obstinate resistance to be encountered by our army, prior to crossing the Chattahoochee, would be in the vicinity of Kenesaw Mountain. Since that was written the position indicated has been occupied and maintained by JOHNSTON for two weeks against the most determined efforts of our combined armies. It was not without a severe struggle that he was driven from Pine Knob, where, on the 14th, 15th, and 16th, Gen. HOOKER, with his invincible corps, fought with great bravery. Gen. GEARY'S division was chiefly engaged, losing 519 men in killed and wounded. The attack was continued until the desired position was attained, and the enemy retreated. On the 17th other divisions came to the active assistance of the heroic division which Gen. GEARY had handled with so much ability. The enemy was forced back through successive lines of works until the 20th, when Kenesaw and its adjacent ridges presented their stern front, bristling with guns and bayonets, to prevent the further progress of the hitherto triumphant army.

Kenesaw Mountain is a huge, isolated, double hill rising boldly out of a country of almost uninterrupted forest-covered ridges – themselves of no mean elevation. In these ridges consist the peculiar adaptation of the country for defensive purposes. Aided by military science, they have been made by rebel engineering absolutely impregnable to direct assault. All the works I have seen partake of the same character. They consist of long lines of rifle-pits, elaborately constructed with good revetments of logs or fascines, and are well drained. These lines following the crests of the ridges, are occasionally broken by forts constructed on the most commanding elevations.

The flanks are always well protected by strong forts. The woods in front of an intrenchment are generally cut down, so as to form an impenetrable abattis. When their lines cross open fields, they are fully guarded by rows of sharpened stakes, driven firmly in the ground, at an angle calculated to impale a horse or man running upon them, and too closely set to permit of passage between. The villainous *chevaux de frise* is also freely used, particularly on roads where our cavalry are expected to charge. This precaution is altogether unnecessary, as it is a well-known fact that we have no cavalry to hurl on rebel works. All we have are required to defend the flanks and rear. Even in the construction of advanced works for skirmishers, the enemy seem to have bestowed time and care. Their forts and lines of intrenchments partake more of the aspect of permanent fortifications than field works for temporary use. The enemy has been driven from them by the flanking process which has been adopted by Gen. SHERMAN with so much success as to earn for him the suggestive appellation of "The Great Flanker."

I will not attempt to record a detailed account of the many assaults and conflicts that occurred between the two armies in the protracted struggle in front of Kenesaw. Suffice it to say that for two weeks Gen. SHERMAN vainly attempted this hill by direct assault. On the 27th of June a general attack was ordered, and in pursuance thereof the Fourteenth and Fourth Corps engaged the enemy's lines near the base of the mountain with great spirit, but could not drive them beyond their breastworks. During the battle, a furious cannonade was kept up on the mountain, enveloping its top and sides in the smoke of exploding shells. The other corps were in readiness to charge the moment the effort should show signs of success. But the attack was not a success, and soon developed the strong position of the foe, proving it to be folly to throw away lives in attempting to dislodge him by assault.

Gen. SHERMAN then turned his attention to other means, and applied to them his never-failing receipt for obstinance – a flank movement. Supplies were replenished at Big Shanty, the new depot. Preparation was made to pass the entire army to the enemy's rear. As the movement contemplated would, if Johnston's lines did not fall back, necessarily leave the railroad at his mercy, the depot was ordered back to

Alatoona Bridge. A strong column, SCHOFIELD'S I believe, was sent westward on JOHNSTONS left, and on the 2d of July other corps followed. During the night of July 2d the enemy was ascertained to be again in retreat, after having obstinately held out against our assaults for two weeks. We pressed rapidly after them, passing through a series of works more formidable than any before captured. We again overtook them at night on the 3rd of July, about two miles south of Marietta.

Marietta deserves more than a passing notice. Prior to the war it was noted throughout the South as one of the centres of Georgian wealth and refinement. Compared with a Northern town its proportions would be diminutive indeed; but in Georgia, with a population of two thousand, it ranked as the sixth town in size in the State. The period of its settlement dates anterior to that of Atlanta, which owes it's superiority in size to the fact of its being a centre for several railroads. Marietta, with no commercial aspirations and no manufacturing interest, had, confessedly, a higher social grade than Atlanta, with all its teeming population, work-shops and warehouses. It boasted a college of considerable importance, not widely known, but well patronized by those of the South, who preferred educating their sons in their own States to sending them to 'Yankee' institutions to be 'contaminated' by the enemies of 'Southern principles.' These watchful guardians of the morality of Southern striplings forgot that their own colleges were almost without exception officered by men of Northern birth and education.

As one might expect, the glory of Marietta College has departed. The buildings are standing gloomily enough upon the hill from whence they overlook the town and beautiful gardens: but the pupils and teachers are gone; the former to the wars to destroy the Union of their fathers; the latter to their Northern homes to escape the persecution of their former pupils. The picture will answer for all Southern colleges. The war has closed their churches and their schools, with here and there a solitary exception.

GENERAL SHERMAN'S ADVANCE. VIEW OF THE PUBLIC SQUARE, MARIETTA (DAVIS). LIBRARY OF CONGRESS.

Marietta presents a spectacle of war's devastating influences. Its fine mansions and lovely gardens, with their shaded walks and arbored seats, still remain but not as they once were – the abode of a happy people, innocent of war. All those have left, and throngs of soldiers are now roaming over the half destroyed gardens or strolling through the mutilated mansions, thrumming on the ruined pianos and lolling on the sofa abandoned by their wealthy proprietors. A few matrons – widowed relics of the war – and their half-scared daughters, still remain in the town. These, with a few old men, striplings and decayed servants, are all that are left of the denizens of the place. At one end of the town a half closed burial ground, with hundreds of newly made soldiers' graves, side by side with marble monuments and mausoleums of the past, reveals the fact that Marietta's dead are more numerous than Marietta's living.

To resume our narrative from which we have digressed. On the 5th of July JOHNSTON moved still further southward, taking position on the railroad about two miles north of the Chattasoochee River. From the tops of the trees on the high blue hills occupied by the Twentieth Corps, we beheld Atlanta's glistening spires and housetops, seemingly about seven miles south of the river. On the 7th Inst. the foe again retrograded and assumed a new position whose contracted limits were speedily ascertained to be in front of the railroad bridge, the flanks resting on the river on either aide of the crossing. It was pretty evident that Johnston was crossing his forces on the pontoons which we knew had been laid in that vicinity. The rebel front was as bold as ever, and no impression was made on their lines. By the morning of the 9th, the last skirmisher had disappeared from our front, and the railroad bridge was discovered to be in flames. We advanced through another series of fortifications to the river-bank, along which our line now rests. The enemy holds the opposite bank and it is not an uncommon sight to see the soldiers of both armies meet in swimming parties and exchange tobacco and coffee, apparently as good friends as though a shot had never passed between them.

As it was currently reported that JOHNSTON commenced to cross the Chattahoochee on the 4th of July, it can be but a matter of surprise to many who view critically the movements of our armies, that he was not attacked at the time when he would have labored under the misfortune of having a river in his rear in very dangerous proximity. This has been a matter of much comment among officers and men, who will canvass such matters whenever opportunity occurs. A battle was pretty generally expected on the 4th, when it was stated that Gen. SHERMAN, in view of the golden opportunity thus presented by the situation of affairs, had ordered a general onslaught to be made by the whole army with a view to drive JOHNSTON in confusion to his crossings. Whether this attack was actually ordered, as the order countermanded, or for some cause rendered inoperative, is a matter for speculation. But one thing all unite in believing; that is had a fight occurred on the "glorious Fourth" there would have been but two alternatives accepted by our army: 'Victory or Death.' It would have fought as it never fought before, so eager and expectant for the fray were commanders and soldiers. There are many who regret the postponement of the battle, which they believe would have been decisive of the result of the campaign. They would have attacked at all hazards of life, though the enemy were never so firm and, to all appearances, secure in their fortifications. Whether these regrets are just or unjust, time will develop. No inconsiderable number believe that JOHNSTON was allowed to cross the Chattahoochee in comparative security to insure important results from combined movements, of which we do not at present know, but in which other armies are supposed to be interested. All unite in endorsing the wisdom and generalship of SHERMAN, and willingly abide by any decision he may make, believing his conduct of the campaign to have been masterly, and productive of the most brilliant results.

Although the Chattahoochee River forms the main dividing line between the opposing armies, we have no inconsiderable force on the other side. Firing is occasionally heard from their direction. Supplies are being accumulated at Marietta from which place they are distributed to the trains of the various corps. No effort is being made to rebuild the railroad bridge, for the reason that a strong fort on the rebel side of the river effectually commands the approaches to the old piers. A general movement to the south side of the river is daily expected. The army is resting and nerving for the severe struggle which will then, in all probability, begin.

Our expectations will be very agreeably disappointed, if the ten miles intervening between our present camp and Atlanta are not more difficult of accomplishment than the one hundred over which Gen. SHERMAN has so successfully led us since we left

J.G.

Special Dispatch to *The New York Times*

Washington, Monday, July 25

The Battles Before Atlanta

Both engagements delivered before Atlanta, namely, that of Wednesday and that of Friday last, have been assaults on the part of the rebels. This is accounted for from the fact that Gen. Hood, Johnston's successor, has been throughout the campaign one of the most bitter opponents of Johnston's retreating policy and he felt impelled, the moment he was placed in command, to pitch in. It does not appear that he has gained any other result than to bring upon himself, in each instance, a loss thrice as heavy as that inflicted on the assailed party.

General Sherman Confident of Success
Gen. SHERMAN'S latest dispatches show an assured confidence in the capture of Atlanta, though the prize may not be won as speedily as the public had anticipated.

What the Historians Say

The battle at Atlanta occurred on July 22, 1864 in Fulton County, Georgia. It was the culmination of the Atlanta Campaign of 1864. The principal commanders were Maj. Gen. William T. Sherman commanding the United States Military Division of the Mississippi confronting Gen. John Bell Hood's Confederate Army of Tennessee. The estimated casualties were 3,641 and 8,499 respectively.

Following the Battle of Peachtree Creek, Hood determined to attack Maj. Gen. James B. McPherson's Army of the Tennessee. He withdrew his main army at night from Atlanta's outer line to the inner line, enticing Sherman to follow. In the meantime, he sent William J. Hardee with his corps on a fifteen-mile march to hit the unprotected Union left and rear, east of the city. Wheeler's cavalry was to operate farther out on Sherman's supply line, and Gen. Frank Cheatham's corps were to attack the Union front. Hood, however, miscalculated the time necessary to make the march, and Hardee was unable to attack until afternoon. Although Hood had outmaneuvered Sherman for the time being, McPherson was concerned about his left flank and sent his reserves, Grenville Dodge's XVI Army Corps, to that location.

Two of Hood's divisions ran into this reserve force and were repulsed. The Rebel attack stalled on the Union rear but began to roll up the left flank. Around the same time, a Confederate soldier shot and killed McPherson when he rode out to observe the fighting. Determined attacks continued, but the Union forces held. About 4:00 p.m., Cheatham's corps broke through the Union front at the Hurt House, but Sherman massed twenty artillery pieces on a knoll near his headquarters to shell these Confederates and halt their drive. Maj. Gen. John A. Logan's XV Army Corps then led a counterattack that restored the Union line. The Union troops held, and Hood suffered high casualties. It was a significant Union victory that affected the outcome of the Campaign and the action in the theater of war.

16

Opequon

The Fifth Major Battle in Sheridan's Shenandoah Valley Campaign

Author's Commentary

Only two correspondents accompanied Sheridan's force at the battle at Opequon, perhaps the most significant battle in Sheridan's Shenandoah campaign. One was from the *Baltimore American,* the other from the *New York World*, a Democratic newspaper. *The New York Times*, a staunch Republican newspaper, chose the reportage of the former newspaper to reprint, perhaps for reasons other than proximity.

Election day was fast approaching, and Abraham Lincoln had been severely demeaned by a press loyal to the Democratic Party. His popularity had diminished considerably.

Following Sherman's victory at Atlanta and Farragut's victory at Mobile Bay, Lincoln's popularity increased. The victory at Opequon helped seal the election for the President. *The New York Times* had national distribution in the northern states, and, with election day fast approaching, the reportage could only help Lincoln's re-election efforts.

Sept. 20, 1864: From the *Charleston Mercury*

Telegraphic – Hampton's Last Dash

Gen. Lee's Official Account

Richmond, September 17 – The following was received at the War Office today:

Headquarters
Army Northern Virginia
September 17

To the Hon. Secretary Seddon: At daylight yesterday the enemy skirmishers west of the Jerusalem Plank Road were driven back on their entrenchments along their whole extent. At the same time HAMPTON attacked his position north of the Norfolk Railroad, near Sycamore Church, and captured about 300 prisoners, some arms and wagons, a large number of horses, and 2,500 cattle.

GREGG attacked HAMPTON, on his return, in the afternoon, at BerrienMill, on the Jerusalem Plank Road, but was repulsed and driven back. Everything was brought off safely. Our entire loss does not exceed 50 men.

(Signed)
R. E. LEE.

Movements in Virginia

Richmond, September 19

A raiding party of Yankees burned the railroad bridge over the Rapidan yesterday afternoon.

Grover's Division, 19th Corps, in action at the Battle in the Opequon (Waud). Library of Congress.

Intelligence from Winchester on the afternoon of the 16th inst. says: 'Our forces hold their ground. The enemy infantry, 30,000 strong, remain behind their entrenchments. Their cavalry, 10,000 strong, display considerable enterpriseand activity. EARLY'S army is in fine condition, enjoying abundant supplies of every kind.'

The *Charleston Mercury*
September 23, 1864

Telegraphic Important from Virginia
A Reverse in the Valley
Richmond, September 20

Information deemed reliable states that the Yankee raiders, after partially destroying the railroad bridge over the Rapidan, returned to Culpeper, where they were ambushed by a force of Confederate infantry and badly cut up.

Official information was received tonight of a severe engagement near Winchester yesterday morning, but the result is not definitely stated. Generals RHODES, of Alabama, and GODWIN, of North Carolina, were killed.

Richmond, September 21

A despatch from Gen. LEE says Gen. EARLY reports that on the morning of the 19th the enemy advanced on Winchester, near which place he met the attack, which was resisted from early in the day till near night when he was compelled to retire. After night he fell back to FisherHill. Our loss is reported severe. Gens. RHODES and GODWIN were killed, nobly doing their duty. Three pieces of artillery were lost. The trains and supplies were brought off safely. An unofficial report says EARLY has fallen back to Strasburg.

Petersburg, September 21

There is no change in the position along the lines. The enemy shelled the city furiously this morning from 5 to 6 o. Our batteries replied, and the roar of cannon was incessant, and deafening.

CUSTER'S DIVISION CAVALRY CAPTURING PRISIONERS NEAR TURNPIKE (WAUD). LIBRARY OF CONGRESS.

Loud cheering in the enemy camp was heard this morning, but the cause has not transpired – supposed to be some news encouraging from the Valley.

Richmond, September 21

Six hundred returned prisoners reached the city tonight, at 8 o. A large crowd of ladies and others assembled at the wharf to greet them, but had mostly dispersed before the arrival of the steamer, which was detained at the obstructions by low tide. The men all in excellent spirits. Four hundred more will be brought up tomorrow.

Lynchburg, September 21

The remains of General RHODES arrived here tonight. The body will lay in state at the city Court House until Friday morning, when it will be interred.

Petersburg, September 22

The *Lynchburg Virginian* has a report of the battle in the Valley on Monday last. The fight is represented to have been very severe. It occurred on the Berryville Road, two miles below Winchester. The early part of the engagement is said to have resulted directly in our favor, but a flank movement of several thousand of the enemy cavalry necessitated a retrograde movement on the part of our forces, which was accomplished in an orderly manner, without hurry or confusion.

The position to which our army fell back is FisherHill, this side of Strasburg. It is said to be a very strong position. The losses on both sides were severe, but enormously so on the part of the enemy. Generals FITZ, LEE and YORK, of Louisiana, were wounded – the latter losing an arm; the wound of the former is said to be not dangerous. General RHODES, while selecting a position for a battery, to fill a gap in our lines, was shot through the head and instantly killed.

All the advantage was on our side, except the loss of ground.

The enemy is believed to have numbered 40,000; and it is reported that GRANT was in command.

Wheeler's Operations

Meridian, September 20

The *Clarion* gives an accountof WHEELER'S operations; MARTIN'S brigade tore up the State Road between Atlanta and Dalton; HUME and KELLY tapped it near Dalton, and Gen. WILLIAMS between Tunnel Hill and Chattanooga; HUME destroyed the East Tennessee Road from Calhoun to Athens. WHEELER was unable to cross the Tennessee River and went around Knoxville, crossing the Holston at Strawberry Plains, came over the Cumberland Mountains via Sparta. Sixteen miles of the Nashville and Chattanooga Road were destroyed – the road being destroyed from Franklin to Campbell Station. Gen. KELLY was mortally wounded in the fight at Franklin, on the 29th WILLIAMS', ROBINSON'S, DIBBRELL'S and ASHBY'S commands have not joined the main command yet.

The *Charleston Mercury*

September 29, 1864

Results of the Summer Campaign

In this campaign, remarks the *Richmond Dispatch*, notwithstanding the two small reverses at Atlanta and Winchester, the balance has been greatly in our favor. We have frustrated the most tremendous combination ever formed against any modern city, and in frustrating it, have slain or wounded, or otherwise put hors de combat, at least two hundred thousand men, of which number GRANT himself lost, under his own eye, at least one hundred and fifty thousand. That General himself acknowledges that he has been awfully beaten when he calls for one hundred thousand fresh troops to finish the job which he expected to finish last June. He is conscious that he does so, and endeavors to explain it away in conversation with one of the toadies that stick to him like a leach in his late journey from HarperFerry to Philadelphia. He only wants them, he says, to make the victory more complete, and to diminish the effusion of blood. Those are the very objects for which all commanders seek overwhelming numbers. To state that object is merely to confess that his present numbers are insufficient to effect the object. Now, taking in HUNTER'S army and BUTLER'S army, GRANT had at least three hundred thousand men engaged in this enterprise. If he still wants one hundred thousand more, it affords the strongest proof that he has been signally and terribly beaten. We say, then, thus far the advantage in this campaign has been prodigiously on our side. We have killed enormous numbers of Yankees, and that is the surest way to bring the rest to their senses. It is far better, indeed, than peace congresses at Niagara or elsewhere. The Yankees are the most mercenary of Gods creatures. And yet the Yankee loves his life better even than his interest; and when the universal nation finds that nothing but death is to be gotten by coming here, they will conclude that it does not pay, and will give it up. The best road to peace lies through the blood of the Yankees. The more we kill, the nearer we approach to peace. Such being the fact, we must be admitted to have made vast progress in this campaign. They have been slaughtered awfully here and every where else.

From *The New York Times*

September 21, 1864

Baltimore, Tuesday, Sept. 20 – 10 P.M.
The following is the *American's* special account of the great battle in the Shenandoah Valley:
Headquarters
Middle Military Division
Winchester, VA, Monday, Sept. 19 – 9 P.M.

Gen. SHERIDAN'S army has this day fought one of the most successful and decisive battles of the war. Victory again perched on our banners, and the rebel army, which so recently threatened the invasion of the loyal North, has been defeated and utterly routed, with the loss of at least three thousand killed and wounded including seven Generals: namely, RHODES. WHARTON, BRADLEY, T. JOHNSON, GORDON, YORK and GODMAN, the first two of whom were killed and the others badly wounded. We have captured 2,500 prisoners, nine battle flags, representing nine different regimental organizations, and five pieces of artillery with caissons.

The recital of the victory ought to make every loyal heart at the North glow with admiration and gratitude to the brave men and gallant officers who have achieved so signal success.

In order to more thoroughly understand the nature of the battle, with all the surrounding influences, it will be necessary briefly to refer to the operations of Sunday.

Sunday morning Early sent Gordon's division of rebel infantry from Bunker Hill, where it had been stationed for the past few days, to drive Averill out of Martinsburg and destroy the bridge on the Baltimore and Ohio R. R. across the Opequon, which they erroneously thought had been repaired. They occupied Martinsburgh for a short time, without doing any damage to the railroad, and were eventually driven by Averill as far as Darkesville.

Gen. Sheridan, learning their movements, ordered the whole command to break camp and prepare to march. Accordingly at 3 o'clock on Sunday the tents were all struck and packed in wagons. The different divisions were all under arms, and prepared to move at a moment's notice, and remained in the state for about an hour, when the order came to go into camp for the night, and everything remained perfectly quiet. About 9 o'clock orders were received from Sheridan for the Sixth and Nineteenth Corps to be ready to start at 3 o'clock, and the Army of Western Virginia, under Crook, at 5 the following morning – the order of march to be as follows: the Sixth Corps to move out on the Winchester and Berryville pike, and move in two parallel columns on both sides of the road, with the artillery, ammunition and supply trains on the road; the Nineteenth Corps to follow on the same road and in similar order; the Army of Western Virginia, under Crook, to move from its camping-ground in the vicinity of Summit Point, and striking across the country in a south-westerly direction, was ordered to form a junction at the crossing of the Opequon, on the Berryville and Wincheater pike, and shortly after 8 o'clock Wilson's division of cavalry crossed the Opequon at the Berryville and Winchester pike. Moving his command rapidly along the road, driving in the enemy's skirmish line, he gallantly charged the enemy's field works with the first brigade, and carried them at the point of the sabre, capturing thirty prisoners. In this charge, Col. BRIXTON, Eighteenth Pennsylvania cavalry, was wounded within a few feet of the enemy's works, while gallantly leading his regiment.

These field-works were constructed at the Opequon, and prevent our passage at that point. It will be seen how signally they failed to accomplish the object for which they were constructed.

Our cavalry having secured a safe passage for the infantry, the Sixth corps was moved across the Opequon, and along the pike toward Winchester – leaving its train to part on the opposite side of the stream – to a point about a mile and a half distant from the ford, where it formed in line of battle and threw out a strong skirmish line. At the same time the artillery opened on the woods into which the enemy's infantry had retired, and kept up an incessant cannonade, the enemy replying briskly with parts of two batteries.

There was a delay of at least two hours, caused by the non-arrival of the Nineteenth corps, who through misconception of orders, had failed to come up at the proper time. Gen.

EMERY had moved his column to the rear of the baggage train of the Sixth corps instead of keeping his command closed up in the rear of the advancing column of the Sixth corps.

Gen. Sheridan, having learned on Sunday that the main portion of Early's forces were encamped to the vicinity of Bunker Hill and Stephenson's Depot, resolved to mass his forces on the Winchester and Berryville pike, and by a rapid movement hurl them on Early's rear. There is no doubt that the enemy were surprised and outnumbered by Sheridan.

Whilst his different columns were being marched to the appointed place of rendezvous, a portion of our cavalry under Gens. Torbett and Averill kept up a strong picket line along the Opequon, and by demonstrating in force at Burn's ford kept a large portion of the enemy at that part of the field, which was nearly twelve miles distant from the point where it was intended our Infantry should operate, and strike a blow which should result in the signal defeat of Early's army.

The delay in the arrival of the 19th Corps enabled EARLY to move GORDON's Division at the double quick from Bunker Hill, distant about ten miles, and bring it up in time to form in line of battle with Breckenridge's, Ramseur's, and Rhodes' commands, who had already arrived, and were formed in a belt of woods skirting Berryville and Winchester.

As soon as the 19th corps arrived, it was formed in four lines of battle, about 300 yards apart, on the right of the 6th corps, and everything being in readiness, the advance was sounded at about 12 o'clock, and the different lines moved forward.

The two corps advanced in splendid style, and just as composedly as though marching at review or on parade, drums beating and colors flying, presenting such an imposing spectacle as has seldom been witnessed in the present war. In fact, some of the oldest and most experienced staff officers present declared they had never before witnessed so truly grand a spectacle.

What the Historians Say

The battle at Opequon, known also as Third Winchester, occurred in Frederick County, Virginia, on September 19, 1864. It was the fifth major battle in Sheridan's Shenandoah

Valley Campaign, which occurred during the months ranging from August through December, 1864.

The principal commanders were Maj. Gen. Philip Sheridan leading 39,240 Union troops pitted against Lt. Gen. Jubal A. Early's 15,200 Confederates. The estimated casualties were 5,020 and 3,610 respectively.

After Kershaw's division left Winchester to rejoin Lee's army at Petersburg, Lt. Gen. Jubal A. Early renewed his raids on the B&O Railroad at Martinsburg, badly dispersing his four remaining infantry divisions. On September 19, Sheridan advanced toward Winchester along the Berryville Pike with the VI and XIX Corps, crossing Opequon Creek.

The Union advance was delayed long enough for Early to concentrate his forces to meet the main assault, which continued for several hours. Casualties were very heavy. The Confederate line was gradually driven back toward the town. Mid-afternoon, Crook's (VIII) Corps and the cavalry turned the Confederate left flank. Early ordered a general retreat.

Confederate generals Rodes and Goodwin were killed, Fitzhugh Lee, Terry, Johnson, and Wharton wounded. Union general Russell was killed, McIntosh, Upton, and Chapman wounded. Because of its size, intensity, and result, many historians consider this the most important conflict of the Shenandoah Valley that resulted in important Union victory.

17

A Casualty of War

Proud to the End
The Charleston Mercury Ceases Publication

Author's Commentary

On February 11, 1865, Union troops closed in on Charleston, South Carolina. It was the five hundred and seventy ninth day of the Federal siege at Charleston Harbor. And it would be the last day a *Charleston Mercury* would be issued during the Civil War. Blue uniformed troops had landed on nearby James Island. More would arrive at any moment. The Rhetts, not wishing to suffer the indignity of being shuttered by occupying forces, elected to leave Charleston and departed for the State capital at Columbia. But the invading Union troops would soon be at Columbia too, and the resultant fire that swept Columbia destroyed the presses of the *Mercury*. It struggled to rise from its ashes in the post war year of 1866, and did so for a short while. But due to financial instability, the *Charleston Mercury* eventually succumbed to the financial malaise that gripped much of the post-war South.

Feb, 11, 1865: The *Charleston Mercury*

Siege Matters – Five Hundred and Seventy Ninth Day

A force of the enemy, believed to be between three and four thousand strong, under cover of their gunboats, made a landing at Grimballplace, on James Island, about 8 o yesterday morning. A brisk fight ensued with our pickets, the latter being finally driven in to our first line of works. Major MANIGAULT is reported to have been killed in the skirmishing, but some doubt is expressed as to the correctness of the report.

The enemy, at last accounts, were drawn up in line of battle and advancing slowly, but no general fight had taken place.

Active demonstrations have also been made along our lines on the Salkehatchie. In an attack there yesterday morning, the enemy were easily repulsed. Another force advanced upon the Charleston road, near Blue House, and opened with artillery, but made no impression on our lines. Everything was quiet at Combahee Ferry.

Spirit of the Army

Headq'rs 1st Regiment S.C.V.
McGowan's Brigade

Trenches near Petersburg, Va., Feb. 3, 1865
To the Editor of the *Mercury*: At a meeting held at the camp of the 1st Regiment S. C. Volunteers, McGOWAN'S Brigade, the following resolutions were submitted and unanimously adopted. Will you be kind enough to publish them in your paper.

Resolutions

The soldiers and officers of the 1st Regiment S. C. V., McGowanBrigade, do resolve:

1. That the war in which we are engaged is a war of self defence; that in the beginning, nearly four years ago, we took up arms in the defence of the right to govern ourselves and to protect our country from invasion, our homes from desolation, and our wives and children from insult and outrage.

ROBERT BARNWELL RHETT, THE GUIDING FORCE FOR SECESSION AND OWNER OF THE *CHARLESTON MERCURY*, AS HE LOOKED IN 1861 (FRANK LESLIE'S ILLUSTRATED NEWSPAPER). LIBRARY OF CONGRESS.

2. That the reasons which induced us to take up arms at the beginning have not been impaired, but on the contrary infinitely strengthened by the progress of the war – outrage and cruelty have not made us love the perpetrators. If we then judge that the enemy intended to impoverish and oppress us, we now know that they propose to subjugate, enslave, disgrace and destroy us.

3. As we were actuated by principle when we entered the service of the Confederate States, we are of the same opinion still. We have had our share of victories, and we must expect some defeats; our cause is righteous and must prevail. In the language of General Greene, during the darkest hours of the Revolution, when he was struggling to recover South Carolina, then entirely overrun and suffering under the scourge of Tarleton: 'Independence is certain, if the people have the fortitude to bear and the courage to persevere.'

4. To submit to our enemies now, would be more infamous than it would have been in the beginning. It would be cowardly, yielding to power what was denied upon principle. It would be to yield the cherished right of self government

and to acknowledge ourselves wrong in the assertion of it; to brand the names of our slaughtered companions; to forfeit the glory already won; to lose the fruits of all the sacrifices made and the privations endured; to give up independence, now nearly gained, and bring certain ruin, disgrace and eternal slavery upon our country.

Therefore, unsubdued by past reverses, and unawed by future dangers, we declare our determination to battle to the end, and not to lay down our arms until our independence is secured. Is life so dear, or peace so sweet, as to be purchased at the price of chains and slavery. Forbid it Heaven!

C. W. McCREARY, Colonel 1st Regt., S. C. V.

CHARLES J. C. HUTSON, 1st Lieut. and Adjutant.

Charleston Courier and Columbia papers please copy.

Telegraphic
War Spirit in Virginia

RICHMOND, February 9 – A great war meeting was held at the African Church today. The building was crowded an hour before the time fixed for the meeting, and thousands wereunable to gain admittance. The assemblage was addressed in stirring speeches by Senator HUNTER, Mr. SHEFFRY, Speaker of the Virginia House of Delegates, Secretary BENJAMIN, and Mr. Gillies, of North Carolina; and then adjourned until seven o.

An impromptu meeting was held at 2 o in the Hall of the House of Delegates, and was addressed by Messrs. GOODE, FUNSTEN and BALDWIN, of the Virginia delegation in Congress.

The deportment of the people indicated a full acceptance of the continuance of the war forced upon them by the refusal of LINCOLN to negotiate for peace.

The following resolutions were admitted by Mr. SHEFFRY, and heartily applauded:

Resolved, that the events which have occurred during the progress of the war have but confirmed our original determination, to strike for our independence; and that, with the blessing of God, we will never lay down our arms, until it shall have been won.

GREAT MASS MEETING TO ENDORSE CALL OF THE LEGISLATURE OF SOUTH CAROLINA FOR A STATE CONVENTION OF DISCUSS THE QUESTION OF SECESSION FROM THE UNION, HELD AT INSTITUTE HALL (LATER TO BE CALLED SECESSION HALL), CHARLESTON, SOUTH CAROLINA, ON MONDAY, NOVEMBER 12, 1860 (FRANK LESLIE'S ILLUSTRATED NEWSPAPER) LIBRARY OF CONGRESS.

Secondly, that, as we believe our resources sufficient for the purpose, we do not doubt but that we shall conduct the war successfully, and to that issue we devote ourselves, and we hopefully invoke our people, in the name of the holiest of all causes, to spare neither blood nor treasure in its maintenance and support.

Thirdly, that we tender our thanks to our soldiers in the field for their noble efforts on behalf of the country, its right and its liberties; and take this occasion to assure them that no effort of ours shall be spared, to assist them in maintaining the great cause, to which we freely devote ourselves and our all.

To Our Readers

The progress of military events, which has occasioned so much public and private inconvenience and suffering, has not spared the newspaper interest. The interruption of railroad communication between Charleston and the interior produces a state of affairs which compels us, temporarily, to transfer the publication office of the *MERCURY* elsewhere; and today's paper will be our last issue, for the present, in the city of Charleston. It is due to our readers that they should be informed of the reasons which necessitate so important a step in the management of our journal. The interruption of the mails on the South Carolina Railroad practically cuts us off from the mass of our country readers, not only in this but all the adjoining States. We consider it highly desirable that the paper should reach this large class; and by the contemplated change we trust to accomplish that end. But a far more important consideration, and one which cannot be overlooked, is the question of our paper supply. Few of our readers have any idea of the enormous quantity of paper required for the daily consumption of our establishment. The paper mill upon which we depend for our supply is situated in Western North Carolina, and as things stand, for want of transportation, there is no chance of a continuance of that supply. So that we have the alternatives presented to us of being obliged to discontinue THE *MERCURY*, for want of the material upon which to print it, or of removing, for a time, our publication office to another more convenient point. Justice to our subscribers, no less than our own preference, impels us to the latter course.

For a few days, therefore, the issue of THE *MERCURY* will be suspended; but soon, we trust, it will revisit all our readers.

18

Appomattox Court House

Grant and Lee Bring a Merciful End to the Civil War

AUTHOR'S COMMENTARY

Journalists, often the cause of great annoyance to general officers on both sides of the War, were coming to the end of their great education. Writing of the exploits of The Army of Northern Virginia and The Army of the Potomac had provided journalists, North and South, with opportunities to develop a rough-hewn craft into a craft many still thought was slightly less than rough. There was still room for improvement. Robert E. Lee thought there was a great deal of room.

After Appomattox and the end of the Civil War, Lee was offered, and accepted, the presidency of Washington College, now Washington and Lee University in Lexington, Virginia. Lee felt that improvement for an aspiring journalist lay in receiving a classical education. Under Lee's direction, Washington College offered scholarships to those wishing to pursue newspaper work as a career. Those receiving scholarships also would work with local printers.

Lee organized committees to coordinate a classical education program in journalism and made the scholarship program known through advertising. After his death in 1870, however, the program was discontinued without explanation. Speculation has it that Washington College abruptly dropped the program due to criticism from the press.

pril 10, 1865: **From *The New York Times***
UNION VICTORY!
PEACE!
SURRENDER OF GENERAL LEE AND HIS WHOLE ARMY
THE WORK OF PALM SUNDAY

Final Triumph of the Army of the Potomac.
The Strategy and Diplomacy of Lieut. Gen. Grant.
Terms and Conditions of the Surrender.
The Rebel Arms, Artillery, and Public Property Surrendered.
Rebel Officers Retain Their Side Arms, and Private Property.
Officers and Men Paroled and Allowed to Return to Their Homes.
The Correspondence Between Grant and Lee.

OFFICIAL.

WAR DEPARTMENT, WASHINGTON,
APRIL 9, 1865 š 9 O'CLOCK P.M.

To Maj. Gen. Dix:
This department has received the official report of the SURRENDER, THIS DAY, OF GEN. LEE AND HIS ARMY TO LIEUT. GEN. GRANT, on the terms proposed by Gen. GRANT.

Details will be given as speedily as possible.

EDWIN M. STANTON, SECRETARY OF WAR.

HEADQUARTERS ARMIES OF THE UNITED STATES
4:30 P.M., APRIL 9

Hon. Edwin M. Stanton, Secretary of War:
GEN. LEE SURRENDERED THE ARMY OF NORTHERN VIRGINIA THIS AFTERNOON, upon the terms proposed by myself. The accompanying additional correspondence will show the conditions fully.

(Signed)
U. S. GRANT, LIEUT. GEN'L.

SUNDAY, April 9, 1865

GENERAL – I received your note of this morning, on the picket line, whither I had come to meet you and ascertain definitely what terms were embraced in your proposition of yesterday with reference to the surrender of this army.

I now request an interview in accordance with the offer contained in your letter of yesterday for that purpose.

Very respectfully, your obedient servant,

R. E. LEE, GENERAL.

Gen. R. E. Lee, Commanding Confederate States Armies:

Your note of this date is but this moment, 11:50 A.M., received.

SUNDAY, April 9, 1865.

In consequence of my having passed from the Richmond and Lynchburgh road to the Farmville and Lynchburgh road, I am at this writing about four miles West of Walter's church, and will push forward to the front for the purpose of meeting you. Notice sent to me, on this road, where you wish the interview to take place, will meet me.

VERY RESPECTFULLY, YOUR OB'D'T SERVANT,

U. S. GRANT,

LIEUTENANT GENERAL.

APPOMATTOX COURT-HOUSE April 9, 1865.

General R. E. Lee, Commanding C. S. A.:

In accordance with the substance of my letters to you of the 8th inst., I propose to receive the surrender of the Army of Northern Virginia on the following terms, to wit:

Rolls of all the officers and men to be made in duplicate, one copy to be given to an officer designated by me, the other to be retained by such officers as you may designate.

The officers to give their individual paroles not to take arms against the Government of the United States until properly exchanged, and each company or regimental commander sign a like parole for the men of their commands.

The arms, artillery and public property to be packed and stacked and turned over to the officers appointed by me to receive them.

This will not embrace the side-arms of the officers, nor their private horses or baggage.

This done, EACH OFFICER AND MAN WILL BE ALLOWED TO RETURN TO THEIR HOMES, not to be disturbed by United States authority so long as they observe their parole and the laws in force where they reside.
VERY RESPECTFULLY,
U. S. GRANT, LIEUTENANT-GENERAL.
HEADQUARTERS
U.S. ARMY OF NORTHERN VIRGINIA

To LIEUT. GEN. GRANT, COMMANDING UNITED STATES ARMIES.

April 9, 1865.
Lieut. Gen. U. S. Grant, Commanding U. S. A.:

GENERAL: I have received your letter of this date, CONTAINING THE TERMS OF SURRENDER OF THE ARMY OF NORTHERN VIRGINIA, as proposed by you. As they are substantially the same as those expressed in your letter of the 8th last, THEY ARE ACCEPTED. I will proceed to designate the proper officers to carry the stipulations into effect.
VERY RESPECTFULLY
YOUR OBEDIENT SERVANT
R.E. LEE, GENERAL

The Preliminary Correspondence

The following is the previous correspondence between Lieut. Gen. GRANT and Gen. LEE, referred to in the foregoing telegram to the Secretary of War:

CLIFTON HOUSE, VA., April 9, 1865.

Hon. Edwin M. Stanton, Secretary of War:
The following correspondence has taken place between Gen. LEE and myself. *There has been no relaxation in the pursuit during its pendency.*
U. S. GRANT, LIEUTENANT GENERAL.

APRIL 7, 1865.
Gen. R. E. Lee, Commanding C. S. A.:
GENERAL: The result of the last week must convince you of the hopelessness of further resistance on the part of the Army of Northern Virginia in this struggle. I feel that it is so and regard it as my duty to shift from myself the responsibility of any further effusion of blood, by asking of you the surrender of that portion of the Confederate States Army, known as the Army of Northern Virginia.
VERYRESPECTFULLY,
YOUR OBEDIENT SERVANT,
U.S.GRANT,
LIEUTENANT GENERAL,
COMMANDING ARMIES OF THE UNITED STATES.

APRIL 7, 1865.

General: I have received your note of this date.
Though not entirely of the opinion you express of the hopelessness of further resistance on the part of the army of Northern Virginia, I reciprocate your desire to avoid useless effusion of blood, and therefore, before considering your proposition, *ask the terms you will offer on condition of its surrender.*
R. E. LEE, GENERAL.

To Gen. R. E. Lee, Commanding C. S. A.:
GENERAL: Your note of last evening in reply to mine of same date, asking the conditions on which I will accept the surrender of the Army of Northern Virginia, is just received.

In reply, I would say that *peace being my first desire, there is but one condition that I insist upon, viz.:*

That the men surrendered shall be disqualified for taking up arms again against the Government of the United States until properly exchanged.

I will meet you, or designate officers to meet any officers you may name, for the same purpose, at any point agreeable to you, for the purpose of arranging definitely the terms upon which the surrender of the Army of Northern Virginia will be received.

U. S. GRANT, LIEUT. GENERAL,
COMMANDING ARMIES OF THE UNITED STATES.
APRIL 8, 1865

To LIEUT. GEN. U. S. GRANT,
COMMANDING ARMIES OF THE UNITED STATES.

APRIL 8, 1865.

GENERAL: I received, at a late hour, your note of to-day, in answer to mine of yesterday.

I did not intend to propose the surrender of the Army of Northern Virginia, but to ask the terms of your proposition. To be frank, I do not think the emergency has arisen to call for the surrender.

But as the restoration of peace should be the sole object of it all, I desire to know whether your proposals would tend to that end.

I cannot, therefore, meet you with a view to surrender the Army of Northern Virginia, but as far as your proposition may affect the Confederate States forces under my command, and tend to the restoration of peace, I should be pleased to meet you at 10 A.M., to-morrow, on the old stage road to Richmond, between the picket lines of the two armies.

Very respectfully, your obedient servant,
R.E. LEE,
GENERAL, C.S.A.

APRIL 9, 1865.

To Gen. R. E. Lee, commanding C. S. A.:

GENERAL: Your note of yesterday is received. As I have no authority to treat on the subject of peace, the meeting proposed for 10 A.M. to-day could lead to no good. I will state, however, General, that I am equally anxious for peace with yourself; and the whole North entertain the same feeling. The terms upon which peace can be had are well understood. By the South laying down their arms, they will hasten that most desirable event, save thousands of human lives, and hundreds of millions of property not yet destroyed.

Sincerely hoping that all our difficulties may be settled without the loss of another life, I subscribe myself,
VERY RESPECTFULLY,
YOUR OBEDIENT SERVANT,
U.S. GRANT,
LIEUTENANT GENERAL UNITED STATES ARMY

The Victory

Thanks to God, the Giver, of Victory.
Honors to Gen. Grant and His Gallant Army.

A National Salute Ordered

Two Hundred Guns to be Fired at the Headquarters of Every Army, Department, Post and Arsenal.

First Impressions of Richmond
The Great Conflagration in the City
Who was Responsible for it?
The Libby and Castle Thunder
Suffering for Food
Distribution of Supplies
Lee's Family

From Our Own Correspondent

RICHMOND, THURSDAY, APRIL 6, 1865.
So many thousand facts are presented to the mind of the visitor here in such a very short space of time, that to record them systematically is almost impossible. The great features of the evacuation, the entrance of our troops, the conflagration, the President's visit and reception, have already been forwarded to you in detail by our corresondents who came in with troops, and I will, therefore, allude to them only in a general way.

Let me say, though, at the outset, that the best part of the city is a ruin. That the awful fire kindled by the enemy, and which at first promised to consume but a few buildings, was so fanned by the rising wind, that before it could be got under subjection, thirty squares, comprising not less than eight hundred buildings in the very best and most valuable business part of Richmond, were in ashes. What the pecuniary loss is no one can estimate. Nearly all the principal mills, factories, warehouses, stores, banks and insurance offices were destroyed, and the losses being so heavy, the insurance companies, perhaps insolvent already from their countenance of the rebel currency, are now more than bankrupted, and thousands of property owners, computed wealthy in their actual possessions three days ago, are now reduced to beggary. It is among the things easily discernable, that this ruin, wrought by their own friends, to whom they have given all, and to whose tyranny they have submitted, with even cheerfulness, is the cause of far deeper gloom among many than that produced by the loss of the city or the defeat of their army. It is apparent indeed that the transfer of the city to the Union flag was not only not distasteful to a very large portion of the people, many of them among the best classes, but even highly gratifying. No captured city, not even Savannah nor Columbia, can present the ruin apparent here in Richmond. It will carry the painful evidences for half a score of years, and the only thing which will speedily alleviate the dire distress that must prevail, and give the city a chance for a speedy recovery from its present stagnation, is immediate peace. It is Richmond's only salvation. The origin of the fire and the incendiaries are so well and positively known that no extended investigation on these points is required. It seems that Gen. Lee was not responsible for it, but that Jeff. Davis and his Secretary of War, Breckinridge, were. The destruction of the supplies and the arsenal involved the destruction of the city, and it was so decided by the leading citizens. Gen. EWELL and Maj. CARRINGTON both protested against it in the most earnest manner, as did also a committee of citizens, but BRECKINRIDGE, in reply, exclaimed that he didn't care a d-m if every house in Richmond was consumed, the warehouse must be burned. Thus this wretched rebel, foisted into a powerful position with no constituents, is responsible for the dreadful ruin, and his master DAVIS is likewise responsible, because he silently countenanced it.

The fire was started in two places, among the supply warehouses near the wharves and at the Danville Depot, where there were 1,500 hogsheads of tobacco belonging to the Confederate Government. This consumed the Danville Depot, also the Petersburgh Depot, and the bridge over the James to Manchester. The famous Libby Prison and Castle Thunder, as I have already informed you, were not burned. They were reserved for a far more appropriate fate. I visited them yesterday, and found Castle Thunder used as a guard-house for factious and thieving negroes caught in acts of plunder, while the Libby contained 700 rebel prisoners, officers and privates, temporarily shut up together. They looked through the iron gratings with gloomy countenances, while the Union guard outside seemed to richly enjoy the transition that the famous building had undergone, evidently having been there himself. The whirligig of time makes all things even, and the thousands of loyal officers and soldiers who have suffered the tortures and horrors of these dungeons may now contemplate their present users with serene satisfaction, and yet without resentment.

A close inspection of Castle Thunder reveals one of the most hideous dungeons that can be conceived. We failed to see it, however, in all its filth and nastyness, for a strong force of men had been engaged two days in carrying out the accumulation of the past three years. The corporal of the guard who conducted us through pointed out a spot on the floor on one of the main halls, not yet cleaned where the dirt was three inches thick and alive with vermin, and yet on this floor, in this condition, prisoners were obliged to sleep either upon the dirt itself or upon pallets of decaying straw.

But I will not descant further upon this vile relic of the rebellion. Its career is too well known. The prisoners confined here, it will be recollected, were those against whom special vengeance was directed – prisoners of State, persons charged with harboring Union prisoners, Union officers charged with being special blockade-runners, &c. Well has it been said that a confinement in Castle Thunder is a foretaste of the tortures of the damned.

This building, together with the Libby, belongs to the estate of JOHN ENDERS and was leased by the rebel Government. They were originally built for stores, but subsequently turned into tobacco manufactories. But their base uses are now at an end.

This is the fourth day of the Union occupation, and the confusion in the city necessarily attendant upon such an evacuation, and such an occupation, is gradually subsiding. Could the ruins of the fire be removed from sight, Richmond would present an attractive appearance, for it is really a handsome city; but, after all, the saddest scenes are at the headquarters of the Provost-Martial, the Commissioners of Subsistence, and the office of Sanitary Commission, the latter being already established here. Gen. WEITZEL had no sooner established his headquarters here than thousands of citizens besieged him for rations. And as the city is now shut out from all supplies from the country, the crowd of applicants for subsistence is rapidly increasing. This morning there was nothing in the markets but a few small fish caught by negroes. The Capitol, the City Hall and the Capitol-square are filled with a great throng of all classes, condition, sexes and ages, with basket in hand and an appealing expression of face. What the regulations yet are in regard to the issue of rations to the citizens, I do not know, but a limited quantity is being supplied them at present.

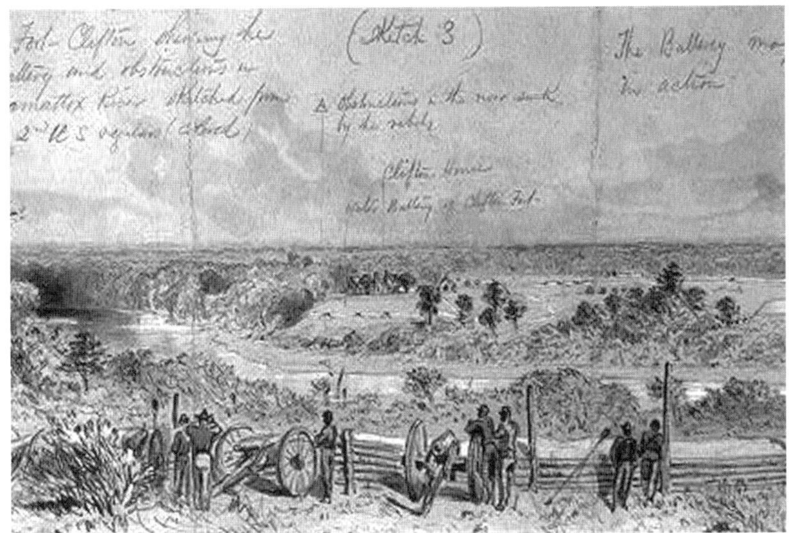

View of Fort Clifton, showing the Water Battery and obstructions in the Appomattox River (Waud). Library of Congress.

In order to study this peculiar social feature of the rebellion, I mingled with these crowds this morning for a short time, to observe their temper, desires and condition. They were, of course, largely made up of what appeared to be the poorer classes, and many negroes were among them, some for subsistence for themselves and some as servants of families. I found many whose intelligent expression of countenance, fair features and attempted gentility of dress, indicated that they were of the higher classes, on whom the demands of want and hunger were as insatiable as upon those of less position. I noticed several ladies approach the officer in charge at the City Hall, genteely attired, and with their faces so closely veiled as to defy the gaze of the keenest eye. They spoke in such tremulous tones when giving their names as to cause us to suspect their names were as foreign to them as the hunger they now sought to appease had been in days gone by. Many of the wealthiest families, however, who had the means, have far larger supplies of provisions on hand than was consistent with the repeated appeals of Confederate officials for such to spare from their bounty to feed the army.

General Robert E. Lee leaving the McLean House following his surrender to Lieutenant General Ulysses S. Grant (Waud). Library of Congress.

The exodus of prominent citizens was confined mainly to those connected with the rebel government, and a few who had made themselves very conspicuous in rebel politics – all the rebel Cabinet and their chief assistants, though not much of their clerical force, got away. The preparations for the evacuation began very quietly among the officials. At noon of Sunday the important records of the departments were boxed up and carted to the depot; but very little suspicion was excited among the citizens as to the real state of the case. A strong guard was stationed at the Danville depot, and four trains were got ready, the first of which left, with DAVIS on board, at seven o'clock in the evening, and the last at midnight. DAVIS' family had gone into the country on the Friday preceeding, but not because of any apprehension that the city was to be given up. Very few families left the city, and there are very few vacant houses – the mansions of JEFF. DAVIS and Gov. BILLY SMITH being among those now in want of tenants. The family of Gen. LEE, consisting of a wife, who is an invalid, and three daughters, are among those who remain. They occupy a stylish house on Franklin street, and for their protection, a well disciplined guard is placed at the dwelling and the family are scrupulously protected from annoyance of any character, the staring gaze of the passer-by hardly being allowed. This is the second time that Mrs. Gen. LEE has been in our hands. She was once captured by our cavalry near White House in 1862, and sent through our lines to Richmond under flag of truce, by order of Gen. MCCLELLAN.

L. L. CROUNSE.

The New York Times

APRIL 11, 1865

Editorials

The New Epoch – The Advent of Peace. This continent quivered yesterday as never since its upheaval from chaos. The lightning flashed peace, and from ocean to ocean, all minds thrilled with the sense of a new order of things. No more deluge of blood. No more whirls of ruin. No more brooding darkness. The republic rested again, and upon foundations as eternal as the hills. The whole heavens were spanned with the rainbow of promise, and every eye saw it.

This tremendous transition has been betokened latterly by many signs, yet its coming was sudden. The terrible trials of the war have weighed so heavily upon the land, and the people have been so often deceived by false appearances, that a confirmed impression existed that the deliverance, if it ever came, would come only with protracted tribulation. Even now, in spite of all we see, it is hard to realize that the rebellion has vanished. But just now it threatened to engulf the nation.

"Glory to the Lord of Hosts, from whom all blessings are." If ever a people under heaven was bound to prostrate itself in gratitude, it's the loyal people of this land. Had it been foretold to them four years ago what trials awaited them, there would have been a universal cry of despairing agony. Human history affords no instance of such a national ordeal. Never could we have endured it but for the strength given from on high, as we had need. The must capacious minds of Europe, schooled to the uttermost limit in all the wisdom of the past, called this war a madness. It was a madness, if estimated by any material standard. Eight millions of Anglo-Saxon rebels, compacted as one man, brave to the last pitch, inhabiting a country peculiarly defensible, having the encouragement of untiring faction beyond their bounds, and a moral alliance with nearly every power in the Old World, according to all the ordinary rules of judging, would surely prevail. But we had a hidden Strength which the world did not understand. It was Faith – a faith that first broke upon us with the first flash of Sumter'e guns, and that ever afterward went on widening and deepening. The people came to feel as by an inspiration from heaven, that the moral elements of the national cause made it irresistible. They were penetrated with the feeling, that as sure as there was an Almighty Father, He would not permit the success of a rebellion that was made only for the benefit of human slavery. It was this which carried them through the struggle. Ten times their physical strength would not have kept them up, in the absence of this sovereign faith. The race of Titans could not have maintained this war, if, too, they had been a race of atheists.

That religious faith is fitly followed now by a religious gratitude. It is wonderful to mark the solemn character of the joy that now spreads the land. There are waving flags, ringing bells, booming cannon, and other national tokens of public gladness. But yet it is plain to see that the dominant feeling of the people is no ebullient exhilaration over human achievement, but a profound sense of a Divine blessing. The popular heart relieves itself, not so much in cheers and hurrahs as in doxologies. Never since the hosannas of that palm Sunday in Jerusalem has such irrepressible praise rolled up from a city street to the pure vault of heaven as from the great thoroughfare of money-changers in New York at the tidings that the rebel capital had fallen. Yet that was but the key-note of the universal anthem. The enemies of this republic may talk as they please of its materializing tendencies, may to their heart's content stigmatize our people as worshipers of the "almighty dollar"; they but waste their breath. Business activities, strenuous as they are, have not stilled the religious sentiment of the American heart. This has been demonstrated in ways without number, but never so grandly as now.

With this gratitude for deliverance is mingled a fresh assurance that Heaven has reserved our republic for a destiny more glorious than can yet be conceived. Americans now feel that it is less than ever a presumption in them to believe themselves a chosen people, appointed to school the world to new ideas of human capacities and human rights. The monarchs of the Old World are trembling with apprehension lest we shall be moved to repay our injuries by turning against them our arms. They have a thousand times greater reason to fear the moral force of our new position. We stand a living proof of the matchless potency of popular self-government. It rivets the attention of the whole civilized world. It will start new thoughts, will generate new purposes, will nerve to new acts. This is as sure as that the human reason shall continue to exist. It is this that the dynastics have need to fear; it is here that we expect our sweetest revenge.

What the Historians Say

The last battle in the Eastern Theater was fought at Appomattox Court House on April 9, 1865, in Appomattox, Virginia. It was the final battle in the Appomattox Campaign, which took place from March to early April 1865.

The principal commanders were Lt. Gen. Ulysses S. Grant commanding the United States forces and Gen. Robert E. Lee leading the Army of Northern Virginia for the Confederate States. The estimated casualties were 700 total with 27,805 Confederate soldiers paroled.

Early on April 9, the remnants of John Brown Gordon's corps and Fitzhugh Lee's cavalry formed a line of battle at Appomattox Court House. Gen. Robert E. Lee determined to make one last attempt to escape the closing Union pincers and reach his supplies at Lynchburg. At dawn, the Confederates advanced and initially gained ground against Sheridan's cavalry. The arrival of Union infantry, however, stopped the advance in its tracks. Lee's army was now surrounded on three sides. Lee surrendered to Grant on April 9. This was the final engagement of the war in Virginia.

LIEUTENANT GENERAL ULYSSES S. GRANT (L. PRANG). LIBRARY OF CONGRESS.

Bibliography

Civil War Sites Advisory Commission Report on the Nation's Civil War Battlefields, Technical Volume II: Battle Summaries, Washington, DC, 1993.

Cutler, Andrew J. *The North Report The War,* Pittsburg, *1955.*

Davis, Elmer, *History of The New York Times, New York, 1921.*

deTocgueville, Alexis. *Democracy in America,Manfield and Winthrop Translation. Chicago, 2000.*

Grant, U.S. *Memoirs, Library of America, New York, 1990.*

Mott, Frank Luther. *American Journalism*, New York, 1950.

Payne, George Henry. *History of Journalism in the United States*, Westport, 1970.

Reynolds, Donald E. *Editors Make War: Southern Newspapers in the Secession Crisis, Nashville, 1966.*

Rhett, Robert Barnwell, Davis, William O *A Fire Eater Remembers*: *The Confederate Memoir of Robert Barnwell Rhett,* Columbia, SC, 2000.

Starr, Louis. *Bohemian Brigade*: Civil War Newsmen in Action, New York, 1954.

White, Laura. *Robert Barnwell Rhett: Father of Secession*, New York, 1931.

Wilkie, Franc, *Pen and Powder,* Boston, 1888.

Other Resources

Charleston Mercury, April 13, 1861.

New York Times, April 16, 1861.

The War of Rebellion: A Compilation of the Official Records of the Union and Confederate Armies.

Papers presented at the 1995 Annual Meeting of the Association for Education in Journalism and Mass Communication: *The First College Journalism Students: Answering Robert E. Lee's Offer of a Higher Education.*

The Kinnochtinny Papers, 1913, Chambersburg, PA. *Dr. John McClellan's extirpation of the parotid gland.*

Letter from Gen. Sherman to Brig. Gen. Blair February 2, 1863.

Letter from Gen. Sherman to Gen. Grant, August 17, 1862.

Harper's Monthly Magazine, October, 1863, L.L.. Crounse, pp. 627-634.

U.S. Census, 1860.

Index

O

P

R

S

Y

Z